Liberating Minds
Liberating Society
Black Women in the Development
of American Culture and Society

Lopez D. Matthews, Jr

And

Kenvi C. Phillips

DEDICATION

To every black woman who fought, struggled, lived and died so that we can be here and publish a book to tell their stories.

CONTENTS

CONTRIBUTORS

Takeia N. Anthony, Ph.D., Edward Waters College

Keisha N. Blain, Ph.D., Pennsylvania State University

Aleia Brown, MA, MTSC Center for Historic Preservation

Cherise Charleswell, MPH, The Hampton Institute

Kelisha B. Graves, Ph.D., Liberty University

Tara Green, Ph.D., University of North Carolina Greensboro

Sheena Harris, Ph.D., Tuskegee University

Amanda L. Higgins, Ph.D., University of Kentucky

Pamela T. Hoff, Illinois State University

Ida E. Jones, Ph.D., Moorland-Spingarn Research Center

Regina V. Jones, Ph.D., Indiana University Northwest

Joshua Myers, Ph.D., Howard University

Anita Nahal, Ph.D., Smithsonian Museum of African American
History and Culture

Zakiyyah Muhammad, Ph.D., Institute of Muslim American Studies

Arlisha Norwood, MA, Howard University

Ashley N. Robertson, Ph.D., Bethune-Cookman College

Crystal R. Sanders, Pennsylvania State University

Jermaine Scott, Ph.D., Northwestern University

Ava Thompson-Greenwell, Northwestern University

Jervette R. Ward, Ph.D., University of Alaska Anchorage

Cait Vaughan, Council on International Educational Exchange

Foreword

"We have to talk about liberating minds as well as liberating society."

Angela Davis

In January 1950 Mary McLeod Bethune then president of the Association for the Study of Negro Life and History penned an article for the *Journal of Negro History* entitled "The Negro in Retrospect and Prospect" In this essay Mrs. Bethune sought to examine the human bridge of successes and necessary terrain yet-to-be covered by the post-war, informed, educated Negro American citizen. The Great Depression gave way to World War II and the world was a different place. The colonized people and modes of imperialism were being challenged across the globe. Mrs. Bethune knew the long history of struggle by the marginalized and oppressed to breathe free. "My splendid audience, here, will join with me in paying tribute to the builders of earlier days, who laid the foundation for today's advance. But we shall not stop over-long to praise our warriors...churchmen...or our educators, Booker T. Washington and Lucy Laney, for their greatest monument to all our black heroes....is the influence which you and I, are wielding in the world today."

Mrs. Bethune weaved history, politics, international affairs and divine accountability into a tapestry of the challenges and responsibility educated and informed Negro citizens needed to maintain as a plumb line. The plumb line was a necessity and cautionary space to temper ego, abandon and recklessness the post-war era could introduce through new opportunities. "My caution would call for acceptance of the responsibility of being informed; for strengthening of moral character; for an increase in formal and informal education at the expense of personal sacrifice...the part of the Negro in both movements [greater unity and fuller democracy] is one of increased strength and significance."

Mrs. Bethune was aware of the important role education played in eliminating stereotypes, creating conversation and instilling confidence. The legacy of education for Black women has been one of educator formally and informally. From the female slave networks, to formation of women's clubs, to benevolent societies, to collegiate sororities, to corporate

i

mentoring programs the need to know and to know how from another woman aided Black women in overcoming obstacles, avoiding pitfalls and lifting up rising generations of women. Angela Davis captures this history in her advice "to liberating mind and liberating society" through education about the prison industrial system. Davis advocates for informing the general public about the devastating conditions in American prisons where Black people are warehoused and made capital gains for a system that never intends to reform, reintegrate or reconsider as full citizens. Mrs. Bethune and Davis echo the issues facing Black people, education and employment both elements are needed to circumvent prison. However, cyclical under-employment/poverty, poor classroom instruction and intra-racial tensions provide breeding grounds for delinquent/extralegal behavior.

Both women believed in education. They engaged in public and organized efforts to advocate for change. In the tradition and spirit of activist scholarship Dr. Matthews and Dr. Phillips continue to promote education. The striking image of Mrs. Bethune stands as a testament to the depths from which Black women have come while Angela Davis represents a far reach into the potential modern society could achieve in true social justice. These essays celebrate this dynamic legacy from Black women, for their children, themselves, spouses and humanity.

Ida E. Jones, Ph.D.

Washington, DC

"If we have the courage and tenacity of our forebears, who stood firmly like a rock against the lash of slavery, we shall find a way to do for our day what they did for theirs."

Mary McLeod Bethune

Cheerleading vs. White Supremacy:
A Summary of Katie Williams' Life of Resistance

TaKeia N. Anthony

Sports are a vital part of the South. Women in sports have largely been omitted from the master narrative, aside from recognizing the black female firsts. One of the major reasons women were omitted from this narrative is because cheerleading was not recognized as a sport. The American Academy of Pediatrics charged schools to consider cheerleading a sport in 2012 to take extra precautions to its dangers.[1] This recognition adds women into sports narratives. In most African American communities sports were significant in the self-development process. Athletes developed skills such as character, teamwork, discipline, and sportsmanship that are used to shape future leaders. This essay demonstrates how cheerleading was used as a self-development tool to alter the method of resistance against white supremacy in the life of one African-American woman, Mrs. Katie Ivery Williams.

Born Katie Ivery on May 7, 1940 in Campbellsville, Kentucky, Williams was the second of four girls to Mr. and Mrs. Rodney K. and Fannie Curry Ivery. "I was born at home. Back then, black people could only go to the colored hospital and there was not one in my hometown. There was one in Louisville, Kentucky but it was too far away."[2] Williams grew up on ten acres of land where her parents taught her and her siblings to be self-sufficient. "We never went hungry at home. We collected eggs from the chicken coop, and my mom snapped beans and peas and canned them for the winter along with pears and apples from our fruit trees. When we wanted meat daddy would go to the smokehouse and cut meat by the slab; that was the best bacon!"[3]

Despite this fond childhood memory of growing up in the Jim Crow south, Williams has a list full of hurtful memories. Her best childhood friend was a girl named Janet. "She was my best friend because we lived close to one another and we were around the same age." During the summer months their friendship was tested daily as Janet was constantly called a Nigger lover; however, when school started they were separated because Janet went to an all-white school and Williams attended Greensburg Colored School.[4]

"One day after school my friend Margie and I went to the ice cream parlor in the downtown square. We could not sit in the parlor and eat ice cream, we had to eat on the steps outside." Williams paused as she was recalling the past and her voice dropped an octave as she told the remainder of the story. "Two white boys rode past us on bicycles and yelled Nigger, Nigger, Nigger!" Her voice carried such hurt and pain. "Margie and I got off the steps, drug them off their bikes, and beat them up! I had nails so I scratched them good. We hit and kicked the boys as hard as we could so they would think twice before they used that word again." Returning to her normal octave, "The people in the square ran out of their businesses and yelled for us to stop hitting them, but no one came to physically break-up the fight. We stopped once we were tired, people went back to work, and we went back across the bridge."[5]

Williams had several similar stories where she chose physical resistance as her method to stop individuals from exercising white supremacy over her. A turning point in this strategy came when she entered Durham High School and became a cheerleader. Sports plays a vital role in developing character and discipline, and Williams, as a cheerleader, was no different. "People came from miles away to watch the

Durham High Hornets! Our basketball team was good but people also came to see the cheerleaders. I did all the gymnastics moves and the splits. Our games were the best." Williams' maturity came her junior year when she was made captain. "When you became the captain you have to think of more than just yourself. You have to be accountable for how others will feel under your leadership. Being the captain is more than just having the spotlight; I did not know this until I was the captain." Throughout the rest of her high school years Williams was conscious to use her position in cheerleading as a learning tool to develop her character and leadership skills.[6]

Sportsmanship was a major lesson taught to Williams. During an away game at Lincoln Institute in Lincoln Ridge, Kentucky the cheerleaders from the opposing school put Williams and her cheerleading squad's clothes in the toilet. After the game the cheerleaders were livid and had to ride home in their sweaty uniforms. A few months later, Lincoln Institute traveled to Campbellsville, Kentucky to play against Durham High School. The cheerleading coach warned Williams that the opposing team's clothes would be locked in the home economics room and would not be damaged. "She told me not to allow them on the floor." Wittingly, Williams told her squad, "Follow me and be ready!" Every time the referee called a time out Williams was the first cheerleader on the floor. "I made sure they did not get a chance to show off their cheers. We hogged that floor and they had to sit back and watch us perform. I thought that was the best "get back" ever but my daddy, the athletic director, did not think so. On Monday morning when we went back to school he suspended me for three games."[7]

The next week Williams felt embarrassment for the first time. One of the referees calling the game informed his parents of Williams' cheerleading talents and invited them to next game, but Williams could not cheer. Her punishment was to sit by the cheerleading coach in her uniform.

"I could not say a word. Everyone knew I was in trouble. Sportsmanship was a hard lesson to learn then, but my daddy was trying to make me understand that you do not have to block someone else to prove you are good. We had to take the high road and not retaliate because eventually their conscious would eat at them for treating us badly." Williams had learned the core message of the non-violent civil rights movement through sportsmanship.[8]

Williams exuded these lessons when she arrived on the campus of Kentucky State College in 1957. Avoiding the shadows of her older sister, Rose, who was a senior and Miss Kentucky State College, Williams, got her own recognition as a cheerleader. "I was still known as Rose's little sister, but I was creating my own identity too and I handled popularity with ease, but it came with a price." Williams chose to use her popularity to make a difference. Her old strategy of physical resistance would not help against the institutional oppression of the Jim Crow south. Her previous lessons of sportsmanship, character, leadership skills, and popularity helped her fight Jim Crow politically. She and four other students were recruited to campaign for the Democratic Party. Their goal was to register students as Democrats. "We went to everyone on campus who had turned eighteen before the November local elections and helped them register to vote in their hometown. It was critical that we made a difference, and this was my new way of fighting."[9]

Williams' absentee ballot caused quite a commotion back home in Greensburg, Kentucky. "I was the first person in my family to register as a Democrat; the republicans were not doing anything for black people any more. They were buying our votes . . . they [republican candidates] would pay every voter four dollars after they voted." Williams was not concerned about the four dollars, she was ready for change. The local election was a close race, and the democratic candidate won by only one vote, Williams'.

"It was a tie race and the last votes counted were the absentees and there was only one, mine. Everybody knew I was a democrat, then."[10]

The newly elected city official visited Williams' mother in her classroom. Showing his gratitude for his newly elected position, he asked Mrs. Ivery, "What can I do for you?" She quickly replied, "You can pave the roads leading to the school and the church." He did just that. The roads in the black community were gravel or dirt roads; when it rained the children had to walk to school or church in the mud. When it snowed the rocks would freeze, leaving a blanket of ice under the snow that was dangerous for the children to walk over. Williams was proud for making a change in her community at home. Not only had she brought better living conditions to the area, she had also shifted her parents' political party allegiance from Republican to Democrat.[11]

Williams' resistance against Jim Crow expanded after her college years. She graduated from Kentucky State Teacher's College in 1961 and immediately relocated to the Deep South in Fort Lauderdale, Florida. During the drive down, the three-car caravan stopped at a service station. "Those homely looking white people stared at us the entire time. We were dressed, you had to be back then." Before Williams returned to the car to continue her trip she wanted some white water. "There were two water fountains. The colored fountain looked like it had never been cleaned, it was starting to rust; but the white fountain was made of porcelain. There was a cardboard sign hanging over them that said Whites Only and Colored Only." As she moved toward the whites only water fountain the men in the other two cars yelled out, "Katie what are you doing?" As she resisted the Jim Crow laws and drank from the white fountain, the white male worker came out with his shotgun and yelled, "That's white only water you Nigger! You uppity Niggers get out of here." She remembered not being afraid and believed, "I was able to get away with it because I was a female, I

5

strongly believe that." Due to her high school sportsmanship lesson, she recalled, "I did not boast about breaking these ridiculous rules as I got back in my car, we didn't have to flash our guns at the white man. I won, I tasted white water and that white man's children and grandchildren have to live with the fact he treated us inhumane."[12]

Once settled in Fort Lauderdale, Williams married James C. Williams in 1963 and had a daughter, Vetria in 1965. She had a teaching job at two all black elementary schools, Charles R. Drew and Rock Island. "I had some of the brightest students. They have gone on to be lawyers, doctors, teachers and principals." In 1970 schools in Fort Lauderdale/Broward County were beginning their desegregation process and Williams was recruited to teach at North Andrews Gardens Elementary School. "North Andrews was in the vanguard in Broward County, it was accepting black students and hired a black teacher in 1969 before the school board forced them to. I do not remember any black and white race issues, but in the 1980's the Spanish-speaking students migrated from Central America."[13]

Williams' leadership skills surfaced once again. "The students and the parents spoke very little English but they wanted to learn and they deserved to learn." After school, Williams and other teachers offered English language activities for the parents and students in hopes to bridge the culture gap and bring equality. Williams encouraged her top students in the class to work with the ESL (English as Second Language) students when they finished their classwork early. "I taught for 25 years at North Andrews Gardens and a total of 34 years in Broward County; I have taught students who are in the NBA, NFL, legislation, teachers, principals, coaches, and many other occupations. My students were the best!"[14]

In 2010, Kentucky State University (KSU) recognized Williams' leadership as a cheerleader and inducted her into the Athletic Hall of Fame.

She is the first cheerleader in university's history to be inducted.[15] "It was an honor to be the first cheerleader inducted into KSU's Athletic Hall of Fame. It illustrates that cheerleading is truly a sport, and it does not omit women from leadership roles. Some people think only football and basketball players were leaders on campus; at KSU the cheerleaders were right there doing our part too."[16]

Discussing life during the Jim Crow era has its joys and pains. Reminiscing about family time, the all black high school and neighborhoods brought joy and excitement as I conducted this oral interview with Williams; however, the pain and hurt was also apparent when she described race relations and discrimination. Williams' early method of physical resistance may have proven itself successful as a child against individuals, but she soon realized white supremacy was institutional and the discrimination was larger than individual white people who used obscenities. As a teacher at North Andrews Gardens, her realization of systematic racial discrimination expanded to the global black and brown world when Central Americans migrated to South Florida. She used her leadership skills to bring equality in education. Williams' story is significant because it adds African-American women to sports narratives with the recognition of cheerleading and it continues the narrative of women's resistance against white supremacy, particularly Jim Crow.

[1] The Associated Press, "Cheerleading Should be designated as a Sport to Improve Safety Rules, Doctors Say" http://www.nydailynews.com/sports/more-sports/cheerleading-sport-doctors-article-1.1190099, accessed September 5, 2014.

[2] Katie Williams, interview by author, Jacksonville, Florida, September 5, 2014.

[3] Williams, interview.

[4] Williams, interview.

[5] Williams, interview.

[6] Williams, interview.

[7] Williams, interview.

[8] Williams, interview.

[9] Williams, interview.

[10] Williams, interview.

[11] Williams, interview.

[12] Williams, interview.

[13] Williams, interview.

[14] Williams, interview.

[15] Kentucky State University Athletic Hall of Fame, http://www.ksuthorobreds.com/hof.aspx?type=class_induction&kiosk=, accessed September 5, 2014.

[16] Williams, interview.

"No Race Has Succeeded Without a Good and Strong Womanhood": Black Nationalist Women and the Politics of Gender in the Negro World, 1924-1927

Keisha N. Blain

Reflecting on the role of women in Marcus Garvey's Universal Negro Improvement Association (UNIA), Black Nationalist leader Maymie Leona Turpeau De Mena argued, "Women were given to understand that they were to remain in their places, which meant nothing more than a Black Cross Nurse or a general secretary of the division."[1] Her statement addressed the complex relationship between gender and Garveyism, Garvey's race-based philosophy of black pride, African redemption, economic self-sufficiency, racial separatism and political self-determination. Garvey, arguably the most influential black nationalist of the twentieth century, was born in St. Ann's Bay, Jamaica on August 17, 1887. His difficult childhood experiences, combined with his extensive travels, shaped the ideologies on which he founded the UNIA in 1914. With the assistance of Amy Ashwood, who later became his first wife, Garvey oversaw UNIA affairs in Kingston, Jamaica before relocating to Harlem, where he incorporated the organization in 1918. At its peak, the UNIA attracted an estimated six million members and boasted approximately one thousand chapters in more than forty countries including South Africa, Cuba, and Costa Rica.[2]

While the UNIA was influential, it neglected to give an equal voice to black women. Despite their substantial numbers in the organization, women held restricted roles and responsibilities, and were often placed in subordinate positions to Garveyite men.[3] Certainly, one cannot overlook remarkable women within the organization such as Amy Jacques Garvey,

Henrietta Vinton Davis, Amy Ashwood Garvey, and M.L.T. De Mena, whose contributions were many.[4] However, these were not typical UNIA women—the average Garveyite woman did not receive the recognition or hold prominent positions as these women activists did.

Despite the limited opportunities to hold visible positions of autonomous leadership, Garveyite women fought to expand their spheres of influence and openly challenged male chauvinism—even as they struggled to abandon some of their Victorian ideals.[5] This essay contributes to the growing literature on Garveyism by focusing on rank-and-file women—a group that historians have often neglected.[6] It addresses how these women used "Our Women and What They Think," the women's page of the *Negro World*, to challenge the prevailing ethos of black patriarchy in the Garvey movement and within black communities at large. In sharp contrast to scholarly works on prominent female figures, this essay highlights the complex, diverse, and sometimes contradictory political ideas of ordinary women in the Garvey movement, who have been largely absent in the historical record.[7]

"Our Women and What They Think"

On April 19, 1924, Eunice Lewis's editorial, "The Black Woman's Part in Race Leadership," appeared on the women's page of the *Negro World*—"Our Women and What They Think." A Garveyite residing in Chicago, Lewis crafted a succinct but powerful article that embodied the spirit of the "New Negro Woman."[8] "There are many people who think that a woman's place is only in the home—to raise children, cook, wash, and attend to the domestic affairs of the house," Lewis noted. "This idea, however, does not hold true to the New Negro Woman," she continued. The "New Negro Woman," Lewis insisted, was intelligent, worked equally with men, had business savvy and most significantly, was committed to "revolutionizing the old type of male leadership."[9] Her comments, which coincided with the Harlem, or "New Negro," Renaissance of the period, signified a shift unfolding on the pages of the *Negro World*.[10]

Published between 1918 and 1933, the *Negro World* was one of the most influential black newspapers of the twentieth century, reaching peoples of African descent throughout the world. Described as the "most effective of Garvey's propaganda devices," the *Negro World* promoted racial uplift, self-reliance, and black unity.[11] Filled with Garvey's speeches, articles, and advertisements, the newspaper addressed practically every aspect of black life and promoted the UNIA's main principles. The newspaper's extensive readership reflected the organization's widespread membership, spanning Africa, Europe, the Americas, and every place where people of African descent resided.[12]

Despite its widespread political influence, the *Negro World* generally neglected to give a voice to black women.[13] When the newspaper did include statements from women prior to "Our Women," they were "often briefly paraphrased, while Garvey's [statements] were usually printed word for word."[14] The inclusion of women's views in the *Negro World* mirrored their actual involvement in the UNIA; they were present but rarely recognized. Described as the "backbone" of the UNIA, women most often participated "behind the scenes," while UNIA men gained public recognition. Garveyite men ran UNIA businesses, served as statesmen and diplomats, while women worked in the background, providing "clerical, cultural and civic support services."[15]

Most women functioned in limited capacities in the Universal Motor Corps and as Black Cross Nurses.[16] Modeled after the American Red Cross, the Black Crosses Nurses auxiliary was established by Henrietta Vinton Davis in 1921 in Philadelphia "for the purposes of providing education, medical aid, and community service" to black communities in the United States and across the diaspora.[17] Operating in their expected roles as nurturers, Black Cross Nurses performed social welfare and organizational functions such as providing clothing for the needy, running soup kitchens and visiting the sick.[18] While men in the UNIA participated in the African Legion, the protective arm of the UNIA, Black Cross Nurses were involved in the 'motherly' duties of meeting the physical and emotional needs of black communities—especially those of children and the elderly.[19]

Similarly, UNIA women participating in the African Universal Motor Corps and Juvenile Divisions of the organization further fulfilled their expected roles as nurturers to the black community, under strict male leadership.[20] In the Universal African Motor Corps, in particular, adult and teenage women learned military drills and a variety of other automotive skills, including driving cars, taxis, and ambulances. However, whether they were Black Cross Nurses or members of the Motor Corps, women held *restricted* leadership positions, and were always accountable to males within the organization.[21]

When Amy Jacques Garvey introduced "Our Women" in February 1924, she made a bold step toward expanding women's spheres of influence within the UNIA. "Our Women" did more for Garveyite women—in terms of consistency, visibility, and significance—than the yearly Women's Day at UNIA conferences, which celebrated women's achievements and accomplishments.[22] The women's page provided Garveyite women with an opportunity to express their views without direct male censorship.[23] It represented an outlet for these women to debate a range of topics, often denouncing "antiquated beliefs" and empowering each other as the organization's leader awaited the result of his appealed conviction on charges of mail fraud.[24] Though filled with advertisements for dinner sets, women's clothing, and hair treatments, the debut issue of "Our Women" also included a politically charged feature article, "Women's Party Wants Not Only Equal Rights, But Equal Responsibilities With Men."[25] The article detailed the National Woman's Party's efforts to introduce eighteen bills to the New York State Legislature, calling for women's labor rights.[26] Ironically, the NWP had already excluded black women from its agenda.[27] Still, the appearance of the NWP article in "Our Women" served as an inspiration to Garveyite women who desired an expansion of women's political rights.

If the NWP article failed to send the intended message, then other articles clarified any possible misconceptions. Written by Carrie Mero Leadett, "The Negro Girl of Today" challenged young black women to build better futures for themselves through innovation rather than imitation.[28] Leadett, who worked as a clerk at the UNIA headquarters in Harlem and for the organization's shipping company, argued that although black women should aim for the same successes as women of other races, they needed to become leaders and not followers.[29] Leadett further encouraged young black women to embrace their dark, natural hair as a sign of their black identity and beauty. Ironically, the *Negro World* advertised light brown dolls with straight or long curled hair, as opposed to natural hair.[30] Nonetheless, Leadett's editorial reflected rank-and-file Garveyite women's desire to pave their own paths and "surpass those of all other races, socially, industrially and morally."[31]

Another article, "The New Woman" by Saydee Parham, challenged women's positions in the UNIA and in the community at large. Parham, a law student who served as Garvey's secretary in 1926, discussed the process of evolution through which all species experience growth and maturation.[32] She argued that women needed to grow in society: "From the brow-beaten, dominated cave woman, cowering in fear at the mercy of her brutal mate…from the safely cloistered woman reared like a clinging vine, destitute of all initiative and independence…we find her at last rising to the pinnacle of power and glory."[33] Certainly, Parham's representation of women differed greatly from Garvey's poetry, articles, and speeches, which reinforced women's responsibility as nurturers and portrayed them as fragile beings that "needed to be uplifted" and protected by their male counterparts.[34] By contrast, Parham's editorial challenged black patriarchy, which reserved "power and glory" for men.[35]

Another writer, Blanche Hall, expressed similar views in a 1924 article, "Woman's Greatest Influence is Socially." Hall addressed the important responsibilities that women held in society, citing men's dependence on women in every aspect of life. "Show me a good, honest, noble man of character" she wrote, "and I will show you a good mother or wife behind him." Consequently, Hall reminded readers that the UNIA could not advance without the assistance of women: "There is much that the woman can do to make this organization a success."[36] Florence Bruce, the wife of John E. Bruce—who served as a contributing editor of the *Negro World* from 1921 to 1924—reinforced this position in her article, "The Great Work of the Negro Woman Today." Citing women's impact in society since antiquity, Mrs. Bruce contended that women's influence would help the advancement of the black community. *"No race has succeeded without a good and strong womanhood,"* she passionately argued, "and none ever will."[37]

While Bruce and others demanded change within the UNIA, they also envisioned a change—albeit a conservative one—in black women's responsibilities within the home. Although women in the UNIA did not completely reject traditional Victorian ideals in the home, they advocated the importance of respecting black women who worked to support their families. Therefore, many UNIA women rejected Garvey's criticism of black homes that deviated from patriarchal standards.[38] Garveyite women

14

recognized the problem facing many black women, both those whose husbands could not fully provide for their families and those who were single mothers. As a result, many of these women entered the workforce in their attempt to assist their husbands or provide for their children. Madame B. Rhoda, an active UNIA member from Nashville, Tennessee, articulated these views in her editorial, "Our Women Think We Should Make Employment." "We Negro Women," she carefully explained, "are compelled to work, for our men can't support us and our children." Rhoda criticized black men, whose failures forced black women to assume many responsibilities in the home that they would not normally fill, including that of breadwinner.[39] Likewise, in her editorial, "Half Million Dollar Churches and No Jobs," Amelia Sayers, a Garveyite from New York, justified black women's decisions to enter the workforce, reiterating, "We are *compelled* to work."[40]

In another article, "The Woman's Part in Race Developments," Vida Horsford detailed the important influence the "Negro Woman" had in the workforce. "By her carefulness, her calmness, her truthfulness, her honesty, her sweetness of disposition [and] her punctuality," she wrote, "she may create a lasting impression on the minds of her fellow workers." Horsford went on to argue that black women in the workforce would help "promulgat[e] racial doctrines" and destroy the misconception that blacks were inferior to whites.[41] While they accepted the importance of raising and caring for children, Garveyite women advocated expanded responsibilities, including women's ability to maintain the finances of the home. This was fully articulated in Rosa Lee Smith's letter to the women's page in 1924. Smith, an activist residing in Pittsburgh, argued that a woman must not only know how to care for her children, but she must also have financial knowledge and budgeting skills. "Since the woman spends most of the money in the home" she explained, "it is necessary that she know[s] how to spend it wisely."[42] Smith's comments, along with the views expressed by Horsford and Sayers, provide glimpses into the general views of rank-and-file Garveyite women who resisted the male insistence that working black mothers indicated a lack of racial progress.[43]

While many women openly resisted male supremacy, this does not imply that all Garveyite women held this conviction, or that these women did not at times accommodate the same male supremacy they fought so passionately against. Women's writings capture the myriad ways they articulated what historian Ula Taylor refers to as "community feminism"— a "territory that allowed [women] to join feminism and nationalism into a single coherent, consistent framework." "At times," Taylor asserts, "community feminism resembled a tug-of-war between feminist and nationalist paradigms, but it also provided a means of critiquing ideas of women as intellectual inferior."[44] Like Amy Jacques Garvey, many rank-and-file women in the UNIA struggled to advance black feminist and nationalist causes.[45]

This dual purpose created at times a "tug-of-war" that is evident in their articles, which reveal both a critique of the UNIA's hierarchical structure and sometimes an acceptance of male supremacy. Amelia Sayers, who had written numerous articles demanding women's expanded responsibilities in the organization, also upheld many of Garvey's patriarchal ideas. In a 1924 editorial, for example, Sayers affirmed traditional gender roles, insisting that "the man is the brain, but the woman is the heart of humanity; he its judgment, she its feelings; he its strength, she its grace, adornment and comfort..."[46] Sayers' statements reinforced sexism and promoted an essentialist view of women as emotional beings, while describing intelligence and wisdom as exclusive male attributes. Sayers also referred to women as the "heart of humanity," thereby echoing Garvey's metaphor of women as "nature's purest emblem," in contrast to men—the "sworn protectors" of their women.[47]

Similarly, other articles affirmed women's responsibility as self-sacrificing wives and mothers and reinforced sexism. One example is "The Ideal Wife" by Vera,[48] which succinctly summarized the perfect woman: "The woman who winds herself into the rugged recesses of her husband's nature, and supports and comforts him in adversity." Describing women as the "softer sex" and "ornament[s] of man" Vera went on to explain that women were responsible for meeting the needs of their men, thereby allowing these men to succeed in the community.[49] Another article, "Thoughts on Matrimony," upheld the patriarchal standards of the home and the importance of wives submitting to their husbands.[50]

Conclusion

On April 30, 1927, the publication of "Our Women and What They Think" abruptly ended. While Jacques Garvey offered no explanation for her decision to discontinue the page, one scholar contends that she may have grown tired of pleading with women to contribute articles.[51] Though short-lived, "Our Women" provides a meaningful contribution to our understanding of rank-and-file women in the Garvey movement of the 1920s. The articles and writers considered in this essay provide a window into these women's ideas. "Our Women" remains a significant chronicle of women in the UNIA, unveiling their views, conflicts, and efforts to foster change in the Garvey movement and within black communities at large. It is a revelation of these women's struggles to balance their feminist ideals with the Victorian patriarchal standards and masculinist visions espoused by Garvey and other black nationalists. Significantly, the women's page of the *Negro World* captures the voices of rank-and-file women who, until now, have remained largely silent in the historical record.

[1] Quoted in Mark D. Matthews, "Our Women and What They Think: Amy Jacques Garvey and the *Negro World*," in *Black Women in United States History*, ed. Darlene Clark Hine (Brooklyn: Carlson Publishing, 1990) vol. 7, 875. In this article, I use the term "black nationalism" to describe individuals who embraced the political view that black people constituted a "separate group or nationality by virtue of their African heritage, their shared historical experiences (slavery, segregation, ghettoization and other forms of oppression), and their distinct culture." Rejecting mainstream white society, black nationalists emphasized African heritage, black economic self-sufficiency, political self-determination, and racial separatism (which often, though not always, meant West African emigration). See Michael O. West, "'Like A River': The Million Man March and Black Nationalist Tradition in the United States," *Journal of Historical Sociology*, Vol. 12, no. 1 (March 1999): 83; Wilson Jeremiah Moses, *The Golden Age of Black Nationalism, 1850-1925* (New York: Oxford University Press, 1978).

[2] See Tony Martin, *Race First: The Ideological and Organizational Struggles of Marcus Garvey and the Universal Negro Improvement Association* (Dover, MA: Majority Press, 1976); Colin Grant, *Negro With a Hat: The Rise and Fall of Marcus Garvey* (New York: Oxford University Press, 2008). While some scholars disagree on the actual extent of Amy Ashwood's leadership in the organization, there is no denying that Ashwood was very instrumental to the UNIA's early success. See Lionel Yard, *Biography of Amy Ashwood, 1897-1969: Co-founder of the Universal Negro Improvement Association* (Washington D.C.: Associated Publisher, 1990).

[3] Barbara Bair, "True Women, Real Men: Gender, Ideology and Social Roles in the Garvey Movement," in *Gendered Domains: Rethinking Public and Private in Women's History*, eds. Dorothy O. Helly and Susan M. Reverby (Ithaca: Cornell University Press, 1992); Beryl Satter, "Marcus Garvey, Father Divine and the Gender Politics of Race Difference and Race Neutrality," *American Quarterly*, Vol. 48, no. 1 (March 1996): 43-76; Bair, "'Ethiopia Shall Stretch Forth Her Hands Unto God': Laura Kofey and the Gendered Vision of Redemption in the Garvey Movement," in *A Mighty Baptism: Race, Gender, and the Creation of American Protestantism*, eds. Susan Juster and Lisa MacFarlane (Ithaca: Cornell University, 1996).

[4] Although they obtained more leadership opportunities than women in other black organizations of the period, only a handful of UNIA women gained prominence and public recognition. Ashwood Garvey, who was Marcus Garvey's first wife, helped to establish the organization and served as one of its first members and secretaries. Amy Jacques Garvey, who became Marcus Garvey's second wife in 1919, served in many capacities including associate editor for the *Negro World* and de facto leader of the UNIA during her husband's incarceration. Henrietta Vinton Davis became the UNIA's International Organizer in 1919 and served on the organization's executive council. Likewise, Maymie De Mena became a member of the executive council, serving as the UNIA's Assistant International Organizer. See Tony Martin, *Amy Ashwood Garvey: Pan-Africanist, Feminist and Mrs. Marcus Garvey No. 1 Or, A Tale of Two Amies* (Dover: Majority Press, 2007); Ula Taylor, *The Veiled Garvey: The Life and Times of Amy Jacques Garvey* (Chapel Hill: University of North Carolina Press, 2002); William Seraile, "Henrietta Vinton Davis and the Garvey Movement," *Afro-Americans in New York Life and History*, Vol. 7, no. 2 (July 1983): 7-

24; Barbara Bair, "Renegotiating Liberty: Garveyism, Women, and Grassroots Organizing in Virginia," in *Women of the American South: A Reader*, ed. Christie Farnham (New York: New York University Press, 1997).

[5] See Martha Vicinus, ed., *Suffer and Be Still: Women in the Victorian Age* (Bloomington:
Indiana University Press, 1972).

[6] One notable exception is Natanya Duncan, "The Efficient Womanhood of the Universal Negro Improvement Association, 1919-1930" (Ph.D. Dissertation, University of Florida, 2009).

[7] Much of the scholarship on Garveyite women centers on prominent women leaders. These works include Martin, *Amy Ashwood Garvey;* Taylor, *The Veiled Garvey*; Seraile, 'Henrietta Vinton Davis and the Garvey Movement"; Karen Adler, "'Always Leading Our Men in Service and Sacrifice': Amy Jacques Garvey, Feminist Black Nationalist," *Gender and Society* 6 (1992): 346-75.

[8] See Deborah Gray White, *Too Heavy a Load: Black Women in Defense of Themselves, 1894-1994* (New York: W.W. Norton, 1999), chapter 4; Keisha N. Benjamin, "How Did Rank and File Women in the Universal Negro Improvement Association (UNIA) Use the Woman's Page of *The Negro World* to Define the 'New Negro Woman'?" *Women and Social Movements, 1600-2000*, Vol. 12, no. 3 (September 2008).

[9] Eunice Lewis, "The Black Woman's Part in Race Leadership," *Negro World*, 19 April 1924.

[10] See Nathan Irvin Huggins, *Harlem Renaissance* (London: Oxford University Press, 1971); David Levering Lewis, *When Harlem Was in Vogue* (New York: Penguin Books, 1979); Houston A. Baker, *Modernism and the Harlem Renaissance* (Chicago: University of Chicago Press, 1987); Kathy J. Ogren, "'What is Africa to Me?': African Struggles in the Harlem Renaissance," in *Imagining Home: Class, Culture and Nationalism in the African Diaspora*, eds., Sidney Lemelle and Robin D.G. Kelley (London: Verso, 1994); Davarian L. Baldwin, *Chicago's New Negroes: Modernity, the Great Migration, and Black Urban Life* (Chapel Hill: University of North Carolina Press, 2007); Anastasia Curwood, *Stormy Weather: Middle-Class African American Marriages between the Two World Wars* (Chapel Hill: University of North Carolina Press, 2010); Erin D. Chapman, *Prove It On Me: New Negroes, Sex, and Popular Culture in the 1920s* (New York: Oxford University Press, 2012); Davarian L. Baldwin and Minkah Makalani, eds., *Escape from New York: the New Negro Renaissance Beyond Harlem* (Minneapolis: University of Minnesota Press, 2013).

[11] Martin, *Race First*, 91.

[12] Tony Martin, "Marcus Garvey and Trinidad, 1912-1947" in *Garvey: Africa, Europe, the Americas*, eds. Rupert Lewis and Maureen Warner-Lewis (Kingston, Jamaica: Institute of Social and Economic Research, 1986), 52.

[13] Bair, "Ethiopia Shall Stretch Forth, 39; Winston James, *Holding Aloft the Banner of Ethiopia: Caribbean Radicalism in Early Twentieth-Century America* (New York: Verso, 1998), 138.

[14] Bair, "Ethiopia Shall Stretch Forth," 48.

[15] Satter, "Marcus Garvey, Father Divine and the Gender Politics of Race Difference," 49.

[16] See Bair, "Ethiopia Shall Stretch Forth," 44-49.

[17] Duncan, "Efficient Womanhood," 125; Bair, "True Women, Real Men," 157. Also, see Anne Macpherson, "Colonial Matriarchs: Garveyism, Maternalism and Belize's Black Cross Nurses, 1920-1952" *Gender and History*, Volume 15, no. 3 (Nov. 2003): 507-527; Leah Michelle Seabrook, "Service in Green and White: The Activity and Symbolism of the Universal African Black Cross Nurses" (MA Thesis, University of California Irvine, 2006).

[18] Bair, "True Women, Real Men," 157.

[19] Rupert Lewis, *Marcus Garvey: Anti-Colonial Champion* (Trenton: Africa World Press, 1988), 68; Bair, "Ethiopia Shall Stretch Forth," 45.

[20] Bair, "Ethiopia Shall Stretch Forth," 45.

[21] Bair, "Ethiopia Shall Stretch Forth," 45.

[22] Martin, *Race First*, 27; Bair, "Ethiopia Shall Stretch Forth," 47.

[23] Taylor, *The Veiled Garvey*, 64-90.

[24] Long determined to deport Garvey, federal officials, under the instruction of J. Edgar Hoover, arrested Marcus Garvey in 1922 on charges of mail fraud for allegedly using the U.S. mail to promote and sell Black Star Line stock for ships that had yet to be purchased. After being sentenced to five years in prison, Garvey was later pardoned by President Calvin Coolidge and ordered to leave the country. Garvey was deported on December 2, 1927. On the reference to "antiquated beliefs," see Amy Jacques Garvey, "No Sex in Brains and Ability," *Negro World*, December 27, 1924.

[25] "Women's Party Wants Not Only Equal Rights, But Equal Responsibilities with Men," *Negro World*, February 2, 1924.

[26] The 1920s was at the beginning of the decade that the National Woman's Party (NWP) moved to center stage, as its leader, Alice Paul, advocated equality for all women. The NWP's endorsement of the Equal Rights Amendment signified a step toward women's expanded influence, and as far as Paul was concerned, it was the necessary step towards the swift attainment of complete equality. However, Paul's call for equality had its limitations. Her appeal for equality extended to white women only; the NWP excluded black women from its agenda. The NWP's stance reflected the position of numerous feminist organizations during the 1920s. See Kathryn Kish Sklar and Jill Dias, How Did the National Woman's Party Address the Issue of the Enfranchisement of Black Women, 1919–1924?" in *Women and Social Movements in the United States, 1600-2000* (1997).

[27] Sklar and Dias, "Enfranchisement of Black Women"; Paula Giddings, *When and Where I Enter: The Impact of Black Women on Race and Sex in America* (New York: William Murrow & Co., 1985), 160.

[28] Carrie Mero Leadett, "The Negro Girl of Today Has Become a Follower—Future Success Rests With Her Parents and Home Environment," *Negro World*, February 2, 1924.

[29] On Leadett's biography, see Robert A. Hill, ed., *Marcus Garvey and the Universal Negro Improvement Association Papers* (Berkeley: University of California Press, 1983-), vol. 6: 418.

[30] Michele Mitchell, *Righteous Propagation: African Americans and the Politics of Racial Destiny after Reconstruction* (Chapel Hill: University of North Carolina, 2004), 191-192.

[31] Carrie Mero Leadett, "The Negro Girl of Today Has Become a Follower—

Future Success Rests With Her Parents and Home Environment," *Negro World*, February 2, 1924.

[32] On Parham's biography, see Hill, *Marcus Garvey and the UNIA Papers*, vol. 6: 406.

[33] Saydee Parham, "The New Woman," *Negro World*, February 2, 1924.

[34] Honor Ford-Smith, "Women and the Garvey Movement in Jamaica" in *Garvey: His Work and Impact*, eds. Rupert Lewis and Patrick Bryan (Trenton: Africa World Press, 1991), 75; On Garvey's poetry, see Tony Martin, *The Poetical Works of Marcus Garvey* (Dover: Majority Press, 1983).

[35] Saydee Parham, "The New Woman," *Negro World*, February 2, 1924.

[36] Blanche Hall, "Woman's Greatest Influence is Socially," *Negro World*, October 4, 1924.

[37] Florence Bruce, "The Great Work of the Negro Woman Today," *Negro World*, December 27, 1924 (emphasis added).

[38] Ford-Smith, "Women and the Garvey Movement in Jamaica," 75-76.

[39] Madame Rhoda, "Our Women Think We Should Make Employment," *Negro World*, March 7, 1925.

[40] Amelia Sayers, "Half Million Dollar Churches and No Jobs," *Negro World*, November 29, 1924 (emphasis added).

[41] Vida Horsford, "The Woman's Part in Race Developments," *Negro World*, September 19, 1925.

[42] Rosa Lee Smith, "Managing a Household," *Negro World*, September 27, 1924.

[43] Rhoda and Sayers' statements, while revealing black women's frustration with men's criticism of working women, failed to address the socioeconomic conditions of the 1920s. Racism in the labor market restricted black men and women from obtaining white-collar jobs, and for the few jobs that they could obtain, blacks received meager salaries. For this reason, a typical working-class black male could not effectively provide for his family without the assistance of his wife. See Sharon Harley, "For the Good of Family and Race: Gender, Work and Domestic Roles in the Black Community, 1880-1930," *Signs* 15, no. 2 (Winter 1990): 336-49.

[44] Taylor, *Veiled Garvey*, 2; Ula Y. Taylor, "Negro Women are Great Thinkers as Well as Doers": Amy Jacques-Garvey and Community Feminism in the United States, 1924-1927, *Journal of Women's History*, vol. 12 (2000): 104-26.

[45] Here I am employing Linda Gordon's definition of feminism: "a critique of male supremacy, formed and offered in the light of a will to change it, which in turn assumes a conviction that it is changeable." See Gordon, "What's New in Women's History" in *Feminist Studies, Critical Studies*, ed. Theresa de Lauretis (Bloomington: Indiana University Press, 1986), 29. Garveyite women's writings on the women's page of the *Negro World* certainly reveal, among other things, a critique of male supremacy within the UNIA and their attempts to change it.

[46] Amelia Sayers, "Man is the Brain, Woman the Heart of Humanity," *Negro World*, November 8, 1924.

[47] Martin, *Poetical Works of Garvey*, 59.

[48] The author's last name is not provided.

[49] "The Ideal Wife," *Negro World*, April 5, 1924.

[50] "Thoughts on Matrimony," *Negro World*, May 10, 1924.

[51] Adler, "Always Leading Our Men in Service and Sacrifice," 358.

War and Redemption in the Cloth

Aleia Brown

The Freedom Quilting Bee (FQB) took life in the Alabama Black Belt. Originally named for the region's black topsoil, the identification reflected the rich and nutrient dense soil along the Mississippi River. Additionally, the enslaved people responsible for cultivating the land were black. Even after enslavement, the sharecroppers and tenants of the land were overwhelmingly black. Their environment was especially oppressive. Beyond living in an area muddied with intense racial disparities, a shared experience among many blacks in the South, they also lived in extreme isolation. The Mississippi River hid them away in one of its bends, surrounding the land on three of its four sides. Even as sharecroppers, the land still confined them, locking them away from other choices for financial gain. Regardless, the women in the community decided against being complicit in their oppression. The Freedom Quilting Bee used their quilts in an attempt to bring financial solvency to their community. They were fierce proponents of the civil rights movement by marching and providing funds for the movement. Quilting for these women was not simply a docile activity taking place in the home sphere. In a sense, the Freedom Quilting Bee used their craft a weapon against injustice used to bring financial solvency to the Boykin community.

Quilting for African American women has never served only as a craft or pastime. This foundation informs the activist work of the Freedom Quilting Bee. Harriet Powers (1837- 1910) two extant quilts, *Bible Quilt* (1886) and *Pictorial Quilt* (1898) provided the earliest example of African American women documenting their history and asserting their identity through quilts. While the Freedom Quilting Bee tended to produce improvisation quilts rather than narrative quilts like Harriet Powers, they still asserted their identity by sticking with an African aesthetic. FQB continued an established quilting tradition. Often left out of critical discussion was the fact that the women in the Bee came from families who had been quilting since the turn of the twentieth century.[1] They used a cultural resource unique to their heritage to create a solution for their community. When the FQB established their quilting cooperative in 1966, they also asserted independence and pride in their identity.

Beyond making quilts, these women also actively fought for their personal rights and their community's rights. Wilcox County officials closed the Gees Bend Ferry in 1962. A strategic move that further isolated the African American community, it deterred them from going to Camden to vote and earn a living.[2] A round-trip to Camden using the ferry service took just 30 minutes, while traversing the roads without the ferry was a two-hour round-trip. A USA Today article dated July 21, 2006 unfolds the story of the county finally reoffering the ferry service since they cut it off in 1962. Willie Quill Pettway recalled operating the ferry, transporting civil rights workers, protesters and voting activist.[3] Quilters like Estelle Witherspoon, were part of the movement, travelling to Camden on the ferry and also as far as Selma to encourage African Americans to rise above government imposed constraints and vote.

The Rural Development Leadership Network even acknowledged that Witherspoon went to jail along with early FQB members for their activities promoting civil rights. Witherspoon's lifelong dedication to social justice established an often-overlooked dimension of the Civil Rights movement. She inhabited a dimension that involved African American women using their creativity to gain justice and fiscal stability for their community. While these women heavily contributed to the collective, they rarely saw individual gain. Estelle Witherspoon died in 2001, six years before the government reinstated the ferry service that gave African

Americans access to political and employment.

Although the quilters lived in the very secluded Boykin, tucked away in Mississippi River's meandering folds, they still captured attention and made interesting connections. Reverend Francis X. Walter proved a tentative but ultimately helpful advocate for the Freedom Quilting Bee. Working with the Selma Interreligious Project during one of the most tragic and intense periods of the movement in the region, Walter struggled to maintain peace after deputy Tom L. Coleman shot and killed fellow Episcopal seminarian and civil rights advocate Jonathan Daniels. As evidenced in his journals, Walter also struggled to fully conceptualize racism as a lived experience. Discouraged, he proclaimed "Today I was plunged into the world of rent, lease, parity, debt... and loans, loans, loans... the tangle of tenant-landlord finance is so artfully constructed that it's impossible to know how a man can owe over $3,000- twice his historical income is hard to grasp."[4] After meeting at a conference, civil rights lawyer Vernon Jordan encouraged Reverend Walter to foster racial uplift through financial stability. This shift in thinking helped him conceptualize relationships, which led to influencing his relationship with FQB.

FQB and Reverend Walter connected over their shared goal to bring Wilcox County to financial solvency. Many of the people in the community had lost their homes and employment due to their work in the civil rights movement. After seeing the quilts and showing them to his wife, who was an artist; he proposed to creating an artistic cooperative with Estelle Witherspoon and Callie Young. Even with his support, the quilters still worked intentionally to relay that the women owned their history, furthering the weight they played in the role of moving their community forward.

Medical Anthropologist and Southern Rural Research Project

(SRRP) field worker Nancy Scheper Hughes stumbled upon FQB while surveying Wilcox County for tenant farmers and sharecroppers health, living and working conditions in 1967.[5] Her primary job was part of a large effort to establish environmental racism as a substantial problem and to hold the government accountable for it.[6] Hughes documented that the area once dominated by chattel slavery, now suffered in the slavery of hunger.[7] Health care and job opportunities were privileges that did not extend to the nearly all black town of Boykin. Even in the mist of degradation, and environmental and social isolation, Hughes looked beyond their living conditions to truly understand the people in the town. In writing about her experience, Hughes attempts to rectify the record, arguing that the people she studied in the Black Belt during the fading civil rights movement were more than just descendants of slaves.[8] The women were deeply spiritual and saw their quilting as a "godsend."[9] They had been quilting long before any scholarship or media covered their work. In their quilting groups, they started uniting around salient issues to their community like education, housing, paved roads and telephone lines.[10] Essentially, through her work, Hughes came to another way to critically conceptualize black women. FQB illustrated how African American women could unite and creatively solve problems in their community regardless of how bleak the situation seemed, even after educating the public about the injustices that every generation faced until the present.

Hughes eventually became an avid supporter of FQB, taking out a loan to facilitate their enterprise even after she completed her assignment as a field worker.[11] Even after moving to Cambridge, Massachusetts in 1968, Hughes still corresponded with Estelle Witherspoon. Witherspoon sent Hughes quilts, hoping that she would be able to sell them to craft and interior decorating shops in the New England states. Despite the small window of commercial success FQB garnered from Bloomingdales and other department stores, the African aesthetic did not thrill the Northerners. Also, their story and their organization's mission did not even move them to consider the purchase.[12] Although the organization did receive financial help from other northern foundations, clearly foundations and collectors alike did not unanimously support them. Perhaps it was their faith in God that carried them through difficult realizations.

Through careful strategy and helpful relationships the Freedom Quilting Bee creatively worked to empower their community. In 1966, the Bee hosted their first two auctions, which also occurred in the same year that they banded together as a cooperative. Reverend Walter and his wife Betty Mitchell Walter used their connections in New York so the quilters' work could gain maximum exposure. A photography studio in Central Park West hosted the show in March 27, 1966. Later the Unitarian-Universalist Community Church of New York hosted the second show on May 24, 1966. After the two auctions, the quilts began fetching $100. In addition to quilts, the quilters produced quilted bedspreads, sunbonnets and potholders. Their marketing and public relations transformed from word of mouth to full-length feature articles in the New York Times. Two years after the cooperative formed, Rita Reif penned an article that shed light on the Bee's mission to overcome racial oppression by creating their own opportunities for financial solvency.[13] This exposure opened new doors for the quilters.

The New York Arts Foundation awarded the Bee $5,000 in 1968 and another $2,500 in 1971. On February 18, 1969 Reverend Walter wrote a letter of gratitude to President of the New York Arts Foundation John Hayman thanking him for donating the funds. This money, along with the profits the quilters earned went toward the construction of the Martin Luther King, Jr. Memorial Sewing Center, where they would employee residents and also provide affordable daycare for working mothers. Profits rolled in from endorsements from the likes of interior decorator Sister Parish.[14] *Vogue* editor Diana Vreeland also used her influence to promote the quilts and their unusually imaginative aesthetic. Ultimately Bloomingdale's and Saks Fifth Avenue both carried quilt lines. The Bee succeeded in transitioning from navigating a minefield that prevented them from participating in civil rights activism through blacklisting their jobs and mortgages, to becoming self-sufficient entrepreneurs. The women carried their community into a new age of independence and new opportunities.

Although the women dramatically increased opportunities for their community, they did not necessarily benefit from the cooperative framework. As noted earlier, the men in the community did not always support the women's newfound independence. Their work disturbed social and economic norms. Reverend Walter offered the insight that "if a man works from sun up to sun down chopping cotton for $2 a day, it is hard for him to see his wife earn as much or more in shorter hours."[15] Outside of social issues, the women also faced the harsh reality that their community made major strides towards financial solvency, while they struggled individually. In 1967, the most skilled and highest paid quilter only made $500 that year after the cooperative took its share.[16] Her family depended on her sole income to support them. Additionally, their individual form of personal expression eventually went out of style. As the early 1980s approached, folk art lost its popularity and orders for their work waned.[17] The quilters never individually maintained financial stability beyond the late 1970s.

Undeniably, the Freedom Quilting Bee fueled their community and a movement through a critical time and space of racial tension and oppression. Their unique place and actions in history stand out because they contributed to the Civil Rights Movement as it began to lose steam and the Black Power Movement began to take its place. Repeatedly, the women of FQB explained their efforts as divine appointment. They were simply doing the work of the God they served. Understanding their guiding principles illuminates why they chose to partner with Reverend Francis X. Walter and Nancy Scheper Hughes. It may also explain why they did not allow their desperate situation to inhibit their faith or creativity.

The women worked tirelessly to improve their community through mastering financial fluency. Revenue from the quilts went toward housing for activists who were kicked out of their houses and jobs at the Community Center for those who lost their jobs. Despite their contributions to the collective, it is not as evident that the women made major individual strides from their efforts. Even in their own racial sphere, African American men did not always support the Bee's efforts. Hughes noted that some of the men verbalized that women were becoming too modern and spent more time advocating in public than fulfilling their traditional responsibilities at home.[18] Beyond their social constraints, the more recent past has presented new struggles. Most of the quilters cannot afford to purchase their own work. Collectors who purchased FBQ work when the quilts sold for $15 have the opportunity to make far more substantial profits than the quilters. Additionally, two quilters associated with the Bee and Gee's Bend have suspected that certain brands are using their quilt images without proper authority to the point that they took major brands to court. Ultimately, the individual quilters do not have control over the tools they used to advance their community collectively.

[1] In "Anatomy of a Quilt: Gees' Bend Freedom Quilting Bee," Nancy Scheper Hughes attempted to offer more insight about how the women contributed to the Civil Rights movement, she mentions makes the point that quilting was an established activity.

[2] In the 2006 USA Today article "Ferry carries symbolic weight," Gees Bend Ferry Commission Chair Hollis Curl cites the official reason for the ferry service discontinuing because they needed to start a service upstream so that the mill workers could get to work. He also noted the unofficial reason, which involved keeping blacks from registering to vote.

[3] Mike, Linn, "Ferry carries symbolic weight," *USA Today*, 2006.

[4] Taken from an oral history first published in Susan Youngblood Ashmore's *Carry it on: The War on Poverty and the Civil Rights movement in Alabama.*

[5] Nancy Scheper Hughes, "Anatomy of a Quilt: Gees' Bend Freedom Quilting Bee," *Anthropology Today 19*, no. 4, (August 2003): 15.

[6] The SRRP was a Student Nonviolent Coordinating Committee (SNCC) affiliated legal rights project. In 1968 the SRRP filed a class action lawsuit on behalf of hungry children, *people v. the US Department of Agriculture.* Though SRRP lost the case, they won a decent amount of media coverage, and landed a documentary on CBS. See Hughes "Anatomy of a Quilt" for more information on the outcomes outside of the courthouse.

[7] Hughes, "Anatomy of a Quilt," 16.

[8] Ibid., 15.

[9] Ibid., 18.

[10] Ibid.

[11] Ibid., 19.

[12] Ibid.

[13] Rita Reif, "The Freedom Quilting Bee: A Cooperative Step Out of Poverty," *New York Times,* 1968.

[14] Sister Parish (1910- 1994) is most recognized for her interior decorator work in the White House during the Kennedy administration.

[15] Rita Reif, "The Freedom Quilting Bee: A Cooperative Step Out of Poverty," *New York Times,* 1968.

[16] Ibid.

[17] Victoria F. Phillips, "Symposium: Commodification, Intellectual Property and the Quilters of Gee's Bend," *Journal of Gender, Social Policy & the Law* 15, no. 2 (2007): 365.

[18] Ibid.

Barbara Christian: Fighting For Black Women's Literary Voices

Charise Charleswell

Introduction

Barbara Christian, esteemed professor, path-breaking scholar, pioneer of contemporary American literary feminism, spent much of her career championing the contribution of Black women's literary voices. She was born in 1943, on the island of St Thomas Virgin Islands, in the Caribbean, just 26 years after the territory was transferred from Denmark to the United States. Christian graduated from St. Peter and Paul's school at the age of 15 as Valedictorian. A year earlier, 1t 14, she won the Virgin Islands-wide High School Oratorical Contest and was invited to skip 12th grade and enter Howard University. However, she declined, preferring to graduate with her high school classmates.[1] Christian graduated with honors from Marquette University in Illinois, and was selected as the keynote speaker for the student body of the entire University. She later completed a master's and doctorate degrees, with distinction from Columbia University, where she was the first woman in the contemporary British and American Literature Program.[1]

She joined the faculty of the City College of the City University of New York in 1965 as a member of the English Department. There she was appointed as an instructor in the pioneering SEEK (Search for Education, Elevation, & Knowledge) program. This appointment and the program were quite significant. The SEEK program is seen as the greatest legislative accomplishment of Shirley Chisholm, who was also Caribbean-American. Chisholm became the first African American woman elected to the New

York State Assembly. Her SEEK program, and the dedicated activist-educators like Christian, paved the way for open admission at CUNY, which provided opportunities for promising, but underprivileged students from low-income, working-class, African-American, Latino, and immigrant backgrounds. The program helped to transform CUNY into a system that is more representative of the city of New York, and it continues to do so today.

Later at the University of California Berkeley, Professor Christian helped to establish the university's first African-American Studies Department, and in 1978was the first African-American woman to be granted tenure at UC Berkeley. Then in 1986, she was the first African-American promoted to full professor, and between 1978 and 1983, she served as Chairperson for the Department of African American Studies at Berkeley. Continuing on this path of academic excellence and leadership, between 1986 and 1989, she was chair of the recently formed Ethnic Studies doctoral program at the university. From 1971 to 1976, she also served as a founding member and teacher with the University Without Walls, a community based alternative college committed to providing education to people of color. She later would go on to be awarded the City of Berkeley's highest honor, the Berkeley Citation.

Her Work & Its Socio-cultural Importance

Professor passed away on July 25, 2000, succumbing to lung cancer. However, within her short 56 years, she was able to have a great impact on American literary culture, where she authored and edited several books, and published almost 100 articles and reviews. In 1980, she published her landmark study, "Black Women Novelists: The Development of a Tradition", which helped to usher in the rediscovery of the work of work black women writers such as Zora Neale Hurston and Nella Larsen. She also helped to focus national attention on the then-emerging writers, Toni Morrison, Alice Walker, and Paule Marshall; earning her praise for doing more than any other person, to bring black women writers into academic and popular recognition. She followed up again in 1998, with another groundbreaking essay, "The Race for Theory", which passionately called for the inclusion of the Black women's writings in critical discourse, and helping to form the foundation of Black feminist literary criticisms.

Other work of Professor Christian include:

1. From The Inside Out: Afro-American Women's Literary Tradition and the State
2. Female Subjects in Black and White Race, Psychoanalysis, Feminism
3. What Do Black Feminist Critics Do? A Look at The Color Purple.
4. From the Inside Out: Afro-American Women's Literary Tradition and the State.
5. Black Women Novelists: The Development of a Tradition, 1892-1976
6. "But What Do We Think We're Doing Anyway?" in Changing Our Own Words: Essays on Criticism, Theory, and Writing by Black Women
7. Diminishing Returns: Can Black Feminism(S) Survive in the Academy
8. Editing the 1970s – 1990s section of the Norton Anthology of African American Literature
9. New Black Feminist Criticism, 1985 -2000

Ultimately, her work was an act of rebellion against the status quo of the "literary elite" who attempted to negate the importance of Black women writers, and who did not deem black critical writers as eloquent enough. Christian was well aware of the fact that social attitudes and mainstream critiques initially down-played the artistic contribution of these writers. Further she found the literature did not accurately reflect the complexity of Black womanhood, and instead focused on stereotypical images such as the mammy, concubine, and conjure woman.

In the text Black Feminist Criticism: Perspectives on Black Women Writers she offers the following commentary about Lutie Johnson's novel The Street, to illustrate this point: "The Street combines some of the characteristics of the various Black female stereotypes of the previous century. She is a domestic working in the rich white folks' home, northern style. She is a mother struggling to protect her child, not only form overt physical danger, but also from the more hidden patterns of castration and debasement sketched by the concrete plantations of the North. She is a "brown, good-looking-girl", plagued by the sexual advances of men, both black and white, who would use her as a sexual object in much the same way the Black female slave was used. She is struggling to survive, working overtime, no longer bearing the legal status of the slave, but a slave nonetheless in the framework of society".[2] Christian would argue that these experiences of Black women, thief suffering of dual oppression—were critical subjects for literature.[3]

One has to understand the role that literature plays in society, in order to truly appreciate Christian's efforts; and to understand why the amplification of the voices of Black women writers is imperative. Literature is purely a reflection of society – its good values, ills, as well as the prevailing attitudes held by members of a particular society. Essentially, what is seen in this "reflection" is what people say, think, and do. For any given society and culture, particularly the American society, there is a sub-culture; and the everyday realities of those within a sub-culture are often ignored or remained unknown. Literature can help to illuminate their stories, and does so by educating the reader. Readers are able to learn about people, communities, and cultures that may be foreign to them or not greatly understood; and what they carry away are new viewpoints, outlook, or knowledge that they can bring to society. Ultimately, it is this in depth understanding that often helps to bring about needed social change. It is for this reason, that Professor Christian worked tirelessly to ensure that the work of Black women writers were able to reach a broader audience.

The work of these Black women writers was indeed ground-breaking and transformative. Christian would note that, "They shattered the stereotypical images of Black women and dealt with 'forbidden' subjects like slavery and the way Black women were shaped by and survived in spite of, its bitter legacy". [3]

Black Feminist Pioneer

Professor Christian was a pioneer of contemporary American literary feminism. She was also well known for her critical presence in the growing debates over the relationship between race, class, and gender; a debate which culminated into the theory of intersectionality, coined by Kimberlee Crenshaw in1989.

Her work, But Who Do You Really Belong to -- Black Studies or Women's Studies?, speaks to this problem of intersecting factors that Black women have to endure; and again in the canonical text The Race For Theory, she states that -- We need to read the works of our writers in our various ways and remain open to the intricacies of the intersection of language, class, race, and gender in the literature. She went on to elaborate on this matter, by pointing out a critical problem within feminism, and that is that "seldom do feminist theorist take into account the complexity of life-- that women are of many races and ethnic backgrounds with different histories and cultures and that as a rule women belong to different classes that have different concerns". [4]

A number of African American intellectuals who argued that the work of Black female writers, particularly Alice Walker, weakened the struggle for Black people by presenting a negative image of Black men. In 1985, Tony Brown, a syndicated columnist and host of the television program Tony Brown's Journal, called the film The Color Purple, based on Alice Walker's novel, "the most racist depiction of Black men since The Birth of a Nation and the most anti-Black family film in the modern era."[5] While Black novelist, Ishmael Reed, a Black novelist labeled the film and book a "Nazi conspiracy". Professor Christian responded to the backlash, controversy, and criticism by arguing the following, "The patriarchal actions of men in these novels are not portrayed as inherent male evils, but as rooted in the oppressive structure of society." [3] In other words, she did not feel it necessary for Black women to silently suffer and not address sexism within their community in their work, in an attempt at solidarity. Instead, this oppression must be acknowledged in order to have meaningful discussions that could bring about needed structural and social changes. Further, it is imperative for Black women writers to tell their unique experiences, including those that are a result of their gender. As pointed out by Christian in the following, there was a need, and continues to be a need to not only create these works, but help them to garner the same amount of acclaim and attention as stories that focus on the hardships and lives of Black men:

Maud Martha, Gwendolyn Brook's only novel, appeared in 1953, the same year that Go Tell It On The Mountain, James Baldwin's first novel, was published.....although she was an established Pulitzer Prize winning poet, Brook's novel quietly went out of print while Baldwin's first publication was to become known as a major Afro-American novel. Brook's novel, like Baldwin's, presents the development of a young urban

Black into an adult, albeit Brook's major character is female and Baldwin's is male. Her understated rendition of a Black American girl's development into womanhood did not arouse in the reading public the intense reaction that Baldwin's dramatic portrayal of the Black male did.

Professor Christian's second book was actually entitled, "Black Feminist Criticism". The book utilized a feminist lens to conduct literary analysis, and made the assertion that literature is simply an abstract representation of Black women throughout the Diaspora and our complex lives. Further the importance of Black feminist writers was to ensure that this complexity is depicted. As a Caribbean-American, Christian understood the need to build bridges between Black feminists and Third World Feminists, and to be actively engaged with Trans-national feminist movements. In carrying out this work of bringing Black American feminism(s) into productive dialogues with Black women and other women of color all over the world, she compiled the teaching volume, "African Diaspora Feminisms".

Activist Scholar

She applied her overwhelming social consciousness not only the sphere of academia, but also engaged in conscious activism. Christian eagerly and vocally engaged in activism in support of affirmative action, as well as issues related to women and gender. She utilized her public-and-international platform to draw attention to these issues. This was done through numerous teach-ins, talks, and of course through her writing; which offered a critical analysis of social conditions and injustice. Often she would make these points through her commentary of the literary work of authors, whose characters were impacted by various forms of oppression – whether it be race or gender-based. She was amongst those in the struggle to save Ethnic Studies within the UC system, and she would stand in solidarity with the students, by leaving her home and standing between them and the police.

Her Legacy

During a career spanning more than 30 years, Barbara Christian's life work was advocating for the inclusion, respect, analysis, and critical discourse on the work of Black female writers, and how their writings offered honest critiques of American society, as well as contributes to American culture. In carrying out this work she helped to make this important and liberating literature of the ignored and oppressed known, respected, appreciated, and loved world-wide. Her literary criticism and efforts supported and continues to legitimize they attempt of African-American women writers to define and express their totality rather than being defined by others.

Her lasting legacy remains her contribution to the development of the fields of African Diaspora studies, feminist studies, and literary theory. In 2001, the Caribbean Studies Association established the Barbara T. Christian Literary Award. If you have read the works of notable Black female authors, such as Toni Morrison, Paule Marshall, Alice Walker, or even Zora Neale Hurston, then you should know that it was partially due to the work and unrelenting commitment of Barbara Christian that those novels made it into your hands, or onto a movie screen. Nobody did more to bring Black women writers into academic and popular recognition. In carrying out this work, Professor Christian notably stated that, "I know, from history, that writing disappears unless there is a response to it", [4] and that is her greatest legacy, her response to and championing of the work of Black female authors, which included commentary that not only provided analysis and critique of the works of literature, but American society as a whole.

Conclusion

In her own words and in the text, The Race for Theory, Barbara Christian shares the following sentiments about why she choose to carry out her life's work, ""I can only speak for myself. But what I write and how I write is done in order to save my own life. And I mean that literally. For me literature is a way of knowing that I am not hallucinating, that whatever I feel/know is." The following poem by award-winning artist, Dr. Opal Palmer Adisa, pays tribute to Christian and speaks to her legacy:

CHANTING BARBARA HOME

you be a talking
seeing righters
sister opening
our eyes and
reading us like
a mirror

you be a
person-loving
giving sister
welcoming all
into a circle
of knowing
and friendship

you be a
generous-door-keeper
fierce tenacious
laughing and
dancing us into
new space

you be
one of us
we be
one of you
you be
creating
space for
us to be
free

you be
our ancestor [6]

Works Cited

1.   Christian C.L.E. (2006). Tribute to my sister: Barbara T. Christian. St John   Source.   Retrieved   on   April   1,   2014   from http://stjohnsource.com/content/community/people/2000/06/27/tribute-my-sister-barbara-t-christian

2.   Christian, B. (1997). Black feminist criticism. Teachers College Press. New York, NY.

3.   Revolutionary Worker. (2000). Barbara Christian (1943-2000): A fierce scholar. Revolutionary Worker #1082. Retrieved on April 1, 2014 from http://www.revcom.us/a/v22/1080-89/1082/bchris.htm

4.   Christian, B. (1988). The race for theory. Feminist Studies. 14(1):67-79.

5.   Bobo J. (1988). Black women's responses to the Color Purple. Jump Cut: A Review of Contemporary Media. 33:43-51. Retrieved on April 2, 2014 from: http://www.ejumpcut.org/archive/onlinessays/JC33folder/CIPurpleBobo.html

6.   Palmer OA. (2000). Barbara Christian, Caribbean American pioneer. Rootsweb-Caribbean-L-Archives. Retrieved on March 31, 2014 from http://archiver.rootsweb.ancestry.com/th/read/CARIBBEAN/2000-06/0962141582

Pushing Daisy:

The Activism, Leadership, and (Un)Respectable Politics of Daisy Bates

Kelisha B. Graves

On the evening of August 22, 1957, Daisy Bates strolled the neighborhood with her dog, Skippy. That evening, her mind churned ceaselessly over the imminent bid of nine Negro teenagers to integrate Little Rock's Central High School. She had only just returned home from walking the dog and was sitting in front of her cherished grandiose picture window when an object erupted through the glass. Bates threw herself to the floor, suffering only a few of cuts. Around the rock that cut a shattered path was wrapped a menacing promise, "Stone this time. Dynamite the next." This merchandise of white aggression to the cause for civil rights revealed the violence, rhetorical and real, that would plague the Bates abode for the duration of the school desegregation struggle of 1957.[1]

That night, Daisy Bates was displayed to the community as a woman of gargantuan grit and guile. "Their aim is damned poor," said the tiny 5-foot 3-inch and 125-pound Bates. "Their luck might run out before mine does."[2] That Bates could dismiss the nefarious aim at her life as "damned poor" disclosed not only her ability to absorb the agonies and accouterments of leadership with remarkable aplomb, but also her reluctance to bare wound or weakness to the enemy. It was this reflexive attitude that "just blew people's minds," according to her friend Brynda Pappas. "Who is this woman sounding like this? Who does she think she is?"[3]

While the explicit goal of the 1957 Little Rock movement was to force the local school board to abide by the Brown v. Board of Education mandate of 1954, the implicit experiment was the leadership of Daisy Bates both as a contradiction to mainstream behavioral norms and a challenge to the traditional panorama of black male leadership in the civil rights movement.

41

Because the seminal nature of her leadership operated against the context of a civil rights struggle that was not singularly focused on advancing gender equality, but rather racial equality, Bates would face the daunting task of creating a novel brand of female leadership without the benefit of a preexisting pattern.

In view of recent historiography, Daisy Bates' life offers a glimpse into the intersections of race, gender, and the myriad recriminations aimed at a black woman who occupied a role outside of patriarchal norms. The idea that Bates' unconventional leadership challenged a canopy of patriarchal ideals is worthy of examination in terms of the ways her leadership shifted ideas about how women should participate in civic and political affairs. Thus, she expanded definitions about what could be achieved in a black female body by using aesthetic as a political instrument of respectability and by defining a role that would allow her to enact her own ire against injustice while also defying the expectations of patriarchy.

Little Girl Lost: Realizing Race and Gender

The tough burden of black folks to eke out an identity against the onslaught of white supremacy is what W.E.B. Du Bois proposed would be the problem of the twentieth century. Trapped in the toil of double consciousness —Du Bois called it a "peculiar sensation…the sense of always looking at one's self through the eyes of others…an American, a Negro; two souls, two thoughts, two reconciled strivings"— it would be the task of twentieth century black folks to discover confidence and courage against the psychological poison of black inferiority that was pumped into their brains.4

The day seven-year-old Daisy Lee Gatson saw herself in the context of color her mother had not been feeling well. "You'll have to go to the market to get the meat for dinner," her mother ordered. Daisy grabbed a dollar, "put on one of my prettiest dresses," and "skipped happily" to the market, keeping in mind the instruction that she was to get a pound of "center-cut pork chops."5 Just when Daisy arrived to the market, several whites were waiting to be served.

Daisy had not immediately noticed that the butcher was ignoring her until a young white girl, who had come into the market after her, was served first. When Daisy pleaded for the specific meat her mother had requested the butcher flung a piece of fatty meat at her and made brutally clear the protocols of race: "Niggers have to wait 'til I wait on the white people. Now take your meat and get out of here!"6

Disgraced, Daisy cried all the way home. Although, "I knew I was a Negro," Bates wrote in her autobiography, she neither understood the sociological implications of race nor the caveats color carried. If Daisy Gatson now understood the reality of racism, then her color shock was compounded by the powerlessness of her parents to avenge her.7

Daisy's father, Ora Lee Smith, was a mill worker, a member of the NAACP, and the first black man she genuinely loved. However, his inability to protect her from the grief of racial humiliation debuted her to the impotency black men faced under the crush of white supremacy. "Daddy, are you afraid?" Daisy innocuously inquired of her father. "Hell, no! I'm not afraid for myself, I'm not afraid to die." He insisted that he could "go down to that market and tear limb from limb…but I am afraid for you and your mother." Ora Lee Smith represented the powerlessness that pressed against the aching yearn and urgency of twentieth century black men to protect the wives and daughters they cared about. That evening, against all formal indoctrination, Daisy prayed that the butcher would die.8

According to historian John A. Kirk, "our lack of knowledge about Bates' personal life is partly because of historians having imposed their own (typically masculine) reading of her role in the movement and concluded that what is important about Bates is her role in public life."9 To be sure, Daisy

Bates' sociological roots cannot be ignored in terms of making sense of the experiences that shaped her racial ecology and incited in her a personal fury against forms of injustice. In the late sixties, the enormously gifted Maya Angelou wrote: "If growing up is painful for the Southern Black girl, being aware of her displacement is the rust on the razor that threatens the throat."10 The idea of "displacement" offers a double discourse because it not only speaks to the social implications of black skin, but also reveals the vulnerability of black female life under the ugly ubiquity of Jim Crow. Ignorance had indeed been bliss for Daisy Lee Gatson and in retrospect she might have preferred ignorance to pain, but if the reality of racial displacement was not enough to pull her self-esteem asunder, the revelation that she did not "belong" to the Smiths would rip to shreds her sense identity and thereby activate a lifelong a crusade to find a "place" and to make it her own.

Daisy had just made eight when she discovered that her biological mother, Millie Riley Gatson, had been viciously raped and murdered by three white men. Her biological father, Hezekiah Gatson, gave her away to his "best friends," Ora Lee and Susie Smith. He fled town and never returned.11 "For Daisy it undercut her emotional growth and development," explained Sybil Jordan Hampton. "She didn't have well-being and she didn't have security."12

The painful lesson learned was that she lived in a world where the bodies of black folks (and black women in particular) were ubiquitously and unanimously unprotected. Bates wrote in her autobiography, "I sat there looking into the dark waters, vowing that someday I would get the men who killed my mother."13 Daisy's interest in the once cherished merchandises of her childhood —"dolls, games, even my once-beloved fishing"— waned as happiness soured into bitterness. She described herself as "so happy once, now I was like a little sapling, which after a violent storm, only puts out gnarled and twisted branches." She confessed, "I now had a secret goal —to find the men who had done this horrible thing to my mother."14

It was this vengeance that gnawed into her personality a deep aversion to all white people. On his deathbed, Ora Lee Smith, counseled his impetuous daughter against the hate she harbored and he encouraged her to find an outlet that would be consistent with his own legacy of community activism. "Hate can destroy you, Daisy," he warned. "Don't hate white people just because they are white. If you hate, make it count for something."15

Activism and the Segue to Leadership

Joining the NAACP was probably not on Daisy's list of priorities as much as finding an escape from her broken childhood environment was. By the time Ora Lee Smith died, Daisy was left to battle a foster mother whose religious fanaticism brushed against her own burgeoning irreverence. Years earlier, she had shocked her mother when she refused to perform in the church Christmas play, arguing, "I don't want no part of that play about a dead white doll!"16 As John Kirk explained in his essay, Daisy viewed "religion as a site of white oppression rather than black liberation."17 Inasmuch as the black church represented the "central focal point of black women's networks and socialization in many southern communities" Bates disillusionment with the institution illumines her yearn to find a form of social expression that did not emanate from a religious or traditional gendered context. Whereas black women routinely found their opportunity to participate in civic affairs through the black church and black women's clubs, this was not the context that sired or inspired the activism of Daisy Bates.18

Against her mother's indoctrination, Daisy pursued the secular more than the spiritual. At fifteen, she found love with a man twelve years her senior and an escape from the repressive policies Susie Smith imposed.19 By the time Daisy Gatson met Lucious Christopher Bates —called L.C. and described as "the kind of man who seemed born old"20— he was still married. That L.C. Bates was a married man with children when they began their relationship would later represent for Daisy Bates —in her mania to remain respectable— a moral blight that her public image could not afford.

Nevertheless, the couple left Arkansas and lived (albeit scandalously) in Memphis, Tennessee before settling in Little Rock in the early 1940s. L.C. Bates launched the Arkansas State Press in 1941 and the couple married in March of 1942.21 In view of her later prominence, it is clear that having a part in the State Press not only pushed Daisy to develop a brain that was pointed beyond the material accouterments she gained through her marriage to L.C., but also enabled her to "have a 'say' in community affairs without working through existing networks of black activism."22 In this way, the State Press empowered her to turn anger into positive activism. "The State Press gave Daisy a platform," recalled Brynda Pappas. "She found her sense of assurance. She came to understand how being a role model and being out front can lead people."23

In time, the Bateses grew in reputation. They built their "dream house" in a predominantly white neighborhood and hobnobbed with local doctors and lawyers. While neither Daisy nor L.C. proclaimed any organic tie to the black bourgeoisie, their status as self-employed black business owners offered them a way into that world.24 Daisy, who particularly enjoyed Little Rock's trendy Ninth Street, joined nearly twenty-two civic and political organizations, although without any particular function. She would later hold a position on the board of the Arkansas Council of Human Relations —a position with access to cross-racial relationships.25

While rumor implied that L.C. was the brains behind the beauty and while it was true that he was Daisy's first tutor, the truth is that she possessed an enormous social genius that could not be taught or caught by L.C. She was naturally friendly and preferred people who "have an outgoing personality."26 Immediately, her effervescent personality and quick laugh rendered her the more visible partner while her husband's relative reclusiveness rendered him more suited to the background. "She was no dummy," Lee Lorch told Bates biographer Grif Stockley, refuting the charge that Daisy was little more than L.C. in svelte miniature. "I regarded her as having a considerable amount of ability."27

By the early 1950s, Daisy had earned her keep as co-publisher of the *State Press*. From this pedestal of rhetorical power, Bates spilled scathing rebukes not only against the white bigotry that expelled black citizens from the precincts of social privilege, but also against the lethargy and pecuniary gluttony of local black leaders. Bates' protégé, Ozell Sutton, has recalled that both Daisy and L.C. were "as condemning of complacent black leadership as they were of what they considered to be reactionary white leadership."28 While Bates used journalism as an artery through which to secrete her own ire against the racism and discrimination that crushed black lives, her willingness to rebuke Little Rock's male leadership pitted her against every gender protocol she had been groomed as a lady to respect.

In 1948, disenchanted with the local NAACP branch because "they weren't doing enough to combat discrimination," Bates spearheaded what the national office deemed a snub to the existing chapter. She rounded up a group of fifty people and attempted to establish a separate Pulaski County chapter of the NAACP, naming herself as president. The national office denied her bid.29

In 1952, she ran again and this round for president of the Arkansas State Conference of NAACP branches. Bates vied for leadership on both the belief that the revolutionary culture of the struggle demanded all able bodies and the "realization that she could not succeed except under conditions that she personally dominated."[30] It was a gutsy grab that angered the established vanguard. Judith and Dennis Fradin noted in their biography on Bates, "Some older black leaders insisted that she was too militant and would cause trouble. One warned she might 'go off the deep end at times' pursuing justice for her people."[31]

While her ego rubbed some the wrong way, by the late 1950s Daisy Bates' aggressive tendencies proved a boon to the NAACP's reputation. Even if the national office did not always appreciate or understand her operational tactics during the Little Rock Crisis, they would revel in the publicity her gargantuan gifts generated toward the organization. Stockley noted, "Bates used what weapons she had: charm and a capacity for guile that might have even surprised her enemies."[32] NAACP Deputy Executive Director Gloser Current confirmed in a phone conversation with Daisy that the sheer force of her personality abetted the goals of the organization, "This is when the Daisy Bates personality is standing us in good stead."[33]

Bending Expectations:
Respectability and the Implications of Leadership

Bates' ascent to the presidency of the state NAACP is essential in the sense that her ambition proved the possibility that women could lead and be effective. Her position as state president of the NAACP and self-appointed role as mentor to the Little Rock Nine is widely documented and will not be discussed specifically in this essay. However, the idea that she deployed respectability as a political instrument of advancement is central to the thesis that Bates shifted ideas about the potency of black womanhood in leadership.

In his treatise on the racial politics in Little Rock, Irving J. Spitzberg wrongly stated, "Daisy Bates was not a charismatic leader... [she] could not be a national personality and a local leader at the same time, for she did not have the charismatic appeal..."[34] By 1957, Daisy Bates was a petite power package of woman with a daunting measure of charm. In fact, the press preferred Daisy to the surplus of male attorneys "pontificating about constitutional rights."[35] Even if Daisy Bates was not the most rhetorically gifted speaker —L.C. wrote most of her speeches and she often dictated to secretaries because of her own insecurities about her educational background— she certainly compensated with a flair for improvisation and an ability to excellently look the part.[36]

Inasmuch as Bates did not habitually mingle with domestics or maids, there was no room to argue that class saved her from the pernicious labels that arched over black womanhood. However, class did allow Daisy Bates to deploy the material accouterments of her social and economic category to the benefit of her race. In this way she was like most African Americans of the early twentieth century who strove to push back the ugly stereotypes that loomed over black progress. In the same way Evelyn Brooks Higginbotham argued that black Baptist women used respectability as a counter-discourse to the malicious manifestos of white supremacy, Bates "promoted respectability as an aspiration, as a cornerstone of racial advancement, and as a responsibility of girls and women."[37] "All I knew was how to be a lady," Daisy Bates told the *Pittsburgh Courier* in 1957. "My father had drilled that into me."[38]

If Daisy Bates used her body as a metaphor for black female survival and success, then she was certainly a cinematographic sensation during the Little Rock Crisis. She carried a magnetic personality that was capsuled in a stunningly svelte size-five frame with "delicate hands," a "doll-like waist" and "child-sized feet."[39] A coiffed bloom of ebony curls cupped a pretty café au lait visage and her occasional hand-on-the-hip stance secreted a haughtiness that was both charming and beguiling. In an era before the black female revolutionism of the 1970s became sexy, Bates was the image of a glamorous revolutionary who was effortlessly elegant in the style of a Lena Horne or a Dorothy Dandridge.

As a young black girl in Arkansas, Janis Kearney, who would work with Bates later in life, was moved by the sheer elegance of a local celebrity. "She was the epitome of...elegant," Kearney recalled of first meeting Bates. "She could easily have stepped out of the pages of *Look*, *Life*, or *Ebony* magazines."[40] L.C.'s first cousin, Lottie Neely, recalled that Daisy "taught me about clothes and how to dress. She loved to wear high heels, 3-inch heels.

Everything was right—her hair, her nails, her clothes."[41] Carlotta Walls Lanier, one of the Little Rock Nine, was similarly flattered. Mrs. Bates "wouldn't be caught anywhere without being perfectly made up, head to toe," said Lanier, "but pity the man who mistook her ladylike ways as a sign of weakness. She was tough to the core, with razor sharp edges."[42] Kearny concurs, "The people who were initially only attracted to her beauty, would soon learn that there was so much more to her."[43]

In view of the growing significance of imagery to the civil rights movement, television and media gave Bates a forum through which to project the potency of positive black female imagery. Janis Kearny considers this much true: "She was smart enough to know that people – both men and women —would pay attention to her, often without knowing what she stood for. They would react to her beauty and style."[44] In this way Bates incorporated the politics of respectability into her fight against injustice and the grace and dignity she secreted evangelized an efficacious message, namely that professionalism nourished self-esteem and helped to shift disfigured images of black womanhood. Even as she was called "a whore," "a commie," "a bitch," and "an instigator," Bates strictly controlled how she presented herself and the precision she practiced in her appearance was a powerful campaign against a legacy of vicious rhetorical labels.[45]

Daisy Bates' insistence on respectability revealed a personal mania for public perfection and a tendency to dissemble when it came to emotion. Bates rarely, if ever, bared her emotions in public. She brandished a concrete persona that cocooned the softer woman. Jefferson Thomas, one of the youngest of the Little Rock Nine, reflected that he saw a side of Bates that few others saw. "She felt she shouldn't show weakness before the public" for fear that "they might think they were wearing her down [or] getting to her, but, I saw her in tears a lot of times for the things that were happening to us."[46]

Bates certainly saw herself as a surrogate mother to the nine children, and while few of them would endorse that label, as one observer noted, Daisy Bates guided the Little Rock Nine with the precision of a "drill sergeant."[47] For Bates, respectability was a point of pride and she understood what Evelyn Brooks Higginbotham phrased as "the significance of individual behavior to the collective imaging of black people."[48] In her autobiography, *Warriors Don't Cry*, Melba Patillo Beals recalled Mrs. Bates' insistence on excellence during a court hearing. " 'Smile, kids.' Mrs. Bates whispered. 'Straighten your shoulders. Stand tall.' [...] 'Melba, we're inside now. Take off those dark glasses.' " When they got distracted, Patillo Beals remembered, Bates promptly corrected them, "Sit up straight. Think about what you'll have to say if you're called to testify."[49] Minnijean Brown Trickey, who was the most tempestuous of the nine, recalled somewhat bitterly in a 2003 interview, "Daisy did all the speaking…I don't know if she thought that people weren't articulate enough, but they were."[50] Brown Trickey added, "Daisy was kind of imperious. She liked to tell people to do this, do that, do this at the point when she became such a heroine, you know at the point that she became the center of it."[51] Ernest Green understood Bates, "I don't think that my mother wanted to be the heroine of Little Rock. Daisy became the logical person…and she wanted to [do it]. [In] 1957 there's no long line of people…trying to step up to be in charge of this."[52]

Thereto, as much as Daisy Bates wanted her name in ink, the details surrounding her private life and early relationship with L.C. Bates remains an enigma. Indeed, Bates preserved respectability to the exclusion of her unrespectable past. Or, in the event that she did not or could not completely exterminate her unsavory geneses, she certainly tweaked it to palatable perfection. She specifically squashed from all narratives the fact that she maintained an affair with a married L.C. Bates from 1932 to 1942.[53] Even her age was negotiable in the fiction she spun around her early life. Moreover, at least for Bates biography Grif Stockley, the story about the rape and murder of her mother is problematic inasmuch it never appeared in the *Huttig News* or anywhere else except for Bates' biography. Stockley wrote, "a possible explanation for this omission is that in her effort to present herself as the 'First lady of Little Rock,' Bates may have been loathed to admit that her birth parents were never married."[54]

From the perspective of respectability, Daisy Bates would have used omission as tactic to eschew public shame and embarrassment. She would discover in 1961 when she started writing her autobiography that telling her story and telling it truthfully would prove painful. Nevertheless, as much as scholars like Grif Stockley find her fibs frustrating, what is clear is that when it came to her persona, Bates erased the dirty truths in order to preserve a respectable public (and posthumous) reputation.[55]

To be sure, Bates' leadership was wrapped in a package that could be accepted for its aesthetic appeal, but in the same way she learned as a child that social shame was the penalty paid for black skin, she learned as Georgina Hickey concluded, "when it came to leadership positions, respectability could work against women in multiple ways."[56] In other words, respectability also served as a kind of patriarchal binary that delimits respectability and unrespectability. The binary distinctions between "respectable" and "unrespectable" behavior offers a gendered discourse in respect to the public and private responsibilities of women. Thus, if respectability is understood as a patriarchal binary or as a construct of patriarchy that defines both *deference* to and *deviation from* the prescribed norm, then one can understand how Daisy Bates, as the first and only female president of a state NAACP chapter in the United States, was considered a deviation from patriarchal norms.

Civil rights activist Rosa Parks, who served as secretary of the Montgomery, Alabama NAACP chapter, offers a tremendous contrast to Daisy Bates. Described as "middle-class, middle-aged, and eminently respectable,"[57] "humble enough to be claimed by the common folk," "dignified enough in manner, speech, and dress to command the respect of the classes," and the embodiment of "proper womanly conduct and demeanor,"[58] Park's taciturn and unassuming nature rendered her reluctant to assume fame or formal leadership and thereby kept her in the good graces of the more ambitious men around her. Similarly, Bates was aesthetically respectable, middle-aged and middle-class, but she was not devout and she was not the taciturn type to turn down an opportunity to shine. Bates cherished the credentials of womanhood —this much was conspicuous in her charismatic femininity— but the same aggressiveness that the civil rights movement demanded of its male leaders was simultaneously deemed taboo in a black female body. **Whereas Rosa Parks' reluctance to fame and formal leadership gave her a bird's eye view into the inner courts of chauvinism and an impenetrable place on the pedestal of respectability,** Daisy Bates, through the assertion of a bold identity that bloomed beyond her black brothers, existed somewhere on the murky median between respectability and the absence of respectability.

Consequently, the public and private discourse of black male patriarchy rebuked women who stepped into the forbidden geography of formal race leadership. The brilliantly brained **Angela Davis** noted in her autobiography that "an unfortunate syndrome" exists "among some Black male activists –namely to confuse their political activity with an assertion of their maleness…These men view black women as a threat to their attainment of manhood — especially those Black women who take initiative and work to become leaders in their own right."[59]

More than once, local male leaders –who Bates described as loathed to follow "petticoat leadership"— attempted to put the woman in her place. In the midst of the '57 Crisis, a group of black male ministers organized a meeting with the decided purpose of putting a cease and desist to Bates. When Bates arrived she quickly discerned their goal and pointedly told them off. Bates made clear that she was only answerable to the NAACP, and the "nine children and their families." She added that she did not need their permission to do "any doggone thing I wanted to do." The ministers were flummoxed. "Of course, they gave me hell," she quipped in retrospect. "I went on about my business and just ignored them!"[60]

On another occasion, I.S. McClinton, president of the Arkansas Democratic Negro Voters League —Bates called him "a low down bastard"— spread a rumor that Bates was not "fit to lead the children" because her private activities were less than ladylike. Indeed, Bates played poker —according to Carlotta Walls Lanier, "Thurgood Marshall, Roy Wilkins, and newsman Ted Poston discovered the hard way that you didn't want to play poker with Daisy Bates if you intended to win"— she drank Scotch, she used curse words, she unashamedly "raised hell," and she occasionally went off the deep end.[61]

Thereto, in view of the disapproval she received from the public sphere, the way her unorthodox leadership affected her private relationship to her husband is also telling in terms of price she paid for the novel leadership pattern she produced. Although L.C. Bates "saw his wife as the best hope for the kind of leadership he had been advocating ever since he started the paper in 1941," there is evidence to suggest that he too might have slightly resented his wife's refusal to play a more traditional female role. Former neighbor Frankie Jeffries recalled, "He [L.C.] would say [to Daisy] 'you got no business' going up there wherever it was...He wanted his wife to stay home."[62]

Indeed, Daisy's "causes" precluded her from being the kind of traditional woman she might have hoped to be and the kind her father had trained her to be. Being an unorthodox woman was not without its personal consequence. The Little Rock Crisis forced L.C. and Daisy Bates to close the *State Press* in 1959 and by the time L.C. Bates died in 1980, the less fiery 67- year-old Bates could admit that she had not been the traditional wife that her husband deserved. She had subordinated her home and her husband to the greater demands of leadership. She revived the *State Press* in 1984 because she felt an obligation to the man who had been her best tutor, but to whom she had not been the best wife. Explained Bates, "I just used my bull-headed determination to keep my promise to L.C."[63]

Daisy Bates had been told as a child, "Your mother was not the kind to submit...so they took her."[64] She perhaps wondered how much of her personality was organic and how much of it had been manufactured by her foster environment? Nevertheless, Bates was an avant-garde black woman who occupied a position of formal leadership in a movement that routinely consigned women to auxiliaries. While jogging against patriarchy and the implications of an unrespectable past, she deployed the discourse of respectability to assert an identity that was an efficacious vehicle against the ugly notions that smote black self-esteem. In this way, she used her body to create a space for black female leadership by putting into print and practice the possibilities of women in the civil rights movement. "Who said I wasn't afraid?" Bates rejected the idea. "You acted in spite of your fear. You acted because you believed, you were committed." For Bates, unconventional leadership was a change that her era demanded. She waved her manicured finger: "Most women who are worth something ought to do something."[65]

[1] Daisy Bates, *The Long Shadow of Little Rock* (Fayetteville: University of Arkansas State Press, 1986), 3-4.

[2] Quoted in Grif Stockley, *Daisy Bates: Civil Rights Crusader from Arkansas* (Jackson: University Press of
Mississippi, 2005), 104.

[3] *Daisy Bates: First Lady of Little Rock,* directed by Sharon La Cruise (Independent Lens/PBS, 2012),
DVD.

[4] W.E.B. DuBois, *The Souls of Black Folks* (Dover Publications, 1994), 2.

[5] Bates, *Long Shadow*, 7-8.

[6] Ibid.

[7] Ibid.

[8] Ibid, 9.

[9] John A. Kirk, "Daisy Bates, the National Association for the Advancement of Colored People, and the 1957 Little Rock School Crisis: A Gendered Perspective," in *Gender and the Civil Rights Movement*, eds. Peter J.
Ling and Sharon Monteith (New Jersey: Rutgers University Press 2004), 19.

[10] Maya Angelou, *I Know Why the Caged Bird Sings* (New York: Random House, 1969), 6.

[11] Bates, *Long Shadow*, 10-12.

[12] *Daisy Bates: First Lady of Little Rock,* directed by Sharon La Cruise.

[13] Bates, *Long Shadow*, 12.

[14] Ibid, 15.

[15] Ibid, 29; Ora Lee Smith had been a member of the NAACP.

[16] Ibid, 20.

[17] Kirk, "Daisy Bates," in Ling and Monteith, 23.

[18] Ibid, 29.

[19] Ibid., 23; Sources that offer information on the background of L.C. Bates (1904-1980); see, for example Stockley, *Crusader*, 22-31; and C. Calvin Smith, "From 'Separate but Equal to Desegregation:' The Changing Philosophy of L.C. Bates," *Arkansas Historical Quarterly* (Autumn 1983): 254-270.

[20] Stockley, *Crusader*, 242.

[21] Ibid, 22-31; In her autobiography, Daisy Bates never wrote about her years in Memphis and barely devotes three paragraphs to her decade-long courtship with L.C. Bates; see, Bates, *Long Shadow*, 32-33.

[22] Kirk, "Daisy Bates," in Ling and Monteith, 29.

[23] *Daisy Bates: First Lady of Little Rock,* directed by Sharon La Cruise.

[24] Ibid. Stockley, *Crusader*, 12, 34, 43, 60.

[25] Elizabeth Jacoway, *Turn Away Thy Son: Little Rock, the Crisis that Shocked the Nation* (New York: Free Press, 2007), 165.

[26] Quoted in Stockley, *Crusader*, 288.

[27] Ibid, 81.

[28] Jacoway, *Turn Away*, 165.

[29] Judith Bloom Fradin and Dennis Brindell Fradin, *The Power of One: Daisy Bates and the Little Rock Nine* (New York: Clarion Books, 2004), 55; *Daisy Bates: First Lady of Little Rock,* directed by Sharon La Cruise.

[30] Carolyn Calloway-Thomas and Thurmon Gardner, "Daisy Bates and the Little Rock School Crisis:
Forging the Way," *Journal of Black Studies* (May 1996): 625.

[31] Fradin and Fradin, *Power of One*, 55.

[32] Stockley, *Crusader*, 58.

[33] Ibid, 124.

[34] Irving J. Spitzberg, *Racial Politics in Little Rock: 1954-1964* (Garland Publishing, 1987) 129.

[35] Stockley, *Crusader*, 132.

[36] Ibid, 44, 132.

[37] Anne Valk and Leslie Brown, *Living with Jim Crow: African American Women and Memories of the Segregated South* (New York: Palgrave MacMillan, 2010), 54. For an in depth discourse on the politics of respectability; see, Evelyn Brooks Higginbotham, *Righteous Discontent: The Women's Movement in the Black
Baptist Church, 1880-1920* (Cambridge, MA: Harvard University Press, 1993), 185-229.

[38] T.W. Anderson "Here's What Makes Daisy Bates Tick," *Pittsburgh Courier*, December 7, 1957.

[39] Janis F. Kearney, *Cotton Field of Dreams: A Memoir* (Chicago, IL: Writing Our World Press, 2004), 275-76; Janis F. Kearney, *Daisy: Between a Rock and a Hard Place* (Little Rock, AR: Writing Our World Press, 2013), xxix.

[40] Kearney, *Cotton,* 275.

[41] Stockley, *Crusader,* 43.

[42] Carlotta Walls Lanier, *Mighty Long Way* (New York: Ballantine Books, 2009), 74.

[43] Janis F. Kearney, e-mail message to author, April 13, 2014.

[44] Ibid.

[45] Kearney, *Daisy,* 53; Daisy Bates Interview, June 21, 1960, Daisy Bates Collection (MC 582), Special Collections, University of Arkansas Libraries, Fayetteville, AR.

[46] *Daisy Bates: First Lady of Little Rock,* directed by Sharon La Cruise.

[47] Stockley, *Crusader*, 139.

[48] Higginbotham, *Righteous*, 203.

[49] Melba Patillo Beals, *Warriors Don't Cry: A Searing Memoir of the Battle to Integrate Little Rock's Central High* (New York: Washington Square Press, 1994), 95.

[50] Elizabeth Jacoway and Minnijean Brown Trickey, "Not Anger but Sorrow: Minnijean Brown Trickey Remembers the Little Rock Crisis," *Arkansas Historical Quarterly* (Spring 2005): 15.

[51] Ibid, 22.

[52] *Daisy Bates: First Lady of Little Rock,* directed by Sharon La Cruise.

[53] Stockley, *Crusader*, 243.

[54] Ibid, 189.

[55] Ibid, 227-29.

[56] Georgina Hickey, "The Respectability Trap: Gender Conventions in 20th Century Movements for Social Change," *Journal of Interdisciplinary Feminist Thought* (July 2013): 2.

[57] Viv Sanders, "Rosa Parks and the Montgomery Bus Boycott," *History Review* (September 2006): 7.

[58] Taylor Branch, *Parting the Waters: America in the King Years, 1954-1963* (New York: Simon & Schuster, 1988), 130.

[59] Angela Y. Davis, *Angela Davis: An Autobiography* (International Publishers, 1974), 161.

[60] Interview with Daisy Bates, 1957 or 1958, Daisy Bates Papers, 1946-1966, Wisconsin Historical Society, Madison, WI.

[61] Lanier, *Mighty*, 254; Interview with Daisy Bates, 1957 or 1958, Daisy Bates Papers.

[62] Stockley, *Crusader*, 242.

[63] Kearney, *Cotton,* 279.

[64] Bates, *Long Shadow*, 15.

[65] Jacqueline Trescott, "Crusader from Little Rock: The Quiet Courage of Daisy Bates," *Washington Post,* March 21, 1981.

Voting is for the Beautiful and the Smart Ones Too: Alice Dunbar-Nelson and the Women's Suffrage Movement

Tara Green

Born in New Orleans in 1875, by the time Alice Ruth Moore Dunbar-Nelson was twenty years old she had published an anthology of fiction and poetry titled, *Violets and Other Tales*. As an active member of the Phillis Wheatley Club of New Orleans and, later, a founding member of the National Federation of Afro-American Women, Dunbar-Nelson focused her energies on empowering Black people in America, but she had a particular interest in uplifting African American women. Before passage of the Nineteenth Amendment and the twentieth-century Voting Rights Acts, Alice Dunbar joined with other women to lay the foundation to secure women's right to vote.

Before she left New Orleans, she voiced her awareness of the impact Black women could have as voters in their communities. In an 1896 article she wrote for *The Women's Era*, a journal founded by and for Black women, she mentioned the Women's Relief Corps required the women of the Phillis Wheatley Club of New Orleans to offer a prayer "that our husbands, brothers, fathers and sweethearts may do their duty Tuesday as true citizens and men." She immediately dismissed this attention to men, which overtly placed women as subordinate to them, and began the next sentence by raising awareness of how the "colored women" have the power to affect the political climate. Women did not have the right to vote, but Black women had an impact on capturing the Black vote, resulting in the "opening of a new public school." As if anticipating the debates that would rage well until the Twentieth Amendment was ratified in 1920, Dunbar became vocal about the rights she felt that Black women should have in influencing social and political decisions, especially in the South. It was not surprising that she took a position as a suffragette and became active in the movement to encourage Black women to seize their right to participate in electoral politics and Black men, in particular, to support them with their power to vote.

As a socially aware woman, she probably knew the history that she had entered. Despite the hope of the promises of the Fifteenth Amendment, both Black men and women had been deprived the right to vote. When the Reconstruction Act of 1867 was passed, requiring Confederate States to hold constitutional conventions, African American men, women, and children attended these conventions en mass. Their presence, especially those of the Black women who outnumbered their male counterparts in states like South Carolina, showed that they were not only interested in exercising a right to vote, but also in seizing political power. There were several prominent debates that emerged after ratification of the Fifteenth Amendment, which granted all men the right to vote. One question was: Should women vote or should they stand in support of Black men, some of whom were able to vote (conditions in Southern states were always precarious) by right of the Fifteenth Amendment? Some women argued that women should stay home and leave the voting to men. While others went as far as taking up arms to protect their husbands and traveling long distances with their husbands and entire families on voting days. Elsa Barkley Brown observes, "African American women, unable to cast a separate vote, viewed African American men's vote as equally theirs" (82). Of course, this could only be said of the women who were married. In such a scenario, unmarried African American women, including widows, would have no man to influence or vote to claim.

Second, should the national movement support Black women,

thereby jeopardizing the chances of all women? The influential National Women's Suffrage Association (NWSA), formed in 1890, was at the core of this debate. Leaders Susan B. Anthony and Elizabeth Cady advocated for "expediency," a strategy that "was to prove that the enfranchisement of White women would further, rather than impede, the power of a White ruling class that was fearful of Black and immigrant domination" (Giddings 124). Threats to Black women gaining the right to vote were obvious at the 1894 convention when the organization expressed placing literacy as a voting qualification. Black leaders, such as Francis Ellen Harper and Ida B. Wells-Barnett, spoke out against this and other tactics that represented class and racial preferences. Segregation amongst the group began to arise. Though Anthony and Wells-Barnett had a respectful relationship, Anthony would not support Wells-Barnett when Black women wanted to form a branch of the NASWA. Tensions rose further when, ignoring the challenges of Black Southern women and their efforts to gain the right to vote, the organization came out in support of state's rights in 1903. This tactic may have gained support from Southern White men and women, but Black women were left to defend themselves, and that they did.

A teacher by day and an activist every chance she got, Dunbar was active with the Republican Party at the time that the twentieth-century suffrage movement was underway. By this time, Paul Laurence Dunbar had died, and even though she left him four years before his death to escape his abuse, she was still regarded as his beautiful and respected widow. Her notoriety among Black people made her popular speaker. In 1915 Dunbar became an organizer for the Middle Atlantic States' women's suffrage campaign. For her part, she was a leader in Pennsylvania's women's campaign to secure passage of an amendment granting women the right to vote. She gave speeches to various African American church groups, club meetings, conferences, and festivals to educate and persuade her audience of voters (men) and potential voters (women). She emphasized two main arguments to liberate a decidedly patriarchal society from its belief that women were incapable of balancing thinking with traditional responsibilities.

First, she addressed the misguided belief in women's lack of intelligence or ability to make informed decisions. Relying on her own experience as a schoolteacher, she informed audiences that girls stay in school longer than boys who tended to leave at the age of fourteen in pursuit of a job. She also addressed the selling of votes by Black men, an action that would not be taken by women she proclaimed: "it would not be of any use to buy a woman's vote, for 'she never stays where she is put'" (*Williamsport Sun*, August 14, 1915). Her direct address to the men was the result of the opposition she reportedly received from "colored men" as she traveled the circuit.

Secondly, she addressed the belief that voting would cause women—if they were married--to be absent from their homes. She reminded the working class men that they had no problem with their wives working to bring in an extra income. In a speech she delivered alongside Mary Church Terrell, she informed the African American audience of men and women at the First Presbyterian Church that women voting would not affect the "home any more than their church activities" (Newark *Evening News*, Saturday October 9, 1915). Dunbar was adamant that women had earned the right to vote based on the contributions they were already making to households and their communities. Her sharpest argument was the wage earning capacity of working women. In a speech she delivered to an African Methodist Episcopal audience, "she showed how the colored women represented equally with their men folks the earning capacity and impressed upon her hearers that had it not been for the women of the race adding their help to the men that the race would not have attained what it has in the way of achievement and moral achievement" (*The Advocate-Verdict*, October 30, 1915). Again, she hoped to convince the men that support for women's suffrage was a step towards further advancing Black communities and families. She also tried to appeal to men's sense of chivalry to entice them to support Black women. Those who were not in support, she argued, "slap [their] women in the face" and "kick themselves" because a vote from women supported the vote of the man.

At times, the press focused more on her beauty than her message. In a statement that proved to subject her to scrutiny not related to her speech, the writer described, "her exceptional beauty has proved irresistible to would-be opponents" (*Ledger* August 7, 1915). Another article described her as "Tall and graceful, a voice beautifully modulated and an easy flow of forceful. Logical arguments could not fail her arguments" (July 30, 1915). The *Williamsport Sun* describes her as "a woman of unusual beauty" (Thursday, August 12, 1915). Since her picture accompanied these articles, there was no need to add any descriptions of her physical appearance. In the cases where the descriptions were part of an announcement, they served the purpose of convincing audiences to attend. Such beauty would disarm her "opponents," as one journalist put it and made her rather radical message more acceptable to men who may have felt threatened by the idea of women voting.

Nevertheless, Dunbar earned the reputation as an intelligent and passionate suffrage speaker and the respect of the Black press. Her presentations were often described as having received "an enthusiastic impetus"; as delivering "heart-to-heart talks" as a "plain truth" and bringing laughter from the audience (*Williamsport Sun* Aug 4, 1915). While recording her appeal and the audience's reception, the news writers also record the depth of her reach. She spoke to relatively large crowds of people. In Washington, PA, for example she "kept more than 400 persons interested for over an hour" evidence of "her power to captivate her hearers." The writer regarded her as "the best suffrage lecturer and one of the most charming speakers ever in Washington." *The Harrisburg Telegraph* begins its article: "Fully 1,000 persons heard Mrs. Paul Laurence Dunbar, widow of the famous negro poet deliver stirring lectures on suffrage…" (October 27, 1915). Alice clearly enjoyed these engagements and the attention that she was given by the press. In some ways she was living in Dunbar's shadow as the poet's widow, but for the first time she redefined herself as a political leader when she leant her voice to a historical political cause. As she did so, she and not Paul Laurence Dunbar, was lauded as the pride of the race. It was printed that "the race should be proud of Mrs. Dunbar; should be proud that one of its members has so thoroughly absorbed the details anent racial advancement, and can so conclusively and conscientiously present them to an audience" (*The Pittsburg Courier*, Friday, October 1915).

Her lectures were to occur during the summer months when she was not teaching at Howard, but she kept a steady schedule up to the date of the vote. As she did so, she continued her appeal to men to vote for passage of the amendment. York papers where she remained posted on the day of the women's suffrage vote, recorded her activities. She continued to address the points she had been making since June: women's place in the home and the impact of men selling their votes, while emphasizing that "intelligent" men are in support of women's suffrage. At this juncture, her addresses became more specific to Pennsylvania as she tried to convince them that the high divorce rate in Pennsylvania would lower if women were able to vote, such a right would make them happier. "The minimum of divorces in the West is undoubtedly due to the equality of sexes, she said" (*The York Daily*, Tuesday Morning, November 2, 1915). On November 2, she remained in York County, Pennsylvania, making speeches and visiting "all the polling places of the city to help boost for votes" (*York Daily*). Unfortunately, the people of York failed to support Amendment One: 5,348 voted yes while 12,090 voted no. According to one article, York was one of three counties expected to vote against the amendment. Most certainly she was in the area to try to change the inevitable. Although the amendment did not pass in 1915, the women's work served to educate people as the country moved closer to passage of the U.S. Constitution's Nineteenth Amendment.

Despite all of her work and the reputation she had garnered, by 1921 she felt hardly satisfied with where she was in her career as a writer and activist. Rosalyn Terborg-Penn reports, "In spite of these efforts to implement their political rights, black women in the South were disenfranchised in less than a decade after the Nineteenth Amendment enfranchised them in 1920, and black women outside the South lost the political clout they had acquired" (19). Probably not by coincidence, this year also marked the decline of her popularity in politics as the suffrage movement had come to an end and new political shifts had begun to take place. In 1921 Alice became chair of the publicity committee of the National League of Colored Republican Women. But by the end of the year, she was no longer very active in this position or as organizer for the Mid-Atlantic States. By 1921, she had lost her position with the State Committee. Yet, she remained active in other areas of politics, pushing for the advancement of racial equality, especially Black women's rights, until her death in 1935.

Works Cited

Alice Moore to Paul Laurence Dunbar. Alice Dunbar Nelson Papers, University of Delaware Library, Newark, DE.

Brown, Elsa Barkley. "To Catch the Vision of Freedom: Reconstructing Southern Black Women's Political History, 1865-1880. "Ann Gordon and Bettye Collier-Thomas, eds. African American Women and the Vote, 1837-1965. Amherst: University of Massachusetts Press, 1997. Pp. 66-99.

Terborg-Penn, Rosalyn. African American Women in the Struggle for the Vote, 1850-1920. Bloomington: Indiana University Press, 1998.

African-American Women and the "Public Sphere"

Sheena Harris, Ph.D.

Women's roles in society have been essential in shaping the outcome of events. Among them are the African-American women activists who were involved in politics from the 1820s to the turn of the century, such as Martha Miller Stewart (1803-1879), Sojourner Truth (c1797-1883), Ida B. Wells-Barnett (1862-1931), and Callie House (1861-1928). Their activism extended beyond distinct female spheres to spaces that men and women shared: political organizations, mutual aid societies, universal organizations and schools. These women also fought for equality and inclusion in the electoral process, although women could not legally vote. This essay will show how black women of the nineteenth-century devoted their lives to changing the political systems of their day and how they were influential in the development of American culture and society.

Notions that African-Americans, both free and enslaved, were barbaric, lacked history, were uncivilized, and unfit to shape public culture, would be challenged by a new generation of black females leaders. Their activism proved that the contributions of black women during the antebellum period were numerous. Women carved out their public sphere for decades, yet their achievements are only recently being explored. Enslaved women, who despite their servitude, created communities and networks that were imperative to their survival, and engaged in many forms of daily resistance – whether it was through preserving their indigenous religion or taking portions of food from the main house, as a means to feed their families – were equally important in creating a collective sphere of resistance for black women. The society in which enslaved, quasi-free and free women operated during the antebellum period, was filled with racism, violence, and murder, yet they struggled to define themselves and fought for the collective interest of blacks.

ENSLAVED BLACK WOMEN

Toward the end of the colonial period and with the onset of the cotton gin, the institution of slavery became more harsh and brutal to black men and women.[1] Enslaved blacks were arriving early in the colonial period, but a substantial growth in the slave population did not occur until the 1790's when planters shifted away from tobacco and indigo production and began to plant cotton on a large scale. Prior to the reign of cotton, enslaved blacks were almost always recognized as persons and not just items or property. By 1820, enslaved blacks made up more than 43.5 percent of southern states population, and by 1860, more than 436,000 enslaved blacks lived in Mississippi alone.[2]

From the 1820s onward, slavery hardened as an institution. The expansion of cotton into new lands in the west, the rising value of slaves, the growing fear of rebellion, and outside interference made slavery at once more permanent and more oppressive. The need for labor increased the likelihood of sales and separation. Emancipation also became more difficult, if not impossible. Slave codes were now being strictly enforced, prohibiting gatherings and reducing almost all liberties of enslaved and free blacks alike.[3]

Despite these deplorable conditions, the women's sphere of influence expanded during American slavery. Black women denote a broader understanding of public discourse. Through their different forms of resistance, black women, both enslaved and free, were influential to the societal structure of America and desperately fought for a public reevaluation of the "women's question."

The role of black women within the slave community was essential in preserving the African-American family structure. Deborah Gray White's

Ar'n't I A Woman, was one of the first studies to explore the role of enslaved women. Unless dealing with childbirth, black women were portrayed as always performing similar tasks. However, White tells the story of the enslaved black woman while emphasizing three main characters – mammy and jezebel and their transformation into the Sapphire myth.

Jezebel represented the black woman who used her body and sexual abilities to manipulate men and to improve her situation. On the other hand, mammy constituted a desexualized woman who was assertive and tireless. She would work diligently for her master and protect him under any circumstances. After slavery, the image of the black women evolved and she became anything but a woman – from that emerged the Sapphire myth. Sapphire consumed men while also taking over their roles. She was assertive like the mammy, but lacked maternal instincts, placing her on the same level as a man.

Many black women embodied these characters as a means of survival. However, they resisted the culture that created them. Since black women were not seen as women during slavery, their attempt to assert their womanhood would fall on deaf ears for decades. Yet, enslaved and free women executed a clear sense of resilience and culture that aided in the abolitionists movements. Although slave women were subject to abuse by their masters, they fought, similar to their freed sisters, to establish a community and sphere in which they could cultivate their culture and shared identity.

Rigid family structures existed within enslaved communities. Because the slave families on many occasions were separated, enslaved women had to create communities amongst themselves, showing their roles as women, as opposed to their role as wives or slaves. Enslaved men were also more likely to escape slavery, leaving women to pursue freedom on their own. Whether they lived on a large plantation or a small farm, the lives of slaves consisted largely of work, short rations, and the fear of frequent violence and forced separation from their families. Enslaved women constantly recreated themselves in order to resist the institution that held them in bondage. They taught their children race pride and used their domestic sphere of influence to help change American culture.

FREE BLACK WOMEN DURING SLAVERY

It was not only a curse to be enslaved, but also the curse extended to free blacks and mulattoes. The laws governing slavery changed over time. These changes made life for free blacks virtually impossible. The rights of freemen and women in the south were almost none existent. They were similar in nature to the black codes that were issued after slavery. Free blacks had to have a license for their weapons. Free blacks and mulattos were not allowed by the law to use offensive language to white persons, regardless of the situation. The list of restrictions that enslaved and free persons endured together were numerous.[4]

Nonetheless, free black women during the era of slavery used the public sphere to influence change, in ways that her enslaved sisters could not. Boston reformer Martha Miller Stewart (1803-1979) approached the "woman question," with her diligent struggle to help educate the masses. Through her life and public persona, she depicted the hypocrisy that existed when men fought for racial equality while demeaning women due to their gender. She was the first American to deliver a public speech to a male audience. She used her life to encourage women to be involved in the larger political and social environment while also seeking economic power.[5] Until 1848, black males generally embraced the rights of women. However, with the passage of the 1850 Fugitive Slave Act, the *Passenger Cases,* along with the Dred Scott decision, the focus of black public culture shifted to issues of race and freedom. Black men argued that during this time and until the Civil War, gender issues had little significance to the larger race issue.

71

AFTER EMANCIPATION

During the Reconstruction years, women expanded their public platform through avenues such as: public speaking, fund-raising, teaching and women's clubs.

With emancipation, black women became more visible in public culture. They opened schools, they joined the teaching staff of local American Missionary Associations, they formed and joined women's clubs, and they spoke out against social injustices to help their men folk in the struggle for human rights, civil rights, political rights, and equality. Black women also wanted suffrage. During an Equal Rights Association meeting in 1867, the ex-slave turned abolitionist, Sojourner Truth, voiced her growing discontent towards rumors of suffrage only being extended to black males. "I feel that I have a right to have just as much as a man... There is a great stir about colored men getting their rights; and if colored men get there rights and not colored women theirs, the colored men will be masters over the women, and it will be just as bad as before."[6] It would take more than five decades for Truth's plea to be heard.

Similar to Truth, black women also formed organizations to demand the government's assistance after emancipation. Born on a slave plantation in Rutherford County, Tennessee, ex-slave Callie Guy, later Callie House, joined the public sphere with her endearing fight for reparations for formerly enslaved blacks. With the demise of the Freedman's Bureau, House garnered the attention of the government after she joined with Isaiah Dickenson and started the National Ex-Slave Mutual Relief, Bounty, and Pension Association in 1894. A few years later she was seen as a threat to national security and sentenced to one year in prison. Although House's attempt failed, influential blacks such as Marcus Garvey and others continued the fight. Callie House was not middle-class; instead, she was considered a commoner, who worked as a washerwoman. Yet, her life offers a glimpse into the struggle and fight of working-class black women in the long struggle for equality in the public sphere.[7]

Black women continued to expand their influence on public spaces throughout the nineteenth-century. The end of Reconstruction, and its ultimate failure, led to the decline in black male authority in the political realm, and the decline of women's religious authority. However, black women remained active in their club affiliations. Organizations such as that seen in their Masons' auxiliary Order of the Eastern Star, which was not subject to the rule of male leaders, and the creation of the National Association of Colored Women (NACW), formed in 1896, showcased how black women remained resilient in the face of Jim Crow laws, disenfranchisement, violence, and continued opposition.

Access to public forums contributed greatly to the public sphere of influence that indirectly brought into question the designated role of black women. In order to prove they were cultured, many middle-class men and women adopted the social norms of the dominant race, subjecting women to domesticity. Black women continuously fought these restrictions and found themselves in a constant struggle for a public and private sphere to rebuild their communities. Although experiences varied due to class, location, and social affiliation, in many regards most black women shared similar discriminations. They all co-existed within a race-based society that placed them at the bottom of the totem pole. While whites were adjusting to their new life under a system not based on "slave" labor, they were also coping with their greatest fear – not that black women were, in their eyes, returning back to their "barbaric" state in the absence of slavery, but rather, that blacks were learning the laws of the land, both in resistance and political power, and disproving arguments of their inferiority and incapable nature to govern themselves without white supervision.

Whites also used laws to chip away at the freedoms of blacks.

However, women represent a sector of society who rarely made appearances at large gatherings or in the textbooks of later generations. They used this undetected radar to singlehandedly fight against injustices, in ways that their male counterparts could not. The story of Ida B. Wells-Barnett exemplifies this very fact. Born a slave in Mississippi, Wells-Barnett went on to become a prolific writer, journalist, civil rights activists and anti-lynching crusader. After the lynching and murder of her three friends at the Local Peoples' Grocery Store in Memphis, Tennessee in 1892, Wells-Barnett used the pen to visually depict the inhumane use of vigilante justice on blacks. Her anti-lynching campaign reached the US Supreme court during the 1920s; however, an anti-lynching bill was never passed. Still, Wells-Barnett started a movement against injustice that civil rights leaders such as A. Phillip Randolph used during World War II and that others carried into the long civil rights movement.

The rhetoric of black female activists and authors such as Well-Barnett's adds considerably to the discussion of the public sphere. Shirley Logan uses the forensic rhetorical theory of Quintilian and Cicero to explain Wells-Barnett's use of "ocular demonstration." Wells-Barnet used this to depict the inhuman horrors of lynching and to make them come alive to audiences who were isolated from the crimes, and to provoke them to take action. The public discourse of African-American women that were produced during the last two decades of the nineteenth century, show the political efficacy of the era. Shirley Logan defines persuasive discourse as "verbal communication toward a particular audience to obtain what Perelman and Olbrechts-Tyecta called 'the adherence of minds'." It was within this definition and sphere that black women addressed and tackled the abundant needs of African-Americans.

Just as Ida B. Wells-Barnett had done, black women used the printing press to distribute information and ignite change. Largely through women's clubs, African-American women were able to voice and meet many needs of the larger black community. The plight and contributions of clubs such as the National Association of Colored Women and the Daughters of Africa and Daughters of America, display black women's candid fight for education, and their ability to use the printing press to promote the betterment of the race.

Ultimately, the role of black women during the nineteenth-century is abundantly rich. Freed women resisted enslavement and un-free persons sought freedom. Within this double paradigm, freedwomen sought to make distinctions from their enslaved counterparts as a means to continue their freedom, while also working towards abolition in a means to better protect all freedoms. Freed women, just as enslaved women, within their own time, forged a meaningful life for themselves and their family, despite the tenuous environment that they both lived within and adds them to the long continued fight for civil rights. With the passing of the 13th Amendment to the United States Constitution, African-American women were forced to redefine their freedom. Women within the professional world, and those who because of poverty were forced back into a new form of servitude – later called Jim Crow, both aided in the social transformation that would take more than a century to unfold. Women used knowledge as a tool of power to advance their realms of influence and to lead the race into social equality.

In summation, women's sphere of influence definitely expanded from the 1830s to the 1900s, but it was still a bounded space and thus continued to be segregated and limited in many ways. Black women used their bodies, their domestic abilities, the printing press, and clubs and organizations join in the struggle for equality. They constantly gave of themselves in an overt attempt to improve their conditions and the conditions of all black men and children. The larger discussion of activism and women's public culture within the nineteenth-century is an important pretext to the long civil rights movement. These women apply a broader understanding to "What a Women ought to be and to Do." Through their different forms of public and private activism, they created a sphere of change and influence and leave a legacy of agency at the turn of the century. While some looked at black women as an inferior sex who were a part of an "inferior" race, black women stood their own ground and proclaimed that "when and where I enter… the race enters with me."[8]

[1] Donald R. Wright, *African Americans in the Colonial Era: from African Origins through the American Revolution* (Wheeling, Ill.: Harlan Davidson, Inc, 1990), 2-6; Darlene Clark Hine, and Kathleen Thompson, *A Shining Thread of Hope: The History of Black Women in America* (New York: Broadway Books, 1998), 9; Deborah Gray White, *Ar'n't I a Woman: Female Slaves in the Plantation South* (New York, London: W. W. Norton & Company, 1985), 2.

[2] Bradley G. Bond, *Mississippi: A Documentary History* (Oxford: University Press of Mississippi, 2003), 65-66; John H. Moore, *The Emergence of the Cotton Kingdom in the old Southwest: Mississippi, 1770-1860* (Baton Rouge and London: Louisiana State University Press, 1988), 520-526; *Freedman's Journal* 1827, 3.

[3] Nancy Woloch, *Women and the American Experience* (New York, NY: McGraw-Hill, 1984), 174-175; *Freedman's Journal,* 1829, 1.

[4] Bond, *Mississippi,* 67; James T. Currie, "From Slavery to Freedom in Mississippi's Legal System," in *The Journal of Negro History,* vol. 65, No. 2. (Spring, 1980), 113.

[5] Shirley J. Yee, *Black Women Abolitionists: A Study in Activism, 1828-1860* (The University of Tennessee Press, 1992), 26

[6] Dorothy Sterling, ed., *We Are Your Sisters,* 411; Yee, *Black Women Abolitionists,* 1.

[7] Callie House, *The Tennessee Encyclopedia of History and Culture,* accessed May 6, 2014.

[8] Paula Giddings, *When and Where I Enter: The Impact of Black Women on Race and Sex in America* (New York: HarperCollins Publishers, 1984), 11.

Pathological Matriarchy?: Black Women, The Moynihan Report, and Black Power Antiwar Activism

Amanda L. Higgins

Women's contributions to the Civil Rights and Black Power Movements have begun to be unpacked through recent scholarship, memoirs, and oral histories. The foundational and sustaining roles women played in creating, maintaining, and moving peace, justice, and freedom forward in the United States have long been relegated to tangential histories or ascribed traditional gendered stories—background support, nurturing, and respectability in the face of opposition. But, as Bobby Seale and others have noted, by 1968 women made up the majority of the Black Panther Party and similar demographics existed in many Civil Rights and Black Power organizations.[1] From the radical life of Rosa Park to the role of sexual assault and violence in spurring Southern civil rights activism, women's place in the Movement is slowly being restored.[2] However, black women's role in antiwar activism remains hidden in plain sight, as scholars of the era focus on the activities of men who risked being drafted or jailed for speaking out against involvement in Vietnam. A few historians have begun to look at the connections between antiwar activism and the nascent second wave feminist movement, but fail to include women of color in their discussion. Moreover, these histories are often reductionist and focus on women who fulfilled traditionally acceptable female roles through their activism as secretaries, note takers, and paper stuffers for organizations headed by men, or focus on women who used their role as mothers to counsel soldiers. While any discussion of women in the organizations is a welcome respite from the male dominated leadership of most antiwar literature, black women's roles in articulating specific arguments about class, race, and gender and their relation to antiwar activism highlight the important intellectual, physical, and emotional work women brought to Black Power antiwar activism.[3]

Like their male counterparts, black women's antiwar activism took many forms and occurred across a number of organizational platforms. Working within already established groups and creating their own outgrowths, women brought the economic and social costs of the war to their activism, tying together calls to end the draft with expansions of welfare benefits and support for black communities in the United States. Facing no threat of being drafted, black women were able to forcefully use their voices and actions to demand change, while also highlighting the intersections of government policies abroad and the lived experiences of African Americans in the United States. Anti-Vietnam War activism proved a fertile test ground for expanded gendered arguments about the effects of race, class, and sex in the capitalist system and the exploitation of poverty to serve the government's agenda.

Black Americans' interaction with the Vietnam War was dramatically shaped by the 1965 Moynihan Report which argued that one of the keys to addressing poverty in black American communities was through providing masculine work, like military service, to black men. To make such an argument, Moynihan denigrated black women, especially female heads of households and bread winners, who, according to the report, were overly dominate in the black family and stripped black male youth of their masculinity or desire to work. The matriarchal structure of black families, according to Moynihan's report, "because it is so out of line with the rest of American society, severely retards the progress of the group as a whole, and imposes a crushing burden on the Negro male and, in consequence, on a great many Negro women as well."[4] Labeling the female led black family a "tangle of pathology," Moynihan warned that a cycle of poverty would continue to exist in the black community until it conformed to the dominate society's (i.e. white) familial mores. He blamed the "tangle of pathology" on the higher educational attainment numbers of black women and their ability to access white collar work at higher levels than black men. The survival tactics and coping strategies employed by black women— working outside the home as domestics, secretaries, and assistants—in order to support families at times when black men were denied jobs or access to advanced training were seen as barriers to black family mobility and success by Moynihan. Ignoring the lack of jobs for skilled black men throughout the country and using the words of conservative African American leaders like Whitney Young, President of the National Urban League, to defend his findings, the Moynihan Report essentially criminalized black womanhood.[5]

The Moynihan Report's focus on gender and attainment highlighted both government racism in dealing with institutional barriers to economic success in the United States and the double-bind of being black and a woman in mid-century America. Historian Carol Giardina argued that the Moynihan Report was also a function of government backlash directed at black women like Fannie Lou Hammer, Ella Baker, and Rosa Parks, who angered white liberals with their militant stances, thus "a report blaming the 'emasculating' independence and strength of such women for their race's poverty and unemployment might help to dampen black women's militancy and keep them out of the black freedom struggle." Moynihan's focus on the pathology of black females served not to quell black women's active participation in the economic and social advancement of their race, but encouraged further involvement and a desire to assert their own definitions of femininity and masculinity.[6]

The use of the report by the U.S. Department of Defense to justify relaxed draft standards and promote hegemonic, white notions of masculinity further denigrated black women by questioning their roles as mothers, wage earners, and community leaders and placing their sons, brothers, and husbands at increased risk for being drafted and sent to Vietnam to prove their masculinity. The Department of Defense failed to realize that removing black men from their community and sending them to fight a war where they could be injured, maimed, or killed, only served to heighten female heads of households, at least in the short run. Moreover, by demanding a hegemonic masculinity, the Moynihan report created a pathological black femininity, challenging generations of work in the politics of the respectability for black women.[7]

To counter Moynihan's criminalization and express their antiwar and anticolonial beliefs, black women used many outlets to reach their intended audiences. Some women worked within the framework of already established anti-war committees in Civil Rights and Black Power organizations. Linking black men's participation in the military to the overall quality of life for black Americans, female antiwar activists tied the war to white masculinity and white leaders' desires to further subjugate black men and women in the mid-century capitalist and neo-colonial system. Gwendolyn Patton of SNCC helped established the National Black Anti-Draft, Anti-War Union (NBADAWU) as an outgrowth of SNCC's antiwar fervor in the fall of 1966. Patton's work with the NBADAWU was multifaceted and relocated her to SNCC's New York City office, where she joined SNCC's women's caucus, chaired by Frances Beal. The women's caucus challenged the masculine rhetoric of SNCC and other Black Power organizations and highlighted what Beal labeled double jeopardy or the challenges of being black and a woman. SNCC's woman's caucus provided a space for women to explore leadership roles, learn gender and economic theory, and express new forms of activism. As a part of SNCC, women's caucus participants were uniquely aware of the intersections of race, class, and gender in the lives of black women in the Movement. Moreover, women like Beal and Gwen Patton knew the Vietnam War exacerbated gender and economic discrimination in the Black Power and antiwar movements, as men focused on the draft and military service, while downplaying the plight of women and welfare recipients.[8]

In order to curb American colonial wars and to end the exploitation of people of color by the capitalist U.S. Government, Patton believed, "the course of action to take is not to simply stop the war in Vietnam, but to radically change this country so that no more horrors and atrocities will exist in this country and abroad." Radically changing the country also meant changing the attitudes of the leadership of progressive organizations, a position Patton articulated in her 1970 essay "Black People and the Victorian Ethos," published in Toni Cade's *Black Woman* anthology. Having spent most of her life in civil rights organizing, elected as class president of Tuskegee Institute, and almost killed in a single car accident in Birmingham while shuttling a draft dodger to a bus station, Patton wrote with the authority of a veteran. She called for black men and women to abandon the white community's notion of Victorian ideals and the politics of respectability. Victorian ethos allowed black men to dominate black women and for black men to be dominated by white men and women, thus it was a mentality of sacrifice, defeat, and desperation. The Victorian ethos created a subservient culture within black homes and communities, denying black women a chance at real political freedom and allowed for government officials to continue to belittle and ignore the needs of women and men of color.[9]

The role of women in creating and defining anticolonial and antiracist activism expanded greatly in the late 1960s and early 1970s. Frances Beal's Women's Caucus officially broke from SNCC in 1969 and by 1971 was renamed the Third World Women's Alliance, reflecting an expansion of the membership to include Puerto Rican, Asian, Chicano, and American Indian women. The Third World Women's Alliance goals included: "creating sisterhood through Third World solidarity; promoting Third World unity around economic, social, educational, and political issues; collecting, interpreting, and disseminating information about the Third World; establishing solid relationships with Third World men based on 'human love and respect'; and training Third World women for leadership in the revolutionary struggle." Their work was not explicitly anti-Vietnam War, as by 1971 American involvement in Vietnam was slowly winding down, but reflected the desire to work collectively with other colonized women to end imperial wars and create independent nations with full equality.[10] The organization's international perspective also reflected the globalization inherent in Black Power rhetoric and the belief that women throughout the colonized world shared similar experiences of oppression.

The Third World Women's Alliance took their mission beyond print activism, sponsoring and participating in a November 4th antiwar march in New York City. At the march, they called for support of the South Vietnam Peace Plan, ending national and racial discrimination, and ending attacks on working people. By linking peace in Vietnam with antidiscrimination action, the women were able to dissect and articulate the intersections of American war policy and the consequences of capitalist imperialism, as experienced by people of color in the United States and abroad. The Third World Women's Alliance and their allies sought to overthrow American capitalism and establish a "socialist society free of class, race and sexual exploitation," and worked to develop coalitions with groups including Black Workers Congress, Third World Youth Movement, and the Black Panther Party to advance their agenda.[11]

Black women's antiwar protests were an integral part in the development of the black and Third World women's movements of the

83

mid and late 1970s and beyond. Black women's contributions to antiwar and feminist organizing has often been ignored, as white, middle class activists of both genders were projected as the vanguard forces in social change. The work of black women to redefine black manhood and womanhood in a light of the Moynihan Report and the Vietnam War were refutations of hegemonic masculinity and femininity based on white standards.

By connecting welfare, war spending, and the plight of black Americans women challenged the economic arguments presented as reasons for black men to enlist in the military. Most importantly, black women's strong stances against the war and encouraging black men to refuse service presented black womanhood not as pathological, but as uplifting and supportive of families, communities, and themselves. Instead of being reduced and degraded by the Moynihan Report and its various implementations across governmental policies, black women showed that black womanhood was made up of "matriarchs, but we have been forced to live in abandonment and been used and abused...Let it be clearly understood that Black women's liberation is not anti-male; any such sentiment or interpretationa [sic] as such cannot be tolerated. It must be taken clearly for what it is—pro-human for all peoples." Black women's focus on keeping black men out of military service served to undermine matriarchal dogma, while also reinforcing the humanistic arguments of a shared Third World mentality and imagined community of colonial subjects.[12]

---

[1] Bobby Seale, *Seize the Time: The Story of the Black Panther Party and Huey P. Newton* (Baltimore: Black Classic Press, 1991); Erika Huggins and Angela D. LeBlanc-Ernest, "Revolutionary Women, Revolutionary Education: The Black Panther Party's Oakland Community School," *Want to Start a Revolution: Radical Women in the Black Freedom Struggle* eds. Dayo F. Gore, Jeanne Theoharis, and Komozi Woodard (New York: New York University Press, 2009), 161-184.

[2] Gerald Gill, "From Maternal Pacifism to Revolutionary Solidarity: African-American Women's Opposition to the Vietnam War," *Sights of the Sixties*, ed. Barbara L. Tischler (New Brunswick, NJ: Rutgers University Press, 1992); Amy Swerdlow, *Women Strike for Peace: Traditional Motherhood and Radical Politics in the 1960s* (Chicago: University of Chicago Press, 1993); Marian Beth Mollin, "Actions Louder than Words: Gender and Political Activism in the American Radical Pacifist Movement, 1942-1972" (Ph.D. Dissertation, University of Massachusetts at Amherst, 2000); Jessica M. Frazier, "Collaborative Efforts to End the War in Vietnam: the Interactions of Women Strike for Peace, the Vietnamese Women's Union, and the Women's Union of Liberation, 1965-1968," *Peace & Change* 37:3 (July 2012): 339-365; Jerry Lembcke, *Hanoi Jane: War, Sex, and Fantasies of Betrayal* (Amherst: University of Massachusetts Press, 2010); James Dickerson, *North to Canada: Men and Women against the Vietnam War* (Westport, CT: Praeger, 1999).

[3] There is a growing literature of black women's contributions and notable exceptions to the masculine discourse of organizing, including Winifred Brienes, *The Trouble Between Us: An Uneasy History of White and Black Women in the Feminist Movement* (New York: Oxford University Press, 2006); Bettye Collier-Thomas and V.P. Franklin, eds. *Sisters in the Struggle: African American Women in the Civil Rights-Black Power Movement* (New York: NYU Press, 2001); Dayo F. Gore, Jeanne Theoharis, and Komozi Woodard, eds., *Want to Start a Revolution: Radical Women in the Black Freedom Struggle* (New York: NYU Press, 2009); Christina Greene, *Our Separate Ways: Women and the Black Freedom Movement in Durham, North Carolina* (Chapel Hill: University of North Carolina Press, 2005); Faith S. Holsaert, Martha Prescod Norman Noonan, Judy Richardson, Betty Garman Robinson, Jean Smith Young, and Dorthy M. Zellner, eds., *Hands on the Freedom Plow: Personal Accounts by Women in SNCC* (Urbana: University of Illinois Press, 2012); Danielle McGuire, *At the Dark End of the Street: Black Women, Rape, and Resistance from Rosa Parks to the Rise of Black Power* (New York: Knopf, 2010); Barbara Ramsey, *Ella Baker and the Black Freedom Movement: A Democratic Vision* (Chapel Hill: University of North Carolina Press, 2003); Belinda Robnett, *How Long, How Long: African American Women in the*

Struggle for Civil Rights (New York: Oxford University Press, 2000); Robyn Ceanne Spencer, "Engendering the Black Freedom Struggle: Revolutionary Black Womanhood and the Black Panther Party in the Bay Area, California," *Journal of Women's History* 20, no. 1 (2008): 90-113; Kimberly Springer, ed., *Still Lifting, Still Climbing: Contemporary African American Women's Activism* (New York: NYU Press, 1999) and *Living for the Revolution: Black Feminist Organizations, 1968-1980* (Durham: Duke University Press, 2005); Anne M. Valk, *Radical Sisters: Second-Wave Feminism and Black Liberation in Washington, D.C.* (Urbana: University of Illinois Press, 2008); Deborah Gray White, *Too Heavy a Load: Black Women in Defense of Themselves* (New York: W.W. Norton and Company, 1999); Rhonda Y. Williams, *The Politics of Public Housing: Black Women's Struggles Against Urban Inequality* (New York: Oxford University Press, 2004).

[4] Daniel Patrick Moynihan, *The Negro Family: The Case for National Action* Office of Policy Planning and Research, Department of Labor, March, 1965, 29.

[5] Patricia Hill Collins, *Black Feminist Thought: Knowledge, Consciousness, and the Politics of Empowerment* (New York: Routledge, 2000), 76-106.

[6] Carol Giardina, *Freedom For Women: Forging the Women's Liberation Movement, 1953-1970* (Gainesville: University of Florida Press, 2010), 89.

[7] Evelyn Brooks Higginbotham explained the politics of respectability through the actions of middle class church women at the turn of the 20th century. Those women "adhered to a politics of respectability that equated public behavior with individual self-respect and with the advancement of African Americans as a group. They felt certain that 'respectable' behavior in public would earn their people a measure of esteem from white America, hence they strove to win the black lower class's psychological allegiance to temperance, industriousness, thrift, refined manners, and Victorian sexual morals." *Righteous Discontent: The Women's Movement in the Black Baptist Church, 1880-1920* (Cambridge: Harvard University Press, 1993), 14; Tanisha C. Ford, "SNCC, Women, Denim, and the Politics of Dress," *Journal of Southern History* 79, No. 3 (August, 2013): 625-658.

[8] Gwen Patton, interview with the author, 1/15/2013; Simon Hall, *Peace and Freedom: The Civil Rights and Antiwar Movements in the 1960s* (Philadelphia: University of Pennsylvania Press, 2006), 42, 143-148, 190.

[9] Gwen Patton, "Black People and the Victorian Ethos," *The Black Woman: An Anthology*, ed. Toni Cade Bambara (New York: Washington Square Press, 1970), 140-148; Gwen Patton, interview with the author, 1/15/2013; Margo Natalie Crawford, "Must Revolution be a Family Affair? Revisiting The Black Woman,"

Want to Start a Revolution?: Radical Women in the Black Freedom Struggle, eds. Dayo F. Gore, Jeanne Theoharis, and Komozi Woodward (New York: New York University Press, 2009), 185-204.

[10] Springer, *Living for the Revolution*, 49; Kimberly Springer, "Black Feminists Respond to Black Power Masculinism," *The Black Power Movement: Rethinking the Civil Rights-Black Power Era*, ed. Peniel E. Joseph (New York: Routledge, 2006), 105-118.

[11] "Third World Antiwar March, Nov. 4," *Triple Jeopardy*, ND, 3.

[12] Maryanne Weathers, "An Argument for Black Women's Liberation as a Revolutionary Force," Oct. 1968, 1-2, Social Action Vertical File, Black and Third World Women's Liberation Alliance, Wisconsin State Historical Society, Madison, Wisconsin.

"Just Like My Momma Use to Say": *African American Mothers as Keepers and Teachers of Culture*

Pamela Twyman Hoff

"Don't forget the bridge that brought you over"

African American culture is a unique blend of African cultures shaped by a shared experience of trauma, resistance and resiliency in the United States (Gates 1988; Stuckey [1987] 2011). Separation from the natal culture and enslavement did not strip Africans of their cultural memories and knowledge that informed their foundational beliefs, values and worldviews. Africans who were enslaved and their descendants had the monumental task of identifying, naming, representing, and responding to the conditions, complexity and contradictions that characterized their very existence (Marable and Mullings 2000). The intermingling of natal cultural memories and knowledge constructed from everyday practices formed an epistemological well from which African Americans would draw to develop culture, create counter ways of knowing that informed and justified resistance to structures of oppression for self-determination.

The African American oral tradition has been a long standing institution for the transmission and preservation of cultural values, knowledge and history (Smitherman 1977, 2001; Hamlet 2011). The narratives, stories, old sayings, parables, metaphors, songs and other creative expressions characterize the ways in which African American people communicated the desires of the heart, will and strategies to live from generation to generation. In the African and African American oral traditions, the speaker and listener are engaged in a style of communication that relies on nonverbal cues, gestures and notations to hold interest, evoke feelings and emotions (Kenyatta 1967, Mosha 2000, Hamlet 2011).

In African American culture, the motherwork of African American women has been critical in the preservation and transmission of the deep structural cultural values (Giddings 1985; Roberts 1997; Collins 1999; Abdullah 2012). The value of oral conceptualist teaching and learning is well documented in the literature, however in the wake of the hegemonic value of education these ways are slowly disappearing with the elders. There is a sense of urgency to study the relational ways in which these ways of knowing most used by African American mothers contributes to the development of her people and communities. Along those lines of reasoning, this discussion focuses on the oral conceptualist motherwork of African American women and their use of *sayin's* to transmit and reinforce cultural ways of knowing in a way that activates thinking about self, others and society.

Sayin's like all language emerges from the need to communicate, express feelings and transmit knowledge. Wrought from dialectical prism of hegemony, resistance, skill and cultural development, *sayin's* function as conceptual tools that stimulate higher level thinking that are meant to bring about an awareness of self and others. The instructional value of *sayin's* in the African American oral conceptualist tradition function similarly to proverbs, metaphors and riddles in African oral tradition. According to Joyce Penfield and Mary Duru (1988) proverbs are conceptual bridges to what is known with the unknown. Like proverbs *sayin's* are replete with multiple meanings that inspire, correct behavior and pass on ways of knowing. Like metaphors, symbols and images, *sayin's* present abstract thoughts and feelings that may be too complex to explain or comprehend. Riddles are word puzzles (Mosco 2000) in which figurative language is used to conceal and convey a concept. The listener is expected to decode the concept from its characteristics to reveal the literal meaning(s). In everyday speech *sayin's* convey thoughts, feelings, ideas, and ways of knowing, belief systems, and codes of behavior, ethics, perceptions and values. Teaching and learning in these ways brings about a conceptual awareness and thought process that make it possible to apprehend the complexity and contradictory nature of the lived experience.

This discussion was taken from a larger study (Hoff & Allen-Brown forthcoming) of African American *sayin's*. What emerged from the study was the overwhelming identification of mothers as the primary users of *sayin's*. Over 50 individuals were interviewed, and the vast majority started their reflections with the phrase, *"my momma use to say ..."* For clarity it is critical to note that my use of the word "mother" is not limited to blood relations. Rather, it is used in alignment with the African American value of mothering borne from a commitment to children for the transmission of culture and wellbeing of the community (Collins 1997; 1999; Wyche 1998). From this cultural vantage point, use of the term "mothers" include biological mothers, othermothers, grandmommas, aunties, and spiritual and community mothers. The motherwork of these women has been to care for, support, pass on cultural values, encourage, advocate for, love and teach to ensure that children become self-determining and productive members of the community. The mothering of these women has included the use of *sayin's* in a way that has sustained and preserved African American culture.

"A Wishbone Will not Suffice Where a Backbone is Needed"

Motherhood in the African American cultural context occupies a well-deserved position of esteem. Black mothers have been on the frontlines in the struggle against systemic domination (Collins 1999; Abdullah 2012). Reverence for Black motherhood was certainly shaped by the experiences in America; however it is equally important to note that this reverence has deep cultural roots in African culture. Runoko Rashidi (1992) makes clear the extent and depth to which ancient Africans valued and respected motherhood as a philosophical and spiritual institution:

> .... the Africans had strongly developed religious concepts in which the female deity played a tremendously important part. Indeed, in the earliest times, she had an all-encompassing influence and was universally acknowledged as the greatest and ultimate seat of power. She was both the giver and sustainer of life. These religious concepts, still powerful today, originated not in the Nile Valley, strange as it may seem, but in the Great Lakes region of East/Central Africa, the continental cradled. Here, in this primordial center, occurred the molding and forming of the religious and philosophical ideas that were to critically shape the world. (p. 72)

Nah Dove (2002) introduces the concept of the mother-centered matrix to articulate the values and communal benefits of a mother-center philosophy. The mother-center matrix values balance between male and female principles where in which there is a shared responsibility and commitment of all to ensure the wellness of the community and preservation of culture for the benefit of children and families. Invasions of Africa from the north and south, colonization and imperialism, chattel slavery institutionalized worldviews that privileges masculine principles while devaluing feminine principles. The historical reverence of Black motherhood in the Black community has a similar tone and tenor of its cultural progenitor confounded by systemic domination. In systems of domination patriarchy and racism are symbiotic concepts (Robert 1993). Patricia Hill Collins (1997) pushes this a bit further, she posits,

> Black motherhood as an institution is both dynamic and dialectical. Ongoing tensions characterize efforts to mold the institution of Black motherhood to benefit intersecting oppressions of race, gender, class, sexuality, and nation and efforts by African-American women to define and value our own experiences with motherhood. (176)

Under the slavocracy, Black women's reproduction was, what Roberts (1993) called, the "quintessential servant" of White patriarchy (p.9). Black mothers, castigated as non-human, had no legal claim to their children and were systematically forced to separate from them. In the White supremacist patriarchal capitalistic power structure the images of Jezebel, Mammy and Sapphire were constructed and purported to rationalize inhumane practices that mischaracterized and defined Black motherhood as pathological (Roberts 1993; 1997). Jezebel, the hyper-sexualized vamp was undeserving and incapable of mothering, as she was controlled by her lascivious desires. Neglecting her own children for the benefit of White children asexual mammy was deemed fit to mother when supervised by Whites. Mean spirited and quarrelsome Sapphire was incapable of sustaining relationships with Black men to create the type of home needed to raise children. She in particular has shouldered the blamed for the so-called destruction of the Black family. In African American culture strength and perseverance of Black mothers has been warped in the social construction of the mythical "strong Black woman" whose struggles are minimized as she places everyone's needs above her own (Collins 1999). The historically distorted images and malignment of Black mothers and motherhood has provided rationale for the unique subjugation of African American women in particular and Black people in general (Abdullah 2011).

Katherine Fouquier's (2011) study of African American mothers' perceptions and experiences of illustrated the guiding principles of Dove's (2002) mother-centered matrix. Mothering and motherhood for these women was a site and source of power and empowerment. In their cultural memories is a powerfully awareness of what it means to raise a Black child in America. Black mothers have the precarious task of passing on this awareness in a way that does not victimization or create fatalistic self-perceptions. To safeguard and protect their children's identity, Black mothers use many strategies, in which Fouquier (2011) discusses under the integrative theme, "preserving our home."

> ... Preserving Our Home illuminates the complex task that African American mothers face in communicating the insidious effects of racism to their children while simultaneously integrating a legacy of pride along with the values, culture, and traditions of the Black community. African American mothers have the monumental task of teaching their children to successfully negotiate racial discrimination and prejudice without damaging their self-esteem or racial identity (151).

To preserve their homes these mothers sought the s guidance and support of the community and relied on the oralist teaching and learning methods learned from mothers and other mothers. Mothers in studies conducted by Dove (1998) and Melina Abdullah (2011) support these claims while adding another task to Black motherwork. Mothers in the Dove and Abdullah studies felt a need to plant and grow in their children a spirit of resistance. For these mothers the nature of the Black lived experience necessitated that their children armed with the counter-cultural knowledge that would allow them to constructively fight back in a society that practices ritualized "dishonorment."

"A Word to the Wise is Sufficient"

The impetus for this study and subsequent collection of over 50 *sayin's* and their corresponding analyzes comes from my experiences learning at supper table, in the car, walking through the store or sitting in the church pews. For me, the learning never ceased as it occurred across my lived experience through my grandmother's use of sayin's. My grandmother had a *sayin'* to fit any situation each delivered with rapid fire precision. For example, I would ask, "Momma can I have ..." she would answer, *people in hell want ice water.* In that one simple phrase my grandmother challenged me to think simultaneously about the things that I knew and did not know at the same time.

There were 30 respondents in the study, all of whom are African American ranging in age from 17 to 92 from southern and mid-western states as well as from the east coast. Of the 30 respondents, 26 were women. A snowball sampling method was used to recruit participants. Recruitment letters were posted on social media outlets and list serves as well as other sites that targeted African Americans. Participants were invited to complete an online survey, and asked to follow up if interested in participating in individual or group interviews (dialogues). Like me, all of the respondents indicated they had grown up with *sayin's*", and credited them with instilling values, guiding behavior, codes of ethics. They were sources of inspiration throughout life, revealing knowledge and insight at each stage of development. Most importantly, *sayin's* laid the foundation to "think" about and how to "be" with the goal of rising above "isms".

Mary Catherine, a 92 year old mother of nine, is most proud that she has lived to see her great-great children. Her narrative suggests the subversive nature of the awareness and knowledge.

> *Mary Catherine*:   .... I remember when daddy [her husband of over 30 years] was in the hospital. He was dying of that cancer that men get. Uh-huh, that's the one. Well, he was dying from prostate cancer. He was in the hospital bed, doctor came in. He was white ... [looks around as if to see if we were alone]
>   *[Laughter]*
>
> Anyway, he [the doctor] was white. He looks at daddy and says, you have diabetes. What he said after that, don't know, he left, I looked at daddy and daddy looked at me, and before I know it, I said, *what white folks don't want they give to us. [laughs]* My auntie and grandmomma used to say that all the time. It's

true too

It means what it says. You got to watch. White folk have always wanted to give us the scraps they don't want. They diseases too, *got to work twice as hard to get have the credit.* Uh-huh that's another one. You got to watch, speak up for yourself, work hard, watch for yourself.

Taught me to speak up for myself, watch out for me and my family. Don't believe everything you hear. They have a way of making you think what they saying best for all. You ain't gonna put that in there, there'll be hell to pay.

One of sixteen children, Etta is 46 year old single mother of two children. She credits her social activism and love of learning to her parents.

> *Etta:* If someone was talking too much, a heated debate needed to end my momma would say, *a word to the wise is sufficient."* She'd use it to mean different things. You could tell what she meant by the way she'd nod her head, a side eye with a nod, not good. She loved a good debate, and wanted us to have those communication skills. If your argument, logic or presentation was off, she'd use that sayin'. I don't know how to say this, but that sayin' compels me to go the extra mile. To know my stuff, go deeper than the surface. Say what you mean and mean what you say, be concise, effective, knowledgeable. Don't let my emotions get the best of me, but to follow my instincts. Be intentional with your thoughts and actions, and purposeful with your action.

Sonny, a spry 70 year old, man, who brags that the more snow on the mountain the wiser he becomes.

> *Sonny:*   My momma use to tell me *to act like a man even, if you don't feel like one.* That has stayed with me for all my life. I've had to say it to myself, many times [repeats the sayin' and pauses]. There have been times in my life when I haven't felt like a man. For all kinda reasons, told I was nothing, felt like I was nothing, not being able to find work, working but not being to make ends meet. Then I could hear my momma telling me, and I'd remember to pull myself up. This too shall pass, I'm made out of stronger stuff things this thing is trying to tell me I am. I got my dignity, my family, my self-respect,

the respect of my family, can't nobody take that away from me. No matter what anybody said or what society told me, you know, I can and should rise up over that thing, that feeling, whatever it was. You know what I mean?

Similar to Etta, Anne, a 40-something graduate student, with a rhythmic southern accent recalled that her momma's *sayin'* has helped her to navigate higher education in a way that keeps her grounded.

> *Anne:* Miss Jean, my momma, use to tell me all the time about the teachers at my school. She use to say, *those teachers are there to make you stupid, so you better get what them teachers telling you and figure out what they ain't.* We have the tendency to believe that education will solve all of issues. It does not. Many teachers thought I wouldn't amount to anything. I've had to take what they say with a grain of salt. I'm a critical thinking because Ms. Jean [her mother]. Really, I

Eat the Meat and Leave the Bones

The institution of Black motherhood is complex and multidimensional, characterized by the dialectics of empowerment and disempowerment. Like all mothers, Black mothers must protect and prepare their children to live and grow in society. However, mothering while Black carries within it the complicated task of preparing children to live in a society in which they routinely debased. Hence, Black mothers are forced to find a way of passing on this existential awareness in a way that does not further victimize or fracture the child's identity. In their triadic roles as teachers, caretakers and cultural brokers Black mothers utilize a number of interrelated strategies and techniques to *mother through the "isms"* (Fouquier 2011). Reliance on community informed by mother-centered values (Dove 2002) have been essential in assisting Black mothers navigate this conceptual tightrope. This research illustrates the ways in which African American mothers use of *sayin's* transmits cultural knowledge that is a source of inspiration, activates conceptual skills to bring about an awareness of self and society. As such, the oral conceptualist teaching of Black mothers as worked to preserved African American culture and transformed communities. As overt controlling processes have morphed into more pervasive culturally controlling processes the awareness of and beneficence of these ways of knowing have waxed and waned depending on cultural and socio-political factors (Hoff, forthcoming). In the wake of post-racial dialogues confounded by the hegemonic rhetoric of formalized education and school it is even more critical that the value and understanding of these ways of knowing and processes of learning are kept alive.

Works Cited

Abdullah, Melina. "Womanist Mothering: Loving and Raising the Revolution." *Western Journal of Black Studies*, 36, no. 1 (2012): 57-67.

Baldwin, James. "If Black English isn't a Language, then tell me, What is?." *Black Scholar* 27, no. 1 (1997): 5-6.

Collins, Patricia Hill. "The meaning of motherhood in Black culture and Black Mother/Daughter Relationships." In *Toward a New Psychology of Gender: A reader,* edited by Mary M. Gergen and Sara N. Davis Gergen, 325-341. New York: Routledge, 2013.

Collins, Patricia Hill. *Black Feminist Thought: Knowledge, Consciousness, and the Politics of Empowerment.* New York: Routledge, 1999.

Davis, Angela Y. *Women, race, & class.* New York: Random House, 2011.

Dove, Nah. *Afrikan mothers: Bearers of culture, makers of social change.* New York: SUNY Press, 1998.

Dove, Nah. "Defining a mother-centered matrix to analyze the status of women." *Journal of Black Studies* 33, no. 1 (2002): 3-24.

Fouquier, Katherine Ferrell. "The concept of motherhood among three generations of African American women." *Journal of Nursing Scholarship* 43, no. 2 (2011): 145-153.

Gates Jr, Henry Louis. *The Signifying Monkey: A Theory of African-American Literary Criticism: A Theory of African-American Literary Criticism.* New York: Oxford University Press, 1988.

Giddings, Paula. *When and Where I enter.* New York: Bantam Books, 1985.

Hamlet, Janice D. "Word! The African American oral tradition and its rhetorical impact on American popular culture." *Black History Bulletin* 74, no. 1 (2011): 27-31.

Hoff, Pamela Twyman and Allen-Brown, Vanessa. *Seeds of fire: African American indigenous knowledge and school preparation,* forthcoming.

Kenyatta, Jomo. *Facing Mount Kenya.* London: Secker & Warburg, 1961.

Mosha, R. Sambuli. *The Heartbeat of Indigenous Africa; A Study of the Chagga Education System*. Shrewsbury, MA: Garland Publishing, Inc, 2000.

Penfield, Joyce, and Mary Duru. "Proverbs: Metaphors that teach." *Anthropological Quarterly* 61, no. 3 (1988): 119-128.

Rashidi, Runoko. "African Goddess: Mothers of Civilization," in *Black Women in Antiquity*. edited by Ivan Sertima, 72-88. New Brunswick, NJ: New Brunswick Publishers, 1992.

Roberts, Dorothy E. "Racism and Patriarchy in the Meaning of Motherhood." American University of Gender and Law, 1, no. 1 (1993) 1-38.

Roberts, Dorothy E. "Unshackling black motherhood." *Michigan Law Review* (1997): 938-964.

Smitherman, Geneva. *Talkin and Testifyin: The Language of Black America*. Detroit, MI: Wayne State University Press, 1977.

Smitherman, Geneva. *Word from the Mother: Language and African Americans*. New York: Routledge, 2011.

Sparks, Elizabeth. "Against All Odds: Resistance and Resilience in African American Welfare Mothers." In *Mothering against the Odds: Diverse Voices of Contemporary Mothers*, edited by Cynthia Garcia Coll, Janet L. Surrey, and Kathy Weingarten., 215-237. New York: The Guilford Press, 1998.

Stuckey, Sterling. *Slave culture: Nationalist theory and the foundations of Black America*. New York: Oxford University Press, [1987] 2013.

Wyche, Karen Fraser. African American Mothers Living with HIV/AIDS. From Coll, Cynthia Garcia, Janet L. Surrey, and Kathy Weingarten (Eds). Mothering against the Odds: Diverse Voices of Contemporary Mothers. The Guilford Press, New York, NY 10012, 1998. 173-189

A Nod to Women of the Race: Seeking to Understand Kelly Miller

Ida E. Jones

> I am anxious about many things concerning the Negro race. I am anxious   about its political rights, its civil privileges, industrial outlook, educational opportunity, but my chief anxiety is that it will persevere in the eternal   moral and spiritual verities…If it will but persevere in these things all things will be added in the fulness [sic] of time.[1]

In April 1950 the *Negro Digest* published an article entitled "America's Greatest Unknown Negro." This article explored the contributions of then 11 years dead Kelly Miller.[2] "A new junior high school in Washington, D.C. was recently christened Kelly Miller in honor of one of the greatest unsung leaders of the Negro race… But few youngsters today have ever heard of this man who wielded one of the most potent pens in America." Throughout the article, the question of "why" had Miller's legacy been relegated to obscurity was presented. Since 1950, scholars and others have asked and answered the same question. There are three are roughly three points of consideration: he left no lasting institution such as Booker T. Washington's Tuskegee Institute, or corpus of work like W.E.B. Dubois *Souls of Black Folk,* or organization like Marcus Garvey's Universal Negro Improvement Association. Therefore, in summation, Miller was a man limited to the issues of his day. However, some aspects of Miller's intellectual prowess have remained prevalent in the minds of scholars, his views on women.

The majority of Miller's writings focused on the condition of the race, yet his pen found time and interest in discussing gender issues. Some scholarship characterized Miller's legacy as misogynistic often citing one of two articles he wrote either "Negro Surplus Women" or "The Risk of

Woman Suffrage." In "Surplus Women," Miller is countering an article by Charlotte Gilman entitled "Surplus Women."

Charlotte Perkins Gilman was born in 1860 in Connecticut. Encouraged by her father, Gilman was a voracious reader and rising feminist. She prided herself on being kin to the Beecher family with great-aunts such as Catherine Beecher, prominent educator; Harriet Beecher Stowe author and abolitionist; and Isabella Beecher Hooker, women's rights activist. Her personal life was plagued by severe depression and a troubled marriage. She found consolation in writing and lecturing about women's independence and self-sufficiency. Her lecture tours contributed to traveling throughout the United States. She became a proponent of temperance, suffrage and labor reform. In her article "Surplus Women," Gilman suggests that women migrate from rural areas to urban centers where opportunities for marriage or independence and exposure were readily available.

Miller's interest in her argument was expressly concerned with Black women involved in the Great Migration. He believed that when these women arrived north and realized the harsh conditions especially in earning a living they might be persuaded or forced into prostitution. Historian Cheryl Hicks explores the social landscape that black women faced in New York during the 1920s. Hicks noted that young women who worked menial jobs and/or were socialized in ways she calls "harmful intimacy" resulted in Black women being arrested on suspicion of prostitution.[3] The stigma attached to most working class women rendered them more susceptible to public scrutiny. During World War I these women were of particular concern to the federal government because they feared the spread of venereal disease yet another gross stereotype. Nevertheless, Hicks asserts that these women continued to live their lives with degrees of wisdom to avoid being arrested or placated as prostitutes.

Miller was concerned that some Black women might believe themselves able to experience the freedom Gilman illustrates in her writing.

> What of the lot of those surplus women who are not white, and not so very free? Is the ennobling sisterhood of woman to be limited to the color line? The struggle of colored woman towards purity and refinement involves as deep and as dark a tragedy as any that marks the history of human strivings...These left-over, or to-be-left-over, Negro women, falling as they do in large part in the lower stratum of society, miss the inhibitive restraint of culture and social pride, and especially, if they be comely of appearance, become the easy prey of the evil designs of both races...The great bulk of colored women in our cities, [are] being shut out from higher avenues of work, must seek employment in domestic service...The Negro woman is handicapped by such an unfavorable environment that it seems almost inhuman to make her the butt of witticism and ridicule as is sometimes done, because from the depth of her lowliness she dares aspire to the highest and best things in life.[4]

Miller's argument holds merit especially when one considers the settlement house movement. The settlement homes sought to provide safe harbor for women moving to the urban north alone, unconnected and unfamiliar with "big city" living. Notably, Victoria Earle Matthews' White Rose Home in New York sought to stave off such abuse of Black women. Matthews noted that the exploitation of migrating black women was a sport of racial cooperation, where blacks and whites abused unsuspecting women. In all fairness Miller's response could be read as condescending toward working class women, labeling them as people of low moral standards. Miller did harbor an element of moral superiority; however, his deepest concern remained with the positive and wholesome progress of all Black people.

In the other alleged misogynistic article "The Risk of Woman Suffrage," Miller proposed a serious examination of women in the political arena. He asserted that politics were an ugly business that could lead to physical and emotional violence irrespective of one's gender. Could women stomach it? Should they have to stomach it? He wrote:

> The human race is divided horizontally by age, vertically by sex and diagonally by race. Each individual passes from the minor to the adult stage in the course of a life time; the cleavage of race is subject to indefinite modification through environment and intermingling of blood; but sex is the one fixed and unalterable separatrix (sic) of mankind...Woman's sphere of activity falls mainly within while man's field of action lies largely without the domestic circle. This represents the traditional and, presumably, the ideal relation between the sexes. It has the sanction of divine authority and the test of human experience. Woman suffrage could not possibly enhance the harmoniousness of this relationship, but might seriously jeopardize it.[5]

Throughout the article Miller cited that women were endowed with finer feelings and higher emotions. To the contrary she lacked the sharp sense of public justice and common good if they run counter to her personal feelings or interest. Miller wrote "Female suffrage has been tried in twelve states of the Union, but so far no genuine public benefit has resulted therefrom, nor has the lot of woman been ameliorated more rapidly than in other states under exclusive male suffrage." Miller seemingly ignored the civic pride the vote inspired in the hearts of enfranchised women. However, being Negro formed a separate and distinct class from other people. Those non-Negro people would not champion the Negro cause, while, men might champion the cause of their mothers, wives and daughters. History informs us that male politicians did not wholly advocate for women's rights, but Miller believed ideally they should have been considered.

It is alleged that Negro suffrage and woman suffrage rest on the same basis. But on close analysis it is found that there is scarcely any common ground between them. The female sex does not form a class separate and distinct from the male sex in the sense that the Negro forms a class separate and distinct from the whites. Experience and reason both alike shows that no race is good enough to govern another without that other's consent. On the other hand both experience and reason demonstrate that the male seeks the welfare and happiness of the female even above his own interest. The Negro cannot get justice or fair treatment without the suffrage. Woman can make no such claim, for man accords her not only every privilege which he himself enjoys but the additional privilege of protection.[6]

The harsh sound of this ahistorical reality for women smacks of misogynist, however, Miller knew the innate power of women to operate outside of the sphere of politics. At the root of the issue for Miller was not that women sought to vote or hold office as civic equals, the feminine agenda sought to make women "artificially identical" to men. This "artificial" identity moved women from their "divinely authorized" position resulting in fallout which he did not articulate. Miller closed the article indicating that if men and women were "artificially identical" and allowed to vote at 21 this ran afoul of biology. Miller wrote: "men are accorded the privilege at that age; whereas according to their physical and mental developments, the sexes have a different order of maturity. If the strictly physiological and psychological basis of male suffrage is placed at twenty-one, female suffrage should be placed at eighteen. If man should be allowed to vote on the first appearance of a mustache, some woman would doubtless demand the same privilege. Male and female created He them; what God has made different man strives in vain to make identical."[7] In careful reading Miller believed that well-intentioned women were commendable while others were seeking to erase all gender distinctions. The dissolution of those distinctions were unacceptable and an affront to the divine order according to Miller's cosmology. The two articles spoke his mind against the stream of popular opinion. He has incurred misunderstanding resulted in being labeled anti-woman. Hopefully, full reading of these articles in the context of my paradigm Miller the private, public and polemic man would allow his writings a renewed perspective.

To the contrary, in an article entitled "The Emergence of Negro Women," Miller celebrated the leadership of Mary Church Terrell. She was born on September 23, 1863 in Memphis, Tennessee. Terrell was born into a family of privilege. Her father's investment in real estate made him a millionaire. Fair complexioned, educated and allowed access to travel, Terrell's sense of racial pride and unity came from affronts she endured because of the virulent racism of the South.

She obtained a degree from Oberlin University in Oberlin, Ohio in 1884. She moved to Washington D.C. and taught at the M Street School. Her growing awareness of discrimination propelled her to intensified study and a consummate desire to speak out on behalf of the unlettered in general and Black women in particular. She was the first president of the National Association of Colored Women's Clubs (NACWC) in 1896. Crafting the NACWC into a social justice organization she helped them create day nurseries, kindergartens and Mother's Clubs. All of these efforts sought to ameliorate the harsh conditions of working class Black women. Her advocacy advanced the race and sought better opportunities for working women and rising generations of young Black women. She wrote articles, lectured and protested for change. In her over 90 years of life, Terrell did not concede to color privilege within the Black community as a place of refuge from empathizing with the economically or aesthetically challenged elements of the African American community. Miller commented on

105

Terrell's 1904 address at the international Congress of Women held in Berlin, Germany. Miller's comments came from a sense of race pride. Terrell attended the conference as part of the American delegation and was the only woman of color. When she arrived in Berlin to deliver her address there had been some concern that speaking in English would lessen its impact, to their surprise she delivered her address in German. She was fluent in German as well as English and French. He wrote:

> This brilliant daughter of a despised race, stood in her place amid this celebrated assembly and pled the cause of her sable sisters in English, French and German, with such ease and eloquence that each delegate from those nations could hear and understand the sad story in her own tongue. The effect of one who herself had come up from lowly conditions which she so eloquently portrayed voicing the miseries and wrongs, as well as, the struggles and triumphs, of black womanhood filled every heart with pity and melted every eye with tears...The case of colored man is often yoked with that of white woman by reason of the common denial of rights and withholding of opportunities on account of race, on the one hand and sex on the other.
> But the case of the colored woman stands alone in its pitiable helplessness. She is the most unfortunate of all the despised elements of our complex society. The sins and inequities of the male portion of both races are visited upon her. She bears the burden of their transgressions. If the situation and circumstances of the colored man awaken such anxious solicitude, and call so loudly for remedial endeavor, what should be said for the Negro woman who staggers beneath the weight of a much severer load? The mere contemplation of her condition fills the soul with infinite pity.
> Under the slave regime her native delicacy was forced into the closest intimacy of contact with the coarsest and most imbruted men of both races. As one of the most thoughtful of her own race has said: But from the day their fetters were broken and their mind released from the darkness of ignorance to which for more than two hundred years they had been doomed, from the day they could stand erect in the dignity of womanhood, no longer

bond, but free, till now, colored women have forged steadily ahead in the acquisition of knowledge, the cultivation of those arts that make for good...These are but samples of the higher aspirations of black, brown and bleached womanhood. Are not such shining emergencies from so dark and forbidden a background, striking and encouraging indications of a higher and better life to which this race is aspiring."[8]

In the same article "The Emergence of Negro Women," he acknowledged Nannie Helen Burroughs. She was born on May 2, 1879 in Orange, Virginia. Her mother's example figured prominent in her life. When her father died unexpectedly, Jennie Poindexter Burroughs, Nannie's mother moved them to Washington, D.C. for a new life. Jennie sought out employment and education for Nannie. While attending school Nannie was firmly entrenched in the Baptist church tradition. She attended the M Street School where she modeled and identified with teachers such as Mary Terrell regarding advancing the race in general and women in particular. Burroughs experienced disappointment at the hands of a high school instructor whose failure to apprentice her left her scrambling for employment. This disappointment opened a window of opportunity for Burroughs whose membership in the prominent Nineteenth Street Baptist Church encouraged her sense of duty to race advancement.

She worked for the Baptist church as a missionary while seeking to apprentice in domestic science/home economics. Unable to apprentice within domestic science, she poured her energy into church work and advancing the position of women. She published articles, lectured and encouraged women. She joined a number of women's clubs and remained an outspoken advocate of social justice as biblically mandated and civically needed. In 1909 she founded the National Training School for Women and Girls. The school motto "work, support thyself, to thine own powers appeal," opted to create opportunities for others she herself was denied. The school offered domestic science and missionary training. The remainder of life was dedicated to racial uplift and the empowerment of women. Miller and Burroughs were close friends. She dubbed him the Sage of the Potomac in part because of his prolific and insightful writings, as well as, his membership in the Bethel Literary Association. Miller wrote:

> As an orator Miss Burroughs is simply irresistible and sweeps all before her with the impetuosity of cyclonic power. Her effectiveness does not end in mere oratory. She is tireless practical worker. By indefatigable energy, she has established in the city of Washington a school for training of Negro girls in household duties and domestic service. When we consider that domestic service is practically the only avenue open to colored girls on an unlimited scale, it will be readily agreed that there is no school in all the scope of Negro philanthropy that is more worthy of aid and encouragement.[9]

Miller's positive perspective on women stemmed from his love and respect he had for his mother. He would father five children two which were girls. He supported his daughters and encouraged them to pursue education. All of his children attended Howard for undergraduate school and all of his children sought post graduate work at a variety of universities. Professionally, Miller maintained cordial relationships with women leaders such as Mary Church Terrell and Nannie Helen Burroughs. He also interacted with fellow educators Mary McLeod Bethune founder of Daytona Educational and Industrial Training School for Negro Girls in Tallahassee, Florida; Charlotte Hawkins Brown founder of the Alice Freeman Palmer Memorial Institute in Sedalia, North Carolina; and Howard's own Lucy Diggs Slowe first dean of women.

Mary McLeod Bethune invited Miller to Bethune-Cookman College in 1927. The financial conditions of Bethune-Cookman precluded her from being able to meet his speaking fee; however, she suggested that he consider a visit to Bethune-Cookman when in the area on other business. Bethune wrote, "Our students and teachers would be so very happy to have you with us, and I would be delighted. If this is not possible, I would not request that you go counter to your usual arrangements, for I know the worth of your message to our people."

Miller also earned the attention of rising notable women such as author Zora Neale Hurston who was a close friend of his eldest daughter May Miller. Hurston wrote him a brief thank you note where she expressed delight in receiving a letter from him. Moreover, she was deeply impressed by "your common sense attitude" towards the radicals. Hurston closed by stating "in a world of changing fashions, you seem to be like "the tree planted by the rivers of water."

He also promoted women writers. He had glowing words for author Sadie Daniel's book *Women Builders.* Daniels work was one of the early titles written by a Black woman about the accomplishments of Black women in professional arenas. The list of women could have spanned more than one volume; however, Daniels was shrewd in limiting the list, as well as, allowing another author to continue the roll call of worthy women. Miller wrote of *Women Builder*: Miss Daniels justifies this limited list by a word of caution:

> Of thousands we cannot write the full story. We shall note here only a few towering personages. This volume will restrict itself to Negro women who are pioneers – those who are builders of educational, financial and social institutions...I do not think that even the women themselves will find occasion to quarrel with the author by reason of the limited list, which, with two unaccountable exceptions, is complete within its category. We are thankful to Miss Daniels for giving us this plain, simple, readable volume and for justly extolling these seven race builders whose work attests

their worth. But we cannot confine our thought to the excellent portrayals presented. We lay down the volume more deeply impressed by what we read between the lines.[10]

His ability to craft words to address the race, nation and world left a lasting impact. Moreover, his passion for considering the contributions of woman led him to give them equal coverage as larger topics of race, politics and cultural criticism. Many of his essays have been reprinted in publications on African American intellectual history. There are several areas of scholarship that could plum the depth of Miller's writings to understand paradigms in independent, activist, and non-partisan thought. Miller was quoted as having distributed over one and half million copies of his publications in some form newspaper/journal article, pamphlet, and book essay. Here is an excerpt from the *Journal of Negro History* wrote:

> He has perfected the epistolary style of the polemic, beyond most writers of this age. His open letters to Thomas Dixon, to President Roosevelt, and to President Harding will take rank with the best literature of this sort of all times...His transient style, logical treatment, and comprehensiveness of presentation give his work a distinct place in the discussion of the race problem.[11]

Miller's writings spawned response and accolades from across the nation. Mary McLeod Bethune from the Daytona Educational and Industrial Training School for Negro Girls wrote Miller on October 6, 1917:

> I read with a great deal of interest and appreciation your letter to Pres. [Woodrow] Wilson. In the "Disgrace of Democracy." We are very happy to know that the race has a man like you to so ably champion its cause. I shall do all in my power to distribute the letter and have as many of them read as possible. I shall place one in the hands of my club women of the state. I am sending you my check for $1.00 for which please send me twenty copies. I shall be glad to get them as soon as possible. I shall be glad to have you visit our work in Daytona sometime and see what we are doing on this end.[12]

There were white people who supported Miller's writings. A white woman Mary O. White sister to Jeremiah Rankin former Howard University president, wrote Miller regarding his position on women. Miller's affinity for Rankin and his serendipitous meeting that spawned his career at Howard welcomed the warm words from White. She wrote:

> I notice you have acknowledged in the course of your letter that 'men are not considered good enough to govern women.' Let me congratulate you on the fact that you have reached this wise conclusion. It is absolutely true that no man, white, black, brown or yellow is good enough to govern women. I have profound respect for the things that women of your race are doing to help other women. I trust that woman suffrage will come to us all soon, and that it will give women of the colored race, who have even more to contend with than the women of the white race, the opportunity they so much need. Hoping you will fight with us and for us to bring this quickly.[13]

Miller's perception of women and gender issues was balanced and critical. He used the same formula in all of his writings. Son of an enslaved mother, father of two daughters, coming of age at time when civil and human rights wrestled for equality Miller remained the daysman/mediator. He sought to mediate consequence before every decision. His perspective on gender is one of the most publically balanced perspectives of his generation. Women of his generation held him in esteem and publically and privately associated with him. Younger women appreciated his scholarship and newspaper columns. In essence his desire for critical and balanced dialogue placed him opposite popular opinion he knew this and remained committed to the polemic position.

[1] Kelly Miller "The Heart of the Race Problem" 1909. This article is an excerpt from *The Heart of the Race Problem: The Life of Kelly Miller* Ida E. Jones, Tapestry Press 2011

[2] Kelly Miller (July 18, 1863- December 29, 1939). Born in Winnsboro, South Carolina, he was the sixth child of Kelly Miller a free Negro and Confederate army veteran and formerly enslaved Elizabeth Roberts Miller. In 1886-1889 first African American admitted to Johns Hopkins University where he did post-graduate work in mathematics and physics toward a Ph.D. On December 18, 1896 Miller, John Wesley Cromwell, Paul Laurence Dunbar and Walter B. Hayson accepted an invitation from Alexander Crummell to plan the formation of a learned Black society initially named the African Academy -- formally named the American Negro Academy. An educator, intellectual, columnist and polemic Miller challenged the ideological camps of Negro thought to embrace a vision beyond petty difference.

[3] Cheryl Hicks *Talk You Like a Woman: African American Women, Justice, and Reform in New York, 1890-1935*

[4] Kelly Miller, "Negro Surplus Women," *Race Adjustment*. 168-167

[5] Kelly Miller "The Risk of Women's Suffrage," p 37-38 *Crisis* November 1915

[6] Kelly Miller " The Risk of Women's Suffrage," p 37-38 *Crisis* November 1915

[7] Kelly Miller "The Risk of Women's Suffrage," p 37-38 *Crisis* November 1915

[8] "The Emergence of Negro Women," Kelly Miller papers, Box 19 folder 3 MARBL, Emory University.

[9] "The Emergence of Negro Women," Kelly Miller papers, Box 19 folder 3 MARBL, Emory University.

[10] *Kelly Miller "Sadie Daniels Extols Seven Women Builders," March 30, 1932 New York Amsterdam News*

[11] Book Review *The Everlasting Stain, Journal of Negro History*, vol. 9, no. 4 October 1924. 573.

[12] Letter from Mary McLeod Bethune to KM, Kelly Miller papers, Box 2 folder 6, MARBL, Emory University.

[13] Letter from Mary O. White to KM, Kelly Miller papers, Box 2 folder 2, MARBL, Emory University.

Nina Simone! A Liberation Artist of the 1960s

Regina V. Jones

Born 1933 in Tryon, North Carolina, Eunice Kathleen Waymon, and (Nina Simone) demonstrated her musical genius and dynamic personality as a three and a half year-old church pianist. As Nina Simone she put a spell on the pubic with her self-confident image, gifted command of the piano, stimulating lyrics, and her mastery of various genres of music. During the 1960s she used her musical talents to describe the sociopolitical realities of Black folk struggling for humane treatment in the USA. As the 1960s ended she reassured the youth that their gifts were accessible and goals attainable. However after two public racist acts of violence that Nina Simone announced "I suddenly realized what it is to be black in America in 1963…" (Simone with Cleary 144). After the slaying of civil rights activist Medgar Evers in June of 1963, followed by another stunning act of terrorism on the morning of November 15, 1963, at the Sixteenth Baptist Church in Birmingham, Alabama, when a bomb claimed the lives of four girls—Addie Mae Collins, Cynthia Wesley, Carole Robertson and Denise McNair—Nina Simone was reignited as an public activist.

Eleven year-old musical child progeny, Eunice Waymon confronted racial segregation at her first musical recital, at Tryon, North Carolina's town hall. As her parents were being shuttled from the front row, "in favor of a white family I had never seen before," she recalled standing on stage and informing the gathering that "if they expected to hear me play then they'd better make sure that my family was sitting right there in the front row where I could see them" (Simone with Cleary 26). Recognition of this act of discrimination caused young Eunice/Simone to acknowledge, "All of a sudden it seemed a different world, and nothing was easy any more. ...But now prejudice had been made real for me and it was like switching on a light" (26). Classical training transported Eunice firmly to a world separate from her working-class Pentecostal family beliefs and practices and beyond the kind white women who supported her.[1]

The recital occurrence embarrassed her parents and "I saw the white folks laughing at me" (26). Good manners and deportment were the cornerstones of well-bred adults and children in Black families. Well-raised African American children were expected to respect their elders, regardless of race, class or gender.

Eunice's sassy public outburst was a bold protest for an eleven year-old Black church girl, who needed the financial support of the community to continue perfecting her talent. Remembering the incident she stated "to hell with poise and elegance" and her parents were returned to their original seats (26). She had taken a direct stand against a common Jim Crow practice and won. This act of resistance made her aware of the casual and accepted practice of racial discrimination and that she could successfully stage a protest, in front of an audience, be heard, and achieve a positive outcome. Eunice's straightforward and outspoken response to racial injustice became characteristic of the candid manner in which she would later presented herself as a musical artist and activist. As she prepared to meet her goal of attending the Curtis Institute of Music, in Philadelphia, Pennsylvania, she relocated to New York and continued to study music at the Juilliard School of Music.

The Curtis Institute told her that her skills were not good enough and Eunice was devastated. However, her uncle—whom her biographer (Cohodas) states was "well connected in certain black and white circles"—

found that, "the Institute wanted to enroll black students, but if blacks were going to be admitted then they were not going to accept an unknown black, that if they were to accept an unknown black then it was not going to be an unknown black girl, and if they were going to admit an unknown black girl it wasn't going to be a very poor unknown black girl" (Cohodas 54; Simone 42). Her lifelong preparation and the conflicting reasons for her rejection to Curtis caused shame, humiliation and anger "at being just another victim of prejudice and at the same time there's the nagging worry that maybe it isn't that at all, maybe it's because you're just no good" (Simone with Cleary 43). The realization of racial, class and gender inequity was a nagging torment that many Black women had to navigate. For Eunice the piercing rejection from Curtis demonstrated that racism, classism, sexism could easily and unexpectedly present an obstacle to one's ambition and training. Shortly after the Curtis rejection Eunice Waymon became Nina Simone.

The classically trained Nina Simone demonstrated her appreciation for many forms of music—folk, jazz, musicals, blues, and gospel for example—and expanded her repertoire to include her compositions, collaborations and on occasion musical favorites where she altered the lyrics. Although she mastered many types of music Simone found that critics classified her as jazz singer. She took umbrage at such a classification—"Calling me a jazz singer was a way of ignoring my musical background because I didn't fit into white ideas of what a black performer should be. ...If I had to be called something it should have been a folk singer, because there was more folk and blues than jazz in my playing" (69). The fact that she was classically trained debunked the racist notions that Black musicians had natural gifts rather than training when it came to music; she asserts "...I put as much of my classical background as I could into the songs I performed and the music I recorded" (91). Simone's music was heard worldwide. She performed in countries on the continent Africa, Europe and in the West Indies. For many people in America and around the world during the 1960s much of her music spoke to the sociopolitical climate in America. Perhaps some of her music should be called consciousness-raising songs or call-to-action tunes as opposed to protest music as "I didn't like 'protest music' because a lot of it was so simple and unimaginative it stripped the dignity away from the people it was trying to celebrate" (Simone 90). Nevertheless, Nina Simone and her some of her music express the frustrations and struggles and occasionally the humor of the civil rights movement during the 1960s.

As previously mentioned the murder of Medgar Evers and the church bombing that killed four little girls in Birmingham, Alabama, provoked Simone to compose a jarring 'show tune,' titled "Mississippi Goddam," in 1963 and "...the entire direction of my life shifted, and for the next seven years I was driven by civil rights and the hope of black revolution" (Simone with Cleary 91). Historian Ruth Feldstein noted that the explicit political song came out "...just one month after the record-setting March on Washington ...and Martin Luther King's famous 'I Have A Dream' speech, she [Simone] provocatively departed from conventional wisdom..." (1352). Feldstein found that Simone is important because of "...the perspectives on black freedom and gender that she among others articulated circulated as widely as they did in the early 1960s" (1352). According to Simone wherever she performed "Mississippi Goddam" the audiences responded enthusiastically; after it was "...released as a single it sold well, except in the south" (Simone and Cleary 90).

Simone supported Dr. Martin Luther King Jr., and the SCLC, (Southern Christian Leadership Conference); SNCC, (Student Nonviolent Coordinating Committee); CORE (Congress of Racial Equality), the Black Panthers and a range of groups involved in civil rights. "I felt non-violence was the way forward in the early sixties because it seemed to get results, but I wasn't committed to non-violence for ideological reasons like Dr. King's organization, the SCLC. I knew a time might come where we would have to fight for what was right, and I had no problem with that:" (Simone with Cleary 94-95). After the assassination of Dr. King, she memorialized that moment on April 7, 1968, three days after the assassination performing "Why? (The King of Love is Dead)" before a live audience; "I think my performance that night was one of my very best, focused by the love and quiet despair we all felt at our loss" (115).

Many of her songs and performances told the stories, fantasies and realities of Black folk; notably she gave voice to the experiences of Black women. For example in "Pirate Jenny," a listener hears the rebellious monologue of a scrub woman; in "Go Limp" a committed young non-violent female activist reveals to her mother how she similarly handled heterosexual sex and peaceful protest; in "Old Jim Crow" she personifies segregation and tells him his time is over.[2]

However, it is Simone's powerful "Four Women" that continues to resonate even today. It speaks to the history and survival of four different Black women—"Saphronia, enslaved; Aunt Sarah, mammified; and Sweet Thing, lecherized. The fourth woman is Peaches, politicized: 'I'm very bitter these days cause my people were slaves—What do they call me? They call me Peee-Chezzz!'" (Bambara 104). Simone stated "Black women didn't know what the hell they wanted because they were defined by things they

117

didn't control and until they had the confidence to define themselves they'd be stuck in the same mess forever—that was the point the song made" (Simone with Cleary 117). She added "The song told a truth that many people in the USA—especially black men—simply weren't ready to acknowledge at that time" (117). As an artist, public figure, and woman Nina Simone collapsed a masculinized heterosexual image of an exclusive male vanguard in the public memory of the civil rights movement of the 1950s and 1960s specifically by her participation and including the voices of Black women. Nina Simone was a woman whose public voice, image, and presence directly and confidently confronted the status quo of American racism, classism, sexism and the Eurocentric perception of beauty.

As a young woman Nina Simone visibly embraced her natural beauty during a period when many Black women were conditioned to reject their natural physical characteristics.[3] Tiffany M. Gill in *Beauty Shop Politics* asserts, "In the 1950s and 1960s, ...For whites to see black women with their hair in its natural state was considered feeding into negative stereotypes of black women as unruly and undeserving of respectable treatment (105-106). Like modern dancer Pearl Primus, her student Maya Angelou, jazz musician Abbey Lincoln, actress Cicely Tyson, South African singer Miriam Makeba many prominent women began to liberate themselves from the stringent and unreasonable beauty regiments designed to diminish the pride and self-esteem of many Black women (Griffin 49). Simone offered an array of natural images from short natural, to head wraps to cornrows. Such images bolstered and encouraged a larger community of Black women to reclaim their natural beauty.

In addition to her natural hairstyles, Simone appeared to be comfortable in her chocolate skin. In American culture African American women are portrayed as the least desirable of all women based on hair, skin color and other Negroid facial and bodily features. As Maxine Leeds Craig points out in her book, *Ain't I a Beauty Queen,* "facial features also were ranked in a racial hierarchy" (26). Even within the African American community the hair texture and skin color of Black women established who possessed beauty for many—lighter complexion and straight or curly hair being the ideal. In the 1960s a Black woman's hair (long or short, kinky or straight) coupled with skin color (dark or light) and finally the accumulation of Negroid facial features (full lips and/or a broad nose) determined how peers, the larger society and even family members, in some cases, responded to Negro girl or woman (Craig 23; Wingfield 8-9; Byrd & Tharps 36-44). Simone's photos on album covers revealed her brown skin, full lips, etc.,—the antithesis of blonde hair, pale skin, thin lips and aquiline noses emblematic of the ideal of the American Eurocentric beauty during the 1950s and 1960s. The concept of beauty is significant because it is political and based on a culture of misogyny (Wolf 150). Simone's image was/is liberating because she conveys an identity of self-love—inner confidence, outer beauty in a public realm—that encouraged many Black women to experience and accept their beauty in positive ways. Even at the beginning of the twenty-first century researchers Jones and Shorter-Gooden prove that skin color is still a source of shame for many African American women (192). During the late 1950s and 1960s when many Black women were trying to make their lips appear thinner, ashamed of their broad noses, and to make their hair as straight and long as possible Simone's poised and self-confident images of womanhood helped claim American space and reinforced an acceptance for black beauty. Simone embodied an infectious Black pride that the public witnessed in her images and in her music.

Simone was as candid with her words as she appeared confident in her appearance.

African American women entertainers who publically challenged the sociopolitical climate of the 1960s were generally silenced and perceived as angry. Eartha Kitt was exiled from the American entertainment scene for ten years once she offered her view on the Viet Nam war at the white house, in 1968. After Abbey Lincoln's lyrical observations about American racism in the 1961 record, *Straight Ahead*, it was twelve years before she was allowed to produce another album.

> ...Black women exist against a backdrop of myth and stereotype, their voices are often distorted and misunderstood. If she is opinioned, she is difficult. If she speaks with passion, she is volatile. If she explodes with laughter, she is unrefined. ...So much of what Black women say, and how they say it, pushes other people to buy into the myth that Black women are inferior, harsh, and less feminine than other women (Jones and Shorter-Gooden 102).

Feldstein observed, "if rudeness in male jazz musicians confirmed their genius, similar behavior confirmed something else about Simone. ...Critics and fans characterized her as notoriously 'mean,' 'angry,' and 'unstable' or as eccentric and beset by 'inner fires. ...As a black woman, however, her status as a demanding diva evoked racially specific kinds of fear" (1359). It is important that Simone is not simply characterized and dismissed as an angry Black woman but as a woman who helped influence politics and cultural of the 1960s. Her commitment in terms of time, money, and artistry, to the civil rights movement is clear; yet, too many historical documents tend to diminish her influence. Loudermilk details Simone's omissions in an essay, "Nina

Simone and the Civil Rights Movement":

> ...Martin Luther King's major biographies (by Oates,
> Dyson, and Carson) fail to credit Nina Simone as the civil
> rights force who sang King's elegy. ...the epic PBS
> documentary *Eyes of the Prize* (Hampton 1987) does not
> mention Nina Simone or play a single one of her songs. In
> the sequel *Eyes on the Prize II* (Hampton 1990), we hear half
> a chorus of "I Wish I Knew How It Would Feel To Be
> Free" during a funeral and that's it. Original SNCC
> director John Lewis, in his memoir of the movement,
> excludes her too, though his successor Stokely Carmichael
> dubbed her the true singer of the CRM [Civil Rights
> Movement]. She may be pictured on the cover of *Chronicles
> of Negro Protest* (Chambers 1968), as part of Chicago's "Wall
> of Respect" mural, but she is not found among the pages
> inside. And you won't find her among *Freedom's Daughters:
> The Unsung Heroines of the Civil Rights Movement from 1830-
> 1970* (Olson 2001). ...she's not part of the Smithsonian
> Folkways compilation *Voices of the Civil Rights Movement:
> Black American Freedom Songs 1960-1966* from 1997 (126).

Black women pay a price to speak; and, Nina Simone confronted de facto and de jure practices of inequality. Simone's choice to challenge racism, sexism and classism was brave and revolutionary. It is expected that she would be characterized as 'angry' during the 1960s diminishing, simultaneously, the ubiquitous racism, classism and sexism that pervaded the country. Perhaps it was her gendered and 'militant' voice that caused Nina Simone to be overlooked in much of the historiography of activists and civil rights protest music during the 1950s-1970s. Nina Simone stood out and stood up to tell the realities of African American existence in America.

121

Finally, Simone ended the 1960s with love by immortalizing her dear friend, playwright, Lorraine Hansberry and contributing to the uplift of Black youth. Hansberry, whom Simone credits with beginning her education on racism and sexism, died before completing a drama titled *To Be Young Gifted and Black* (Simone with Cleary 87). Simone co-created a song using Hansberry's title. As an artist and entertainer who sought to raise public consciousness Nina Simone ends the decade with the release of a single song that encouraged young folk to understand their value—"To Be Young Gifted and Black" (1969).

---

[1] Mrs. Miller was Mary Kate Waymon's (Simone's mother) employer who agreed to pay for early piano lessons with Muriel Mazzanovich otherwise known as "Miz Mazzy." Miz Mazzy also stressed the expected poise and refinement of a concert pianist on stage to Simone. She also "helped her appreciate that every note had to be executed properly or the entire effect would be lost" Nadine Cohodas *Princess Noire* 35.

[2] For an historical examination of "Mississippi Goddamn," "Pirate Jenny" and "Go Limp" see Feldstein "'I Don't Trust You Anymore:'"

[3] Literary scholar Farah Jasmine Griffin in *Harlem Nocturne*, finds that "Black modern dancers would be among the first notable black women to wear their hair natural" and that innovative dancer Pearl Primas "...would pave the way for a different kind of physical type" with ..."unprocessed hair styles [that] were born of necessity" (49).

Works Cited

Bambara, Toni Cade. "Reading the Signs, Empowering the Eye." *Deep Sightings and Rescue Missions: Fiction, Essays, and Conversations*. New York: Pantheon Books, 1996. 89-138.

Bicknell, Jeanette. "Just a Song? Exploring the Aesthetics of Popular Song Performance." *Journal of Aesthetics and Art Criticism*, 63.3 (Summer 2005): 261-270.

Byrd, Ayana D. & Lori L. Tharps. *Hair Story: Untanagling the Roots of Black Hair in America*. New York: St Martin's Griffin, 2001.

Cohodas, Nadine. *Princess Noire: The Tumultuous Reign of Nina Simone*. New York: Pantheon Books, 2010.

Craig, Maxine Leeds. *Ain't I A Beauty Queen: Black Women, Beauty, and the Politics of Race*. Oxford University Press, 2002.

Feldstein, Ruth. "'I Don't Trust You Anymore': Nina Simone, Culture, and Black Activism in the 1960s." *The Journal of American History* 91.4 (2005): 1349-1379.

Gill, Tiffany M. *Beauty Shop Politics: African American Women's Activism in the Beauty Industry* . print. Urbana: University of Illinois Press, 2010.

Griffin, Farah Jasmine. *Harlem Nocturne: Women Artists and Progressive Politics During World War II*. New York: Basic Civitas, 2013.

Harris, Duchess. *Black Feminist Politics from Kennedy to Obama*. New York: Palgrave Macmillan, 2011.

Jones, Charisse & Kkumea Shorter-Gooden, Ph.D. *Shifting: The Double LIves of Black Women in America*. Harper Collins, 2003.

Loudermilk, A. "Nina Simone and the Civil Rights Movement: Protest at Her Piano, Audience at Her Feet." *Journal of International Women's Studies* 14.3 (2013): 121-136.

Simone, Nina with Stephen Cleary. *I Put a Spell on You the Autobiography of Nina Simone*. New York: Da Capo Press, 1991.

Simone, Nina, perf. "Four Women," *Wild is the Wind*. By Nina Simone. Philips, 1966. LP.

---. "Go Limp," *Live at Carnegie Hall*. By Alex Comfort and Nina Simone. Philips, 1964. L.P.

---. "Mississippi Goddam," *Live at Carnegie Hall*. By Nina Simone. Philips, 1964. L.P.

---. "Pirate Jenny," *Live at Carnegie Hall*. By Kurt Weill from *Threepenny Opera*, Lyrics by Marc Blitzstein. Philips, 1964. L.P.

---. "To Be Young Gifted and Black," By Weldon Irvine with Nina Simone." 1969. 45 record.

---. "Why? (The King of Love is Dead)," *Nuff' Said!*. By Gene

Taylor. RCA, 1968. L.P.

Walker, Susannah. *Style and Status: Selling Beauty to African American Women, 1920-1975*. University Press of Kentucky, 2007.

Wingfield, Adia Harvey. *Doing Business with Beauty: Black Women, Hair Salons, and the Racial Enclave Economy*. New York: Roman and Littlefield, 2008.

Wolf, Naomi. *The Beauty Myth: How Imags of Beauty Are Used Against Women*. Anchor Books, 1992.

African American Women and the Niagara Movement 1905-1909

Anita Nahal and Lopez D. Matthews Jr.

In 1905, between July 11 and July 15, twenty nine African American men met in Buffalo, New York to launch a new movement, the Niagara Movement. Spear headed by W. E. B. DuBois, the Niagara Movement lasted just four years and became the precursor to the National Association for the Advancement of Colored People, also led by DuBois, in 1909. While no African American women were part of the original group of twenty nine that formed the Niagara Movement yet, in many ways Black women became an integral part of the movement. This article will present their story.

Black women were the gender capital of the Niagara Movement, though perhaps that was not the intention of the 29 men who came together to form this meeting. This article is divided into four sections in order to create the story of the women in the Niagara Movement: Mary Burnett Talbert, Carrie W. Clifford, Gertrude Morgan and the Membership Lists.

Mary Burnett Talbert

The first meeting of the Niagara Movement opened on July 11, 1905 at the house of Mary Burnett and W.M Talbert. A graduate of Oberlin College, Mary Talbert became one of "the most widely known activist[s] in Buffalo" by the turn of the century.[1] Talbert was an active participant in many different organizations in Buffalo including those created within and outside of the church. In her lifetime, she held such high positions as the President of the Buffalo Phyllis Wheatly Club in 1899, President of the

National Association of Colored Women in 1916, and led the National Association for the Advancement of Colored People's anti-lynching crusade in 1922 as the National Director of the Anti-Lynching Committee and became the first woman to speak before the Norwegian House of Parliament in 1920. As a result of her many years of hard work in support of the improvement of the lives of African Americans and her work with the Anti-Lynching campaign Talbert became the first woman to receive the highest award given by the NAACP, the Spingarn Medal in 1922.[2]

Mary Talbert was also an acquaintance of Booker T. Washington, as well as DuBois. Washington sought Talbert's assistance in keeping him informed of the actions of the participants in the Niagara Movement. In a letter dated July 8, 1905, Washington wrote to his wife Margaret asking her to, "write to Mrs. Talbert to keep you closely informed about proceedings and names of people connected with the Buffalo meeting next week." [3] Expressing her usefulness as an informant in another letter dated the same day, Washington wrote, "Tell Crosby look after Buffalo meeting sharply. It is to be held next week. Inside data can be gotten from Talbert..."[4]

Washington seemed to have been aware that the meeting was to be held at the Talbert's residence from a latter correspondence by Clifford H. Plummer to Washington. In the letter he states, "My dear Mr. Washington: I arrived home this morning and called you up first thing...the report was not true; in fact there really was no conference in Buffalo where delegates were in attendance...I was located near 521 Michigan Avenue from Wednesday morning until Friday and I can state positively that none of the men named in the report were present except DuBois."[5] It is not certain as to which report this was, however, 521 Michigan Avenue was the Talbert's address. The meeting began at their residence on July 11th and the next day moved to the Erie Hotel on the Canadian side of the Falls. Washington's spy arrived at the residence a day late.

The fact that the Niagara Movement meeting began at the Talbert's residence on July 11, 1905 is corroborated by other contemporary sources. A letter dated June 13, 1905 written by DuBois to Mr. W.M. Talbert, Mary Talbert's husband informs him of the proposed meeting. DuBois writes to him about finding the gentleman who would be coming to Buffalo for the meeting accommodation for their stay. The letter has the address, 521, Michigan Avenue at the top. This letter proves that the Talberts knew DuBois and that they were aware of the impending Niagara Movement. It also confirms that the address 521 Michigan Avenue belonged to the Talberts.

Contemporary newspaper accounts also confirm that the Niagara Movement meeting began at the Talbert's residence on July 11, 1905. The *Buffalo Enquirer* reported on July 12 that the, "Colored men from eighteen states held a national conference at No.521 Michigan Street yesterday..."[6] On July 13, the same newspaper reported that the meeting, "...opened Tuesday," and that it was being held at "...the Erie Beach Hotel."[7] This supports three points, that the Niagara Movement started on July 11, 1905, at the residence of the Talbert's and that it moved to the Erie Beach Hotel on the second day—July 12.

The *Buffalo Commercial* also noted on July 12, 1905 that, "A national conference of Negroes is being held at 521 Michigan Street...The leader of the meeting is Prof. W. E. B. DuBois..." The Buffalo Daily also noted on July 12, 1905 that, "...a national conference of colored men from eighteen different states held at 521 Michigan Street, the opening session yesterday...."[8] And the final proof of the meeting having begun at Mary

Talbert's residence is the official address given on top of the page of the list of members and program of the first Niagara meeting. It reads,

NM
First Annual Meeting
Place: Erie Beach Hotel, Ontario and 521 Michigan Ave., Buffalo, N.Y.
Time: July 11, 12 and 15 1905.[9]

While at the time the notation of Mary Talbert's address on the meeting list probably had no great significance for Black women, in retrospect it is a very significant part of Black women's history in the movement for the race. Mary Talbert was a willing partner with her husband to allow DuBois and the other men to meet at their house to form a new movement, one that was in opposition to Booker T. Washington. There was a risk involved in this as Washington also knew the Talbert's and had already been in correspondence with them to gain information on the meeting. The Talbert's did not inform him of the fact that the meeting was going to convene in their residence. In the process the Talbert's signaled their support of DuBois's new radical movement. Mary Talbert was already an active race supporter and did not object to the meeting being convened at her residence even though she was not invited to be a signatory to the Niagara Movement's birth. We do not find any contemporary documents that reveal her taking credit for allowing the first 29 men to gather at her residence. Nor do we find any minutes of the Niagara Movement Meeting acknowledging her name in relation to the formation of the Niagara Movement. Thus Mary Talbert's silent contribution to the foundation of the movement is saluted.

Carrie Clifford

Carrie Clifford, an activist, a reformer and a writer of the Harlem Renaissance is the second woman to be associated with the Niagara Movement, though openly, unlike Mary Talbert. Clifford was from Ohio and Washington and a longtime friend of DuBois. Clifford was also on the committee of one hundred that founded the NAACP in 1909 and a president of the National Association of Colored Women. Through sketchy contemporary documents Clifford's role in the Niagara Movement can be gauged. She was made, "in charge of appeals to women for the Niagara Movement."[10] A letter head for the Niagara Movement carries her name at the top. It says, "Secretary for Women (South)."[11] In another account it is stated that, "in 1906, DuBois asked several women to lead a national committee for a female auxiliary of the Niagara Movement. Clifford assumed responsibility for encouraging women to join later that year at the Niagarites second meeting held in Harpers Ferry, West Virginia. Although women were denied admission to the sessions until the third meeting held in Boston the following year, they met among themselves. In 1907 at the Boston meeting, half of the eight hundred delegates were women. Thus, it is obvious that the campaign led by Clifford to persuade more women to join the Niagara Movement was most successful."[12] And a final document states that she was to work "…jointly with Mrs. Morgan."[13] Mrs. Morgan was later appointed in charge of the women's auxiliary to the Niagara Movement.

Clifford was also the person who suggested in 1906 that race organizations ought to work together and said that the Niagara Movement and the Afro-American Council should join forces and work together.[14] However many were suspicious that she belonged to the Washington camp, thus her ideas were ignored as possible attempts by Washington to infiltrate and influence the group.[15] However, she was known to be a radical. She was a poet of the Harlem Renaissance and in her vibrant poetry she appeared very much the rebel. "In her poetry and in her life, Carrie Clifford did indeed speak with a determination and resolve that would not be quenched by America's accomodationist desires for its black constituency."[16]

In two of her poems Clifford exhorted women to work for the race. The first one is directly addressed to women and in the second there is a reference to women that inspire Black women to struggle for the common cause of the race. The first poem is titled, *Duty's Call*.

> Come, all ye women, come!
> Help till the work is done,
> Help to uplift!
> We must sin's blight remove,
> By deeds of kindness prove
> The wondrous power of love,
> God's greatest gift.
>
> We must remove the ban
> Placed on our fellow-man,
> Thro' Satan's power;
> Let us as one unite,
> Darkness and wrong to fight,
> Then will the glorious light
> Break in God's hour.
>
> "Tis now, we must begin;
> If we our cause would win;
> The foe is strong;
> But we can make him quake,
> His forces swerve and break
> When we old earth shall shake
> With victory's song."[17]

In the second poem titled, *Marching to Conquest*, she stresses upon the noble virtues of women.

> We are battling for the right with purpose strong and true;
> "Tis a mighty struggle, but we've pledged to dare and to do;
> Pledged to conquer evil and we'll see the conflict thro'
> Marching and marching to conquest.

> All the noble things of life we'll teach our girls and boys,
> Warn them of its pitfalls and reveal its purest joys,
> Counsel, guide and keep them from the evil that destroys
> As we go marching to conquest.

> Loving confidence and trust must mark our intercourse,
> Harmony and unity will our success enforce;
> Seeking guidance from the Lord of good, the boundless source
> As we go marching to conquest.

> Come and join our anthem then and raise a mighty shout,
> Sing it with such fervor as will put our foes to rout,
> Sing it with conviction strong, dispelling every doubt,
> As we go marching to conquest,

> Women, when our work is o'er and we to rest have gone
> May our efforts doubled, trebled, still go sweeping on,
> And the voices of millions swell the volume of our song,
> As they go marching to conquest.

> Hurrah, hurrah, we'll shout the jubilee;
> Hurrah, hurrah, we'll set the captives free,
> Ignorance, distrust and hate at our approach shall flee,
> Marching and marching to conquest.[18]

Gertrude Morgan

In early 1906, DuBois decided to organize a woman's auxiliary to the Niagara Movement. DuBois chose Gertrude Morgan, the wife of his old friend Clement Morgan to head the woman's auxiliary and it was decided that Mts. Clifford was to work "...jointly with Mrs. Morgan."[19] Mr. Clement

Morgan was a lawyer and a classmate from Harvard and also one of the 29 men who joined the Niagara Movement in 1905. Trotter it is said rejected the creation of a woman's auxiliary. William Trotter, also one of the 29 founder members of the NM and the owner of the newspaper *Boston Guardian*, has been considered to be adamantly opposed to women becoming involved in the movement and skeptical of the women's rights movement.[20] However, had that been the case then why would Trotter let his wife Dennie Trotter join the Niagara Movement? The Niagara Movement was riddled with difficulties from the beginning. The movement was plagued by two "fundamental" issues "it lacked coherence, both intellectually and organizationally and it lacked the power to challenge the Tuskegee hegemony."[21] With Morgan's appointment as the head of the woman's auxiliary a tension also developed between the Trotters and Morgans.

Trotter's opposition to DuBois's decision to form a woman's auxiliary to the Niagara Movement may have stemmed from DuBois's choice of the person to head it, Mrs. Clement Morgan. Trotter and Morgan did not get along and DuBois was aware of the tension between the two men and attempted to resolve it, albeit unsuccessfully. According to Stephen Fox, the appointment of Gertrude Morgan to head the women's auxiliary to the NM was, "the first sign of breach"[22] between Trotter and DuBois and this affected the smooth functioning of the meetings of the NM and the relationship between its key members. It is said that after Trotter, Clement Morgan was "the most prominent anti-Bookerite in Massachusetts." He was also the State Secretary of the Niagara Movement's local branch. He had also been Trotter's attorney in the Boston riot trials.[23]

A paper written by DuBois in 1906, titled *"A Brief Resume of the Massachusetts Trouble in the Niagara Movement"*, enumerates the tension between

Morgan and Trotter. The first line of the paper reads, "July 1906—Trotter opposed admission of women to the Niagara Movement, and opposed Miss Baldwin and Mrs. Grimke in particular. Mrs. Morgan favored." Initially he seemed to be in favor of Mrs. Morgan according to the above noting made by DuBois. Besides being opposed to Miss Baldwin and Mrs. Grimke, (for which no reasons are found in the contemporary documents), another woman mentioned in the records, whom he opposed, was Mrs. Forbes. The rift between Trotter and Morgan widened so much that it became one of the causes for Trotter's resignation from the Niagara Movement.

The above paper written by DuBois can be divided into three parts for a deeper understanding of what exactly appears to have transpired between Trotter, Morgan and some of the other women. These divisions include:

1) The staging of a play in June 1907 at Massachusetts before the Third Niagara Movement Meeting at Boston in July 1907
2) The meeting itself
3) A discussion on the election of new members to the Massachusetts meeting.

The Staging of the Play

In a noting in April 1907, Mrs. Morgan's name first appears in relation to the staging of a play in order to raise money for the next meeting to be held in Boston, Massachusetts. "General Secretary has sent out a call for raising state quotas of Legal Defense Fund." Mrs. Morgan replies making first mention of the 'Peter Pumpkin –eater Play' and urging Boston as a meeting place in August.[24] Both Mr. and Mrs. Trotter are said to have opposed the staging of the play. The opposition centered on personal jealousies. "…Mrs. Trotter was not invited to cooperate until late, and that the Forbes were allowed to help."[25] The paper goes on to give the reply of the Morgans, "Counter-charge of Morgans that Trotters refused to let their boy take part, blocked arrangements, and that without Mrs. Forbes work in gathering children the play would have failed."[26] Ultimately the play did take place, without the Trotters involvement and brought a total of $65 to the Movement.[27]

The Meeting Itself

Tension over Trotter's perceptions of the Boston meeting also became a cause of tension between the Trotters and the Morgans. DuBois tried hard to achieve reconciliation between the two, but failed. Trotter blamed Morgan for being bossy, while the later labeled him as domineering. DuBois urged Morgan to put Trotter on the Committee of Arrangements for the annual meeting to which he later agreed. However, the Trotters gave a "...written document of 22 pages, virtually rescinding agreement and demanding an official reprimand of Morgan."[28] DuBois refused and as a reaction, Mrs. Trotter resigned from the Niagara Movement. In July, Trotter too resigned from the Committee of Arrangements and presumably criticized Mr. and Mrs. Morgan. In the paper it is noted that, "Policy of Secretaries Morgan and Mrs. Morgan attacked.'[29] DuBois urged Morgan to reinstate Trotter. Morgan did so and Trotter rejoined but refused to cooperate.

Election of New Members

The third part of the paper deals with the charges made against the induction of new members to the Massachusetts Niagara chapter. DuBois goes to great lengths to assert that the balloting had been free, secret and under no pressure at all. For those out of town at the time of the vote, Mr.

Morgan and Mrs. Morgan sent the ballot papers to them. DuBois says at one place in the paper that he appealed to Morgan and Trotter to get those men to join that they knew best and urged Mrs. Morgan to get those women to join that she knew best. Trotter, however, signaled that the elections had not been fair. To which DuBois replied, "Mr. Morgan was State Secretary of the Niagara Movement; the election was necessarily in his hands. Mrs. Morgan is at the head of all Niagara Movement women. The election as far as the women were concerned was necessarily largely in her hands. I could not have usurped the place of these secretaries in conducting the elections even if I wanted to and I did not want to. I could see that the vote was fair and this I did."[30] The last sentence is an addition to the typed version made by DuBois in his own handwriting. The elections were voted as fair and valid.

Mrs. Gertrude Morgan continued to enlist Black women into the movement, thereby greatly helping in the proliferation of the membership and the movement itself. Under her efforts the Massachusetts branch of the Niagara Movement's third meeting at Boston had a total of 38 women members out of 91. Though a list of the total members of the Niagara Movement is not available, 1909 records are available of payments made as dues by the members. From these it is known that 38 female members paid their dues out of a total number (men and women) of 74. Another list of members that paid money for the special Jim Crow Fund shows that out of the total of 17 members that paid, nine were women.[31] Mrs. Morgan's selection by DuBois for the position of Secretary of Women created to a wedge between the Morgans and Trotters. This added pressure on an already weak movement that had been handicapped from the beginning by lack of funds and infighting between its members.

Membership Lists

Besides information available on Talbert, Clifford and Morgan, a study of the limited sources available on membership records of the various NM meetings from 1905-1909 reveals a growing interest of Black women in the movement. During the second meeting at Harper's Ferry, the Niagara Movement began to open its doors to female members. This was indeed a landmark decision considering that in the original 29 members there were no women members and that the Declaration of the Principals stressed on Black male membership. In the minutes of the second meeting, it was stated that, "properly qualified persons may be admitted to the Niagara Movement without distinctions of sex..."[32] Two types of membership existed; full and associate and women were allowed in both. In a member list dated August 15, 1906, there were four women members and they had all paid their dues. In another list dated August 18, 1906, two more women are mentioned who had paid their dues. Another list gives the names of the associate members (those who did not have the right to vote at the annual meetings and hold office), who were primarily women—39 out of 51 listed and all had paid their dues.[33] These lists are useful in collating the number of African-American women that were involving themselves in the activities of the Niagara Movement as membership opened up to them.

One very important document that supports the inclusion of women to the Niagara Movement is a paper dated 1906 (no month is mentioned) entitled, *"Women and the Niagara Movement."*[34] This paper offered three types of membership to women. These included, "Full Membership: The Niagara Movement welcomes to full membership on invitation both men and women...Associate Membership: Women who sympathize with the Niagara Movement...Affiliated Membership; Any women's club may as a club become affiliated with the Niagara Movement..."[35] The change in DuBois's decision to include women members may have resulted from either the realization that Black women were essential for race reform or that they were short of members. Perhaps it was a combination of the two.

In this paper it is also mentioned that Mrs. Gertrude Morgan had been appointed as the National Secretary for Women.[36] The paper also had the names of the various other secretaries and the committees. In the women's committee there were six members besides the secretary and they were all women. In the other committees except for the Arts Committee there were no women! The other committees consisted of Legal, Army and Navy, Crime, Health, education, The Press, Pan-African, Students, Suffrage, Civil Rights, Economics and Ethics. Presence of women in these committees might have held a more significant meaning. The Arts Committee was the only other one that had a woman member, Mrs. M. A. McAdoo, who in 1907 became the chairperson of the committee, as the minutes of the third NM meeting noted on August 27, 1907 in Boston.[37] The minutes of the third meeting also noted that the group did not feel that women were doing "a great deal of work."[38] What is the precise implication of this sentence it is not clear. For women had begun to join the movement only a year earlier. It could mean that not much work was done for the women, or that women in the NM had not done much work for its cause or that not too many women members as yet had been enrolled in the Niagara Movement.

The lists of members available for 1907 are not complete. For Baltimore, the list shows twenty members, however, there were no indications of how many in this group were women. From New Bedford, 18 members are listed, again not indicating how many of the members were female. And the District of Columbia branch showed two full women members out of a total of 14 and 57 Associate members out of a total of 68.[39]

Contemporary newspapers carried news about the NM from its inception. Though nothing substantial can be gained about the role of women, snippets about the presence of women and some of their work are available. For example the Boston Guardian reported in its August 25, 1906 issue about the women in the Second NM meeting at Harper's Ferry. A picture of seven women is given with their names, specifying in some the work or the place they came from. And they have been referred to as, "...pioneer women members." The picture and the statement indicate the media's acknowledgement of the presence and specific roles of the Niagara women. However, this was the only paper that carried this news item. And the owner of the newspaper was Mr. Monroe Trotter, who was a member of the NM. W. E. B. DuBois papers include two pictures—one of the second NM meeting in 1906 and the other of the third meeting in 1907. The first does not show women, while the second does. This was because though the NM encouraged women to join the movement, they were officially recognized as members only from the third meeting. It needs to be mentioned here that Mary White Ovington, a journalist and a socialist became the first white member and first white women to be invited by DuBois to join the NM in 1908. She played a very important role in the founding of the NAACP. This paper is addresses only the role of Black women in the Niagara Movement.

Thus the above lists and the minutes of the NM meetings, the few primary sources that exist and the sparse newspaper accounts, are witness to the role of the African-American women in the Niagara Movement. From no women members in 1905 when it started, to women as members and as chairpersons of some committees, Black women played a significant role in the growth of this new radical Black movement at the turn of the twentieth century.

Desirous of achieving primary race status, Black men have tended to ignore the role of Black women in race movements, with the emphasis being on the contributions of Black men. Further the struggle for gender parity within the Black community was submerged in the larger interests of the race. As such the actual goals, programs, policies and agendas of race movements have centered on the role and encouragement of Black men. Yet when given a role, Black women fulfilled it with enthusiasm and commitment, for they too viewed it as their contribution to race reform. Their aim was to seek empowerment for the race and in the process if they had to neglect their own needs as women, so be it. From the churches to schools, to factories, to women's clubs, to their own national women's movement, to finally race movements like the Niagara Movement, Black gave quietly and strongly. The above article is an example of their important role that few know about, but history records.

[1] Lillian S. Williams, *And Still I Rise: Black Women and Reform, Buffalo, New York, 1900-1940* in Darlene Clark Hine, Wilma King and Linda Reed (eds.), <u>We Specialize in the Wholly Impossible</u> (New York: Carlson Publishing Inc., 1998) p. 523

[2] Cynthia Neverdon-Morton, *Afro-American Women of the South and the Advancement of the Race 1895-1925* (Knoxville: The University of Tennessee Press, 1989), 226

[3] Louis R. Harlan, Raymond W. Smock (eds.) *The Booker T. Washington Papers*, Vol. 8, 1904-6 (Urbana: University of Illinois Press, 1979), 321

[4] Ibid.

[5] Ibid.

[6] *Buffalo Enquirer*, 12 July 1905

[7] Ibid.

[8] *Buffalo Commercial*, 12 July 1905

[9] W.E.B. Du Bois Papers, Reel 2, Frame 853, State University of New York at Binghamton Library, Binghamton, New York. Henceforth referred to as WEBDB, R, F

[10] W.E.B. Du Bois, *Correspondence of Du Bois, Vol. 11*. Herbert Aptheker, ed. (Boston: University of Massachusetts Press, 1973)

[11] WEBDB, R2, F 1037

[12] Jessie Carney Smith, (ed.), *Notable Black American Women, Book II* (New York: Gale Research Inc., 1996), 105 – 108

[13] WEBDB, R 2, F 979

[14] Elliot M. Rudwick, *The Niagara Movement* <u>Journal of Negro History</u>, Vol. XLII, 1957, 188.

[15] Ibid.

[16] P. Jane Splawn, *Writings of Carrie Williams Clifford and Carrie Law Morgan Figgs* (New York: G.K. Hall & Co., 1997), 148

[17] Ibid.

[18] Ibid.

[19] WEBDB, R 2, F 979

[20] Stephen R. Fox, *The Guardian of Boston, William Monroe Trotter* (New York: Atheneum, 1970), 103.

[21] Kathryn Kish Sklar, *Gender and the Color Line in the Founding of the NAACP,* paper read at the Berkshire Conference in Women's History, Chapel Hill, North Carolina, June 1996, 6. and David Levering Lewis, *W.E.B. Du Bois: Biography of a Race, 1868-1919* (New York: Henry Holt, 1993)

[22] Fox, 103-105

[23] Ibid.

[24] WEBDB, R 2, F 962.

[25] Ibid.

[26] Ibid

[27] Ibid.

[28] Ibid.
[29] Ibid.
[30] WEBDB, R 2, F962
[31] WEBDB, R 2, F969, 1004-1005
[32] WEBDB, R 2, F 872
[33] WEBDB, R 2, F 874, 883 and 884
[34] WEBDB, R2, F 893
[35] Ibid.
[36] WEBDB, R 2, F 893
[37] WEBDB, R 2, F 911
[38] WEBDB, R 2, F 913
[39] WEBDB, R 2, F 922

Muslim African American Women: "The Qur'an, Human Excellence and the Four Rivers"

By Zakiyyah Muhammad

Since 1931 Muslim African American women have liberated minds in American society in unprecedented ways. Easily identified by their classic long garments, covered hair and respectable behavior, Muslim African American women have not deviated from that representation in nearly a century. They live by the adage that woman is the "Mother of Civilization"[1] and "Where there are no decent women, there are no decent men."[2] While maintaining the importance of modesty and dignity, they live by their example adhering to the protections from smoking, alcohol, drugs, gambling and sex only with a lawful husband in marriage. Approximately four decades ago, (1975) these basic physical and moral distinctions gave way to evolved spiritual and intellectual distinctions, still surprisingly ambiguous to large populations in the country. To date, neither academia nor American culture has appropriately addressed those distinctions.   Rather, the image that continues to be projected is one of *black protest, the disenfranchised, and anti-Christian* and at worst, one conflated with *abused immigrant Muslim women in a radical illegitimate Arab religion*. With the increased population of Muslims and a barrage of external influences, clarity is needed.

This article, at the intersection of religion, gender and race, presents the intellectual thought and practice of Muslim African American women in their quest for human excellence. Human excellence is the capacity of the moral, intellectual and spiritual faculties to conform to the created pattern God has put in human nature. Education, culture, economics and governance referred to as The *Four Rivers* are the life streams of human society through which human excellence manifests. We will address what Muslim women have and continue to contribute to the liberation of minds and society highlighting significant aspects of the Muslim historical record.

The intellectual thought in this article represents the leadership of Imam W. Deen Mohammed, *father of the Muslim American Experience*. His parents Clara and Elijah Muhammad, builders of the Nation of Islam, and spiritual mother and father to Muslims who embraced Islam (Al-Islam) nearly a century ago are also referenced. They represent the original, independent, most influential and enduring Muslim communities that have impacted America and the international world.

Muslim women support the leadership of Imam W. Deen Mohammed because they choose to. For thirty-three years he proved to be a champion for women. His unprecedented insight of the Qur'an, religious texts and the human condition made it an easy but intelligent choice. He taught, as did other women scholars,[3] that women played a great role in Islamic history and must learn to read the Qur'an for themselves.

Imam W. Deen Mohammed changed America enabling Muslims to claim their "shared freedom space" as a legitimate religious community. He was a signatory to the Williamsburg Charter Foundation[4] "First Liberty" Reaffirmation Ceremony for the Freedom of Religion June 25, 1988. Joined by Presidents Jimmy Carter, Gerald Ford, Reverend Billy Graham, Coretta Scott King and other luminaries, he officially changed America from the Judeo-Christian tradition to the Judeo-Christian-Muslim tradition. His participation and subsequent invitation from Pope John Paul II to address millions from the pulpit at the Vatican[5], October 29, 1999, re-solidified Al-Islam and included Muslim African Americans as a dignified part of the world religious community. Muslim women were in attendance at each of these events and worked seen and unseen to ensure their success.

For Muslim women everything begins with education - enlightenment of the intellect - which informs ones sense of self and how one navigates the world. Education expresses itself in culture, the transmitting mechanisms by which a people's collective life survives. Culture produces economics, a system to exchange goods and services. And economics must have *governance*, cooperative consensus direction. In social language these processes are called *The Four Rivers*. In scriptural language they are called *Sacred Sanctuaries*. The Qur'an (3:28)[6] says those things that are sacred should never be left under the control of others. One can cooperate with others, but the *Sacred Sanctuaries* must be guided and guarded by sacred principles to ensure they keep the integrity of Gods purpose and benefit for human society. *The Four Rivers* may span continents but their origin is Mother.

For these reasons, Muslim women realize that The *Four Rivers* must be consistently observed to ensure they begin with consciousness of The Creator and that any input remains pure. If *The Four Rivers* remain pure they are able to feed and nourish the human being - especially the young - towards human excellence contributing to civilization and the evolution of that people. When *The Four Rivers* are polluted, they can only corrupt a people and poison whatever they contact. One can observe *The Four Rivers* in a society and determine the intellectual and spiritual development of that people. The notion that one can display vulgarity, demean others or violate the law and defend such as jokes, entertainment or culture is an anathema. Humor can be enjoyable, inspiring and elevating.

For Muslim women there is no separation between the intellectual and the spiritual; everything is interrelated and interdependent. The principle of Oneness - *Tawheed* – Unity overrides and underpins everything in the natural world and human society. In the Qur'an (49:13)[7] God says: "O Humanity, Every human being is born from a male and female in excellence and was created in diverse colors and tribes that they may learn from each other not despise each other. The best are the ones most righteous."

Beginning February 26, 1975, the Qur'an was introduced to the African American consciousness by Imam W. Deen Mohammed. For the next thirty-three years, the eyes of America and the world witnessed the transformation of a people and were themselves transformed. The most oppressive issues that had plagued humanity for millennia were crumbling. The Qur'an, the final Revelation, revealed by Prophet Muhammad, broke the chains of white supremacy, anthropomorphism, black superiority and female inferiority. It validated scripturally the existence of African Americans as dignified human beings equal to all others in the "sight of God". This excoriated previous scriptural references/interpretations that Black people were inferior, cursed and cast out with the complicity of God and the Prophets[8]. The Qur'an clarified that God, The Creator, was not black, white, male or female;[9] and women were not responsible for the fall of man and society. This knowledge set free the collective intellect and souls of women from male dominance and a people from white supremacy that had plagued them since enslavement. Imam W. Deen Mohammed produced the largest conversion to Al-Islam in Islamic and American history.

Maxine Salaam said, "I felt like my soul had been set free. I sort of

146

knew some of those things; the Nation of Islam helped me with my sense of self, but Sistaaah when The Imam started speaking.......[10] Rawiyyah Khatib, commented

I felt very liberated because of the knowledge he brought and because he respected the women. He opened the door to the intellectual side; it was not just a rote situation. Now, I admired the Honorable Elijah Muhammad too, he was the foundation. I remember the last Saviors Day when he had white people and the man from Turkey on the stage.....he said to respect everybody. He gave us dignity and respect as women and mothers. But Imam Mohammed allowed women to hold positions and their voices to be heard among the men and women, not just the women. It gave me courage to go to the warehouse [fish distribution center]. And I got a job giving orders to men.[11]

Agency for Muslim women comes from what God has said about them which is why the Qur'an is vital to their life. Their self-discovery, self-definition and self-direction confirms they are special in the "sight of God" created with a special purpose. Each woman navigates that space for herself but collectively is freed from the burden of the designation of temptress and intellectual and spiritual inferiority. The Qur'an says, "Oh, Mankind!... reverence the wombs that bore you..."[12] Woman is not responsible for the damnation of society, Woman is society!

The Qur'anic word referenced is Arham and means womb and much more. She is the womb of life that gives life to all. But woman is more than biology she is the *Womb of Mind*[13] because woman and mother are unified entities. Every woman born is also a mother whether she births physical children or not. Mother is a principle best represented in the

147

biology of the female but is greater than the human female.[14] Mother permeates the entire natural creation. Woman is Mother!

The bifurcation of the image of woman in contemporary society offers a sexualized seductress as the epitome of representation. Sexuality has a place and that place is private, in order to protect children, families and society. Muslim women are not seducers, they are civilizers. The humbleness of their manner is not timidity. They fight for what is right but they prefer peace. Their humble manner is the conscious reverence for God that comes from praying five times a day. They know that all good comes from God.

Muslim women are not in competition with men, because men are not the standard by which they measure themselves. God's criterion is the standard. Women birth men, including prophets, educate them, encourage them, correct them and sometimes *make* them do what needs to be done to move towards human excellence.

In 1931, Clara Muhammad became the moral foundation for the evolution of a people. She heard a man speak, Fard Muhammad, and took her husband Elijah to hear him. Within one year they were co-builders of the Nation of Islam, the organization that broke the chains of psychological enslavement to white people. It took the psyche of Black people out of America to enable it to clean up, stand up, think for itself and do for itself. It instilled unity, courage, morality, dignity, discipline, pride and the skills necessary for men and women to establish strong family life and community responsibility. As Mother of the Nation and first member of the MGT&GCC – Muslim Girls Training and General Civilization Class, Clara Muhammad is credited with the instruction of women and the establishment of Muslim education.

From 1931 to the 1960's after great sacrifices, *The Four Rivers* of the Nation of Islam flowed with abundance throughout the Black community. *Education* soared with more than 40 independent University of Islam schools; *Culture* exploded with poetry, music and intellectual discourse all celebrating beautiful black women and fine black men. Muslim women's fashions created a new industry. James Brown said Elijah Muhammad inspired him to write, "I'm Black and I'm Proud." Health food stores, herbs and juicing, bean soup and bean pie, inspired by the outstanding health regiments of Muslims impacted America. *Economics* expanded collective buying, buy black business establishments and Black Family Bazaars. And *Governance* cultivated Black mayors and politicians. Major newspapers and television stations employed Black journalists for the first time, as they had access to Muslims that others did not. The historical record of the Nation's 40 year achievements is clear.

In 1976, Alex Haley, author of Roots, said, If I had to pick the single person who has been the most important figure for blacks in the black thrust from post-World War II, I would unequivocally pick Elijah Muhammad. Because it was he who ....was like a lightning bolt in opening up the consciousness of black people...... from this just blank psychic wall of just total fear of the structure in which we live. And I am saying these things clinically. Underneath him I would put Malcolm X and Dr. King on equal basis. They appealed....to broadly different groups...Dr. King...the church structure...Malcolm...the grass roots.[15]

The end and the beginning of a new phase of evolution were signified by the passing of Clara and Elijah Muhammad. They laid the foundation but a new knowledge was needed to take a people to their destiny. In 1975 the Nation of Islam did not "fall" the Nation "evolved". The Qur'an came to correct false ideological concepts, provide universal knowledge that has no end and take a people to destiny-human excellence. What was consistent with the Qur'an was kept and what was not was let go.

The education of women expanded. Qur'anic Arabic, Muslim Women's Development Class-MWDC and CERWIS–Committee to Enhance the Role of Women in Society were established. Women learned to formally pray salah; to eat zabiha/halal meats; to fast during Ramadan and to make Hajj. Janazzah burial service classes were instituted; requiring washing/shrouding the deceased and burial within 3 days. And the learning of Qur'anic laws that affect marriage, divorce, inheritance and all social and religious matters remains a consistent study.

The disparate identities of African, Muslim, African American and American were reconciled as Muslim African American. But Imam W. Deen Mohammed cautioned, "We are not to support any foreign government Muslim or other, only the good they do. We are never to forget that no government came to our rescue......"?[16]

Muslims remain at the forefront in the establishment of independent schools which remains the model for independent education[17]. The University of Islam offered what Dr. Carter G. Woodson said was missing in his seminal, *Mis-Education of the Negro*, 1933. Today Clara Muhammad Schools; so named to honor a Muslim woman of courage, represent an elevation of that effort educating all students.

Muslim women's impact on the *Culture* and *Economics* of the billion dollar fashion industry has expanded. They now appear in American and Parisian fashion shows as entrepreneurs and designers not just consumers. Many women also own their own businesses. Their activism in *Governance* has resulted in the election of male and female Muslims in local, state and federal positions. Strong families, healthy eating, discipline and moral behavior continue as hallmarks of their life.

Education

One of the most successful efforts to impact American society was CRAID. Falsely interpreted as anti-Christian, Muslim women in 1978 throughout America supported the *Committee to Remove All Racial Images that Attempt to Portray the Divine* - CRAID. A series of national lectures, articles and conferences from a clinical perspective explained the deleterious psychological effect of portraying the Divine in Caucasian flesh. Muslim Journal newspaper continues to run a notice on page 4 entitled, "A Message of Concern" explaining the detriment of this practice. Muslim women paraded in silence in front of churches with signs regarding this condition. Today, in most churches, particularly African American, the Caucasian image of God is gone, removed, due to this effort. The Association of Black Psychologists in 1980 headed by Dr. Na'im Akbar successfully approved and adopted the following resolution[18] (partially presented):

RESOLUTION

APPROVED AT THE 1980 ANNUAL MEETING OF THE ASSOCIATION OF BLACK PSYCHOLOGISTS

WHEREAS: The Association of Black Psychologists has condemned the negative portrayal of Blacks in media presentations in the past, we recognize the portrayal of the Divine as Caucasian as the most pervasive assertion of white supremacy. We see such grandiosity on the part of Caucasian people as destructive to themselves and damaging to people who accept white supremacy images as subliminal elements of their religious beliefs;

THEREFORE, BE IT RESOLVED: That The Association of Black Psychologists recommends the removal of all Caucasoid images of Divinity from public display and from places of worship particularly in settings where young Black minds are likely to be exposed.

RESOLVED: That the Association of Black Psychologists provide copies of this Resolution to national religious bodies, national civil rights organizations and to select religious leaders for the purpose of opening up an educational dialogue for change.

Today, four generations of Muslims continue to promote the programs popularized by the Nation of Islam that promote unity, independent thinking, authentic self-identity, independent education and cooperative economics. Those programs have significantly impacted the larger African American community and American culture. The following women continue in that inheritance.

Precious Rasheedah Muhammad

In 2010, at the Annual State Department Iftar (Breaking of fast during Ramadan) then Secretary of State Hillary Clinton recognized Precious Rasheedah Muhammad and her research on the presence of Islam in America from 1776 – 2011. Those in attendance included nearly 70 members of the diplomatic corps, 40 members of Generation Change and 150 others from civil society, academia, government and business. In 2011, Precious Rasheedah Muhammad gifted the Department of State with the special research project on Islam in America.

Precious Rasheedah Muhammad is a third generation Muslim African American, scholar, wife and mother. Dedicated to tolerance, fellowship and understanding, she is founder and president of Journal of

Islam in America Press. A 2001 graduate of Harvard Divinity School with a Masters of Theological Studies, she founded the Islam in American conferences at Harvard. Dr. Henry Louis Gates says of her, "Precious Rasheeda Muhammad is a first-rate scholar who has quickly established herself as an authority on the history of Islam in America, especially with regard to the African American community."

Mrs. Muhammad discovered that the intellectual excellence of the Qur'an was respected by the Founders[19] and contributed to the making of America and its great Constitution and historic documents. Both the Library of Congress and the United States Supreme Court honors Al-Islam, the Qur'an and Muhammad the Prophet. In a mural in the dome of the rotunda of the Library[20] and in the north wall frieze of the Supreme Court[21], each depiction cites the excellence of Al-Islam's contributions to law, science, mathematics and the uplift of human society. Precious Rasheedah Muhammad has produced a seminal book outlining those and other treasures, *Muslims and the Making of America 1600 – Present, 2013.*

Okolo Rashid

Okolo Rashid is the Co-Founder and Executive Director of the International Museum of Muslim Cultures, Jackson Mississippi. A Muslim for thirty 30 years, Mrs. Rashid founded, the Museum in 2000. She said, "I was watching TV one morning and a promo of 'The Majesty of Spain' exhibition was coming to Jackson's Mississippi Arts Pavilion. It was expected to attract half a million people. I was thrilled and began to look for components in the exhibit that would highlight the Muslim or Moorish era in Spain. The exhibit only focused on Spain 1700 onward, skipping the whole story of Muslim contributions to Spain and European Renaissance.

This inspired me to feature an exhibit on Islam's presence and contribution in Spain."

Time was the biggest challenge initially. We just had five months to do everything! What started off as an all-Black institution, Masjid Muhammad, now included people of various ethnic backgrounds on its board. Had it not been for the contribution and work of this diverse group, including new immigrant and indigenous Muslims in Jackson, we would not have forged ahead. . This is how, with Allah's blessing and help, we were able to establish this museum in five months, a project that would normally take two years to complete. We call it a "Miracle Project.

Agina Carter-Shabazz

Agina Carter-Shabazz is an entrepreneur and the owner of Agina's Natural Hair Salon, and Agina's Herbal Hair and Skin Products, Philadelphia, PA. She attended LaSalle University with a desire to major in Criminal Justice, but a stronger voice pulled her away. She enrolled at Wilfred Academy Beauty School for Cosmetology. Her beau at the time wanted to marry her but said she had to become Muslim. She did. The marriage did not last but Agina Carter-Shabazz did. She has been a Muslim for thirty-five years beginning in 1974 in the Nation of Islam. She opened her first salon in 1978 and her motto is "Building Healthy Hair and Healthy Investments."

Sensitive to the lack of products for African hair, she followed the tradition of Madam C. J. Walker and formulated and distributed her own. Her clientele are not all Muslims but are 98% African American. Agina is a mentor to aspiring cosmetologists and on the assessment panel -Wharton School of Business Young Entrepreneur Program at the University of

Pennsylvania. Awarded the 1996 Madam C.J. Walker Award - National Coalition of 100 Black Women, Inc., she was appointed by Governor Ed Rendell to the state board of cosmetologist.

Her new project is the Sister Clara Muhammad in Business Project which will provide Vocational Education Programs to young women evolving the skills learned in MGT&GCC to a higher level.

Fatima El-Amin

In April, 2014, Fatima El-Amin was appointed Full Judge - DeKalb County Juvenile Court, Georgia. She is 38 years old and attended Clara Muhammad School and W. D. Muhammad High from pre-school to the 12th grade graduating co-Valedictorian in 1993. Judge El-Amin says that those schools gave her self-confidence and a sense of identity when she entered Harvard University and Emory University Law School. "When I compare myself to some of my peers who went to exceptional schools - that certainly had more resources than the Muhammad Schools - I saw the insecurities, particularly from students of color, going into a majority Caucasian environment. They did not have the sense of identity with their culture or community that I had. We had such an infusion of pride in our heritage that said you are equal, not better than, but equal to your counterparts of different skin complexions.

I call it indoctrination, sometimes positive and negative, but it was pride in oneself and abilities that said I have a right to be here, I am not inferior". She continues, "The greatest benefits of the Muslim schools were a sense of identity, community and history." "We were concerned whether our academic program was rigorous enough and it was." "My first year was a normal transition from high school to college, but after I got my first C, I

155

figured it out."

Judge El-Amin served as a senior child advocate attorney and an assistant district attorney as well as an associate in private practice. She says, "Islam has given me an overwhelming sense of gratitude and the knowledge that God is always in control".[22]

Muslim women believe that the ultimate mercy of God was to give to a people who were stripped of their human dignity - for 400 years - the prophetic gift "to be the moral conscious to America and the world"[23]. Reclaiming the Qur'an permits that. Such undertaking requires Muslim women to be teachers and courageous truth tellers but also to live by example in harmony with other faith traditions. Their goal is human excellence and the beauty of *The Four Rivers*.

Works Cited

Du Bois, William E.B. *Correspondence of Du Bois, Vol. 11.* Herbert Aptheker, ed. (Boston: University of Massachusetts Press, 1973)

Fox, Stephen R. *The Guardian of Boston, William Monroe Trotter* (New York: Atheneum, 1970)

Harlan, Louis R., Smock Raymond W. (eds.) *The Booker T. Washington Papers*, Vol. 8, 1904-6 (Urbana: University of Illinois Press, 1979)

Kathryn Kish Sklar, *Gender and the Color Line in the Founding of the NAACP*, paper read at the Berkshire Conference in Women's History, Chapel Hill, North Carolina, June 1996.

Lewis, David Levering *W.E.B. Du Bois: Biography of a Race, 1868-1919* (New York: Henry Holt, 1993)

Neverdon-Morton, Cynthia *Afro-American Women of the South and the Advancement of the Race 1895-1925* (Knoxville: The University of Tennessee Press, 1989)

Rudwick, Elliot M. *The Niagara Movement* The Journal of Negro History, Vol. XLII, 1957

Smith, Jessie Carney (ed.) *Notable Black American Women, Book II* (New York: Gale Research Inc., 1996)

Splawn, P. Jane *Writings of Carrie Williams Clifford and Carrie Law Morgan Figgs* (New York: G.K. Hall & Co., 1997)

W.E.B. Du Bois Papers, Reel 2, Frame 853, State University of New York at Binghamton Library, Binghamton, New York.

Williams, Lillian S. *And Still I Rise: Black Women and Reform, Buffalo, New York, 1900- 1940* in Darlene Clark Hine, Wilma King and Linda Reed (eds.), We Specialize in the Wholly Impossible (New York: Carlson Publishing Inc., 1998)

[1] Phrase coined by Elijah Muhammad,

[2] Source unknown; Saying in African American culture.

[3] Wadud, Amina. *Qur'an and Woman*, Oxford University Press, New York, 1999.

[4] http://www.freedomforum.org/publications/first/findingcommonground/CO2. WilliamsburgCharter.pdf.

[5] See: You Tube - Imam W. Deen Mohammed addresses the Vatican

[6] Paraphrase of Qur'an – 3:28, Ali Imran (The Family of Imran)

[7] Paraphrase of Qur'an – 49:13 Al Hujurat (The Chambers).

[8] See Genesis 9:24-27; 21:8-20.

[9] Qur'an - 112:1-4 Al Ikhlas (The Purity of Faith)

[10] Maxine Salaam, Telephone interview New Jersey, May 31, 2014.

[11] Rawiyyah Katib ,Telephone interview, , New York, May 28, 2014.

[12] Qur'an –Al Nisa, (The Women) 4:1.

[13] Muhammad, W. D. The Man and The Woman in Islam. Muhammad Mosque # 2, Chicago, 1976.

[14] Muhammad, Zakiyyah. Ummology: The Study of Mother - The Original Feminine Principle (Unpublished Manuscript).

[15] Black Scholar, Vol. 8, No. 1, September, 1976, p. 37-38.

[16] From "What the Imam Taught Us" by Agieb Bilal, 2008.

[17] See C. Eric Lincoln, The Black Muslims in America and Rashid, Hakim and Zakiyyah Muhammad, "The Sister Clara Muhammad Schools: Pioneers in the Development of Islamic Education in America". The Journal of Negro Education, 61 (2), pp.178-185.

[18] See the full 1980 Resolution of the ABP in their archives and in Chains and Images of Psychological Slavery, New Mind Productions, New Jersey, 1984,

[19] Muhammad, Precious Rasheeda, *Muslims & The Making of America: 1600's - Present,* Muslim Public Affairs Council, Los Angeles, 2013

[20] Ibid. p. 35.

[21] Ibid, p. 36.

[22] Fatima El-Amin, Telephone Interview, Georgia, May 29. 2014.

[23] Attributed to Frederick Douglass, Martin Luther King, Jr. and other African American leaders.

The Growing Need of Light on Race Origins: On Drusilla Dunjee Houston's Philosophy of History

Joshua Myers

What Ngugi wa Thiong'o calls a "quest for wholeness" animates much of what we institutionally trained minds might call Black historiography and/or philosophy of history.[1] In fact it is this training—often in academic disciplinary areas—that seems to inhibit more fruitful imaginations of this search for a "new land, the new society, the new being."[2] Yet it must always be remembered that attempts to elide the worst parts of this training are legion. Marked by the clarification of not only our identity, but also our ultimate destiny—a purpose impossible under Western knowledge structures—was a renegade intellectual tradition that emerged as a necessary confrontation with and ultimate distancing from the intellectual foundations of the idea of the West. A well-worn tale, this act of intellectual separation was not an act of isolation, for as Cedric Robinson argues, those who made it merely discovered a tradition that was already "all around them."[3] Over the course of the twentieth century in particular, African-descended scholars were to discover that there was a larger tradition of thinkers with no formal training, but armed with the necessary tools for enlisting and extending the motive forces of a Black intellectual resistance, that developed and cultivated the spaces that were the logical foundation from which to engage the world and imagine a liberated society. They were to discover, that for their forebears, academic licensure was the map—one of many—not the ultimate destination. They were to discover that quests for wholeness need not be subsumed under the politics of the academy.[4] How to resist such incorporation of Black intellectual traditions

159

continues to be a central problematic for those of us mired in academic modes of thought, as in many respects, such acts of discovery have been abandoned.[5] The search for exemplars whose models we might emulate presages the attempt to generate a grander vision, and as such, represents a viable starting point for the conversation.

I

The breadth of thought that structured Black commitments to knowing and doing has been catalogued in disciplinary areas other than history, but it has been individuals who historian Earl Thorpe dubbed, the "historians-without-portfolio,"[6] that have helped to galvanize a Black public that spawned the various intellectual and socio-political movements of the past two centuries. For this reason, history remains one of the most popular intellectual areas associated with Black movements for social change, particularly prominent in the formation of the political identity of what Greg Kimathi Carr calls "African nationalist" political and community work. In exploring the intentionality around the philosophies of history that have animated the same intellectual traditions discussed in this essay, Carr argues that at their core they asserted the imperative of placing African collective memory in a context necessary for orienting futures modeled on the ways of knowing interrupted by the *maafa*.[7]

Standing squarely in this tradition is Drusilla Dunjee Houston. Born in 1876 to formerly enslaved parents in Harper's Ferry, Virginia, and Houston's upbringing exuded all of the trappings of the Black elite, but like many, she exemplified the qualities of the "race woman." The prominence of her family oriented her to a particular tradition of activism and advocacy, but her embrace of the craft of Black history has its own particular genesis in the intellectual tradition to which she would join—for her the two were never separate. An Oklahoman migrant, institution builder, editorialist, schoolteacher, and finally a historian, Houston was able to extend a philosophic-historiographical approach bequeathed her by thinkers like Hosea Easton, Martin Delany, Pauline Hopkins, and W.E.B. Du Bois, whose *The Negro* (1915) at the very least sparked her to more concerted action.[8]

Geographically isolated from the Eastern literary enclaves, the Oklahoman's magisterial self-published *Wonderful Ethiopians of the Ancient Cushite Empire* (1926) contained a well-researched elucidation of what later thinkers have labeled the "African presence"[9] in the ancient world. In this text, the first of three planned volumes,[10] Houston argues that there was a definite "Ethiopian" influence upon the ancient cultures of Eurasia or what Jacob Carruthers calls "tri-continental antiquity."[11] Though it was well received in many circles, despite questions of methodology,[12] it was not until its resuscitation by booksellers F.H. Hammurabi, Paul Coates, and historian James Spady, along with historians and scholars associated with the Association to the Study of Classical African Civilizations, that Houston's work was reread by recent generations.[13] Largely as a result of the nationalist community evoked by Carr, Houston is now a household name—an "old scrapper"[14]—and well-revered among organizations like the Association of Black Women Historians which offers its annual Drusilla Dunjee Houston Award to recognize "emerging Black female scholars" in the field of Africana history.[15] The above-mentioned thinkers all converge around the idea of the importance of Houston's contribution to our understanding of Africa and the ancient world. In various ways their work considers how Houston uniquely challenged the prevailing assumptions around Black invisibility in what could be called "Western civilization" and perhaps more importantly how such knowledge could determine how Africana communities might better confront modernity.

The most-studied Houston scholar, Peggy Brooks-Bertram, author of the sole extended study on her historiography, has argued that Houston's historical scholarship, with its emphasis on deconstructing normative ideas about "race" inherent in Western classical historiography, helped set the stage for what would eventuate as Africana Studies in the late 1960s.[16] If this is true—and we suggest that it is—Africana Studies theorists would do well to recommit to the imperatives that underpinned the philosophy of history employed in *Wonderful Ethiopians*. But first some clarifications on the question of disciplinarity are in order.

The discipline of Africana Studies is often erroneously conflated with the subfield of African American or African Diasporan History.[17] These sorts of mischaracterizations stem from the importance assigned to the past by Africana Studies theorists. For some, the historical subfield represents the foundation or "core" of Africana Studies.[18] Commenting on this relationship James Turner, in his widely cited foreword to *The Next Decade*, wrote that history was indeed a foundational methodology, but argues that it was necessary for understanding the fundamental relationship between Black peoples and the political economy of modernity. Similarly, the influential *Introduction to Black Studies*, authored by Maulana Karenga argues for a propaedeutic role for history asserting that it is "indispensable" to all other subject areas.[19] But it should not follow, as some seem to believe, that Africana Studies is merely a collection of historical disciplines, for it does not share the same methodological or academic comments that emanate from history departments. While the past is crucial, there is no one-to-one correlation between History[20] and the disciplinary purview of Africana Studies and neither is the importance of knowing the past an endorsement of the function of History as it operates in Western knowledge communities.

Those who conflate the two do not properly take into account History's historicity, that is, the ways in which its disciplinarity has rendered the Black subject—in fact, all subjects[21]—and how these renderings have imputed particular, if not flawed readings of Africana experiences within the historical subfields devoted to them.[22] These readings tend to reflect an outsized role of modernity in the evocation of the Black experience, imprecise or Western-centered temporal and spatial considerations of Black life, and the epistemological and methodological reductions of the Black experience to the written text, among many others. These issues stem not merely from intellectual choices, but from disciplinary practice, and they mirror the very intellectual agendas that History does, namely, the elevation of the nation-state and its civil religion.[23] Along with early protestations from Lawrence Reddick and later ones from Vincent Harding, the most consistent critics of Western historiography's depiction of Africana realities has been the "Chicago School of African History," led by Anderson Thompson and Jacob Carruthers, and most recently the Association for the Study of Classical African Civilization's African World History Project Planning Committee.[24]

It is out of these ruptures with History that we also begin to see the process leading to the development of "disciplinary Africana Studies," which has its foundation the study of both "phenomena and experience" on terms set by Africans' ways of knowing them.[25] Disciplinary Africana Studies is characterized by the disengagement and recontextualization of Western structures of knowledge, so that we might more completely recognize ourselves in our own contexts. Far from eschewing the study of the past, disciplinary Africana Studies is premised on rendering historical memories in ways more recognizable and identifiable.[26] This essay shows that Drusilla Dunjee Houston's exposition of a "philosophy of history" dovetails with this larger objective. Where other scholars have rightly showed her contribution to our knowledge of the African past, here I will argue that her statements about the *meaning of the past* represent a uniquely Africana Studies tradition, one that can be extended only through "disciplinary suicide."[27]

II

Perhaps our first clue as to what made Drusilla Dunjee Houston's approach so significant is her embrace by significant portions of nationalist intellectual communities and her continued marginalization by the larger historical community.[28] It is clear that her understanding of the historical experiences of the "Ethiopian" does not necessarily fit with what Anderson Thompson's derides as the "Sambo historiography" that still has its grip on the dominant culture's consciousness.[29] All the more important to clarify the central premises underlining her approach and the ultimate purposes she ascribes to her writing which she articulates in the preface to the volume. These prefatory remarks represent a quintessential declaration of intellectual space, one that finds resonance within a highly visible genealogy of Black historical thinking.

The trajectory joined by Houston extends a continuum dating back to at least a century before her birth in 1876, its sharpest enunciation being what has been termed "Ethiopianism" in the middle of the nineteenth century. Houston, like Ethiopianist thinkers in the nineteenth century, attempted to locate the historical continuities of ancient Africans using both biblical sources and empirical studies, politically attuned toward the future.[30] But her declaration of space to think about the meaning of history, articulated in her preface, also mirrors similar articulations from figures like Arturo Schomburg, whose 1913 tract, *Racial Integrity* and his widely-cited "The Negro Digs Up His Past" (1925) both argued that contemporary history be intimately linked to the long African past and taught and disseminated.[31] Her preface also anticipates the later statements by W.E.B. Du Bois and Lawrence Reddick by helping to contextualize the ways in which the dominant historical schools have organized themselves against the pursuit of the full knowledge of Africana experiences. Du Bois's and Reddick's broadsides helped to concretize the need for a more potent approach to understanding the past, at that time being popularized by Carter G. Woodson and others.[32]

While we know the impact of the Woodson school and the ways in which Du Bois helped to extend to the 1960s Africana Studies movement essential methods for writing and teaching in the discipline, scholars have yet to draw similar parallels between figures like Houston and George G.M. James and other thinkers that find resonance with her approach.[33]

After outlining the inclusive chapters of the volume,

Houston's preface continues with a section titled "The Growing Need of Light Upon Race Origins," in which she sets the theoretical agenda of widening the knowledge of Africana experiences as well as explicitly championing the need for a historical interpretation that placed primacy on how African peoples both contributed to world civilization and uniquely conceptualized their own. This methodological approach to the work underscored the explicit political commitment of restoration or what Martin Delany and others called "regeneration;" that is, the work that needed to be done for African liberation in the present.[34]

This effective uncovering of the content necessary to fill historical gaps and its concomitant alternative interpretation are goals that Houston animates with two particular thematic thrusts that we find throughout the preface. The first speaks to the roots of the modern breakdown of Western society, which she reads as essentially the ubiquity of racial prejudice coupled with economic inequality and the rise of the "spoliation of "the weak."[35] Writing in the aftermath of the Great War and a time where other thinkers had predicted a "decline of the West," Houston articulated a theory of its causes.[36] For Houston, as it was for Du Bois, the origin of world conflict was the battle over the imperial pursuit of resources, conflicts unduly affecting and involving people of African descent and the geopolitics of the continent.[37] Furthermore, Houston places emphasis on the fact that it was indeed false readings of history that made possible this exploitation; further making possible for the construction of the West resting on the underdevelopment of Africa.[38] In a much-cited passage Houston outlines what we can call *Wonderful Ethiopians'* raison d'être:

We are sending forth this information because so few men today understand the primitive forces that are the root of modern culture. So superficial and prejudiced has been most modern research, that many important and accepted theories of universal history have no actual basis in fact. The average modern historical book contradicts what the ancients said about the nations that preceded them. We cannot solve the stupendous problems that the world faces until we can read aright the riddle of the evolution of the races. Uniformed men make unsafe leaders. That is the primal cause for so many errors of judgment in state and national councils. (8)

Here, Houston argues that at root of the racial antipathy so enveloping contemporary society was the willing, blissful ignorance of the true sense from which races developed, a silence supported by "modern research." She argues that racial capitalism was indeed justified, if not made possible by a "worldwide conspiracy in literature to conceal" that which *Wonderful Ethiopians* sought to uncover (8). The development of the idea of racial superiority was the co-conspirator. But she also gestures to the fact that these issues also stem from various forms of nationalisms, also co-conspirators, in that they lead to the kinds of histories that tend to uplift certain groups over others. Speaking largely of the American condition, Houston argued that:

This [ignorance] is not the nature or intention of the better men of the civilized nations but we are uninformed about alien peoples. We are narrow and provincial in our views. The hatred of the races springs out of misunderstanding. The men of the world who have traveled, and read and thought, upon ethnological problems are the men who have cultivated instincts of human brotherhood. (9)

Houston seems to give "the men of the world" the benefit of the doubt, underplaying the role that such ignorance has played in the subjugation of Africans, a condition no less assuaged by those "who have traveled, and read, and thought." But perhaps this is also an appeal to the average American or Westerner, who has been inexorably affected by the ignorance used to create inequality and make war.

If ignorance was the cause of widespread human suffering, then enlightenment might be the solution. This idea was the second general theme, which is inextricably connected to the first. As shown above, Houston anticipated many of the critiques heaped upon Western knowledge of the non-Western other that would come to dominate the academy in the late twentieth century, manifesting in History as the subfield of "social history."[39] But this theme also continued a Black critique of historical silences that had as its corrective the use of historical knowledge to eliminate the intellectual foundations for Black suffering. Houston was not merely a deconstructionist content to "historicize or relativize," her work extended an "agonistic imperative" to the problem, a need to resolve it.[40] She continued:

> The tragedy of human misery increases, the increase of defectives, the growing artificiality of modern living, compels us to seek and blazen forth the knowledge of the true origin of culture and the fundamental principles that through the ages have been the basis of true progress. Only by this wisdom shall we know how to lift human life today. (8)

This is a patent reminder of the true work of historical recovery. Houston principally affirms that cultures were part of the human cargoes of the *maafa* and that intellectual justifications for colonization included erasures of identity.[41] The denial of the former and the impact of the latter rendered Africans broken from "the thread of remembrance" (10). As such, social change had to do more than eliminate the cause, the project of restoration was a necessary measure of human liberation. For Houston, history, aided by the empirical sciences were tools useful for this important aim. Where history up until then had been characterized by written sources, both primary and secondary, Houston begins to place importance upon the works of archaeologists and others specializing in the study of material culture. In this sense, her philosophy of history paralleled that of William Leo Hansberry, who also believed that we might use material culture to fully apprehend what historical writing had chosen to ignore or misrepresent.[42] Further, Houston believed that knowledge of the past would settle forever any questions of "equal opportunity" (9). But as Du Bois, too, would affirm in 1960, that was not the end goal.[43] Houston winds up linking the recovery of historical knowledge to a loftier objective, which she characterizes as "a greater consecration to the high idealism that made the masteries of olden days" (11). The story to follow was not meant to "stir the pride" (11) of African people but to—in Du Bois's 1897 words— help engineer a contribution "which no other race can make."[44] Against the reductionist and postmodernist critique that such histories were merely "African" copies of Western hegemonic constructions of fact, what Houston outlines is a need to restore the human values lost and affirm that the meaning of history was about their recovery *and* their use in a collective construction of a better world, with each race "its rightful place in the consummation of God's plan of the Ages" (11).

Houston's philosophy of history was a clarion call to know more about ourselves, an assertion that the quest for human amelioration might be fulfilled with more knowledge, but unlike the Enlightenment thinkers who uttered similar ideas, she did not consider other human communities outside of History, or "Unhistorical."[45] In many ways, it was a call to envision a history where such readings were no longer normative. *Wonderful Ethiopians,* then for Africans was about a pathway home, and for the wider human community it urged that the key to resolving the questions raised by the recent war included a need to act on the basis of more information. For what the world needed was a truthful rendering of the human past such that would allow us to realize "our common brotherhood and to reach out to solve unmastered problems and unfulfilled duties." Failure to do so would only lead to more "modern crimes of injustice" (12).

Drusilla Dunjee Houston has been justifiably remembered as an original contributor to our understanding of the impact of African cultures on the ancient world. Her work helped to generate more concerted efforts to restore the consciousness of the "riddle of the evolution of the races" (7). But her work portends more. Houston was not writing to elicit favor in the academy or to extend the reach of the discipline of History. Her intellectual contributions ranged to greater heights. For Houston, writing this story was part of an impulse to rewrite the central assumptions of history itself. Indeed, as discussed above, her work shares this critical objective with ASCAC's African World History Project Planning Committee. Their 2000 document, titled "The ASCAC Atlanta Declaration"[46] is an extension of the ideals put forth in Houston's prefatory remarks to *Wonderful Ethiopians*. This document—written 74 years later— in that it recognizes the centrality of African civilizations in antiquity to both the modern world *and* to visions of liberated futures, continues Houston's grand quest for wholeness. Let the circle remain unbroken.

---

[1] Ngugi wa Thiong'o, *Something Torn and New: An African Renaissance* (New York: Basic Civitas, 2009), 35.

[2] Vincent Harding, *Beyond Chaos: Black History and the Search for the New Land* (Atlanta: Institute of the Black World, 1970), 26.

[3] Cedric Robinson, *Black Marxism: The Making of the Black Radical Tradition* (Chapel Hill, NC: University of North Carolina Press, 2000), 170.

[4] See for instance, the discussion of the Institute of the Black World in Derrick White, *The Challenge of Blackness: The Institute of the Black World and Black Political Activism in the 1970s* (Gainesville, FL: University Press of Florida, 2011).

[5] On questions of abandonment and incorporation, see Greg Carr, "What Black Studies is Not: Moving From Crisis to Liberation in Africana Intellectual Work," *Socialism and Democracy* 25 (March 2011): 179 and Roderick Ferguson, *The Reorder of Things: The University and its Pedagogies of Minority Difference* (Minneapolis, MN: University of Minnesota Press, 2012), 1-40.

[6] Earl E. Thorpe, *Black Historians: A Critique* (New York: Morrow, 1958), 143-144.

[7] See Greg Kimathi Carr, "The African-Centered Philosophy of History: An Exploratory Essay on the Genealogy of Foundationalist Historical Thought and African Nationalist Identity Construction" in *The African World History Project: The Preliminary Challenge,* eds. Jacob H. Carruthers and Leon C. Harris (Los Angeles, CA: Association for the Study of African Civilizations, 1997), 292-295.

[8] On their relationship see, Peggy Ann Brooks-Bertram, "Drusilla Dunjee Houston: Uncrowned Queen in the African American Women's Literary Tradition," (PhD diss., State University of New York at Buffalo, 2002), 39 and Herb Boyd, "The Wonderful Historian Drusilla Dunjee Houston," *Amsterdam News,* March 20, 2014, Accessed July 24, 2014, http://amsterdamnews.com/news/2014/mar/20/wonderful-historian-drusilla-dunjee-houston/?page=1.

[9] Ivan Van Sertima and Runoko Rashidi have popularized the study of the "African presence" throughout the world over the past thirty or so years. See Ivan Van Sertima and Runoko Rashidi, eds., *The African Presence in Early Asia* (New Brunswick, NJ: Transaction Publishers, 1987) which republished portions of the work of Houston (Ibid, 54-57).

[10] For a discussion on the lost volumes see Peggy Ann Brooks-Bertram, "Drusilla Dunjee Houston," 48-50. Brooks-Bertram published what she believes to be a second volume. See her discussion in "Editor's Comments," in *Wonderful Ethiopians of the Ancient Cushite Empire: Book II: Origin of Civilization from the Cushites,* ed. Peggy Brooks-Bertram (Buffalo, NY: Bertram Publishing, 2007), xxxvii-xxxix.

[11] Jacob Carruthers, "An African Historiography for the Twenty-First Century," in *The African World History Project: The Preliminary Challenge*, eds. Jacob H. Carruthers and Leon C. Harris, 55.

[12] These critiques were based upon the fact that Houston did not utilize the disciplinary conventions of Western historiography (i.e., footnotes, bibliography,

and an index), its claims to "scientism." For some, this made the text impossible to evaluate. According to Brooks-Bertram, Houston was unable to include these due to space considerations. She however attempted to correct these errors in later editions. See Peggy Ann Brooks-Bertram, "Drusilla Dunjee Houston," 22-23.

[13] Ibid, 54-56. Black Classic Press republished the volume in 1985. In this edition, Coates and Asa Hilliard offer an introduction and afterword, respectively, while Spady adds a commentary. See Drusilla Dunjee Houston, *Wonderful Ethiopians of the Ancient Cushite Empire* (Baltimore: Black Classic Press, 1985).

[14] A term used by Chicago-based historian Anderson Thompson to characterize the pioneers of Black history in the nineteenth and early twentieth centuries.

[15] See "Drusilla Dunjee Houston Award," Association of Black Women Historians, http://www.abwh.org/index.php?option=com_content&view=article&id=106%3 Adrusilla-dunjee-houston-award-information&catid=42%3Aawards&Itemid=157.

[16] She states: "We know that the *Wonderful Ethiopians* series was partly written to refute the false premise of inherent Black inferiority, to vindicate African American ancestry in the arena of public opinion and to rekindle the dying flame of collective race consciousness. Along with these issues, Dunjee Houston intended to demonstrate the vital cultural significance of ancient African matriarchy and its direct link to the Racial Uplift work of elite African American female leaders," Peggy Brooks-Bertram, "Editor's Comments," xii.

[17] The struggle over Africana Studies at HBCUs reflects this tension. Many HBCUS do not have Africana Studies departments, but most channel teaching and research on the Africana experience toward their History departments. Many offer minors under the aegis of these departments.

[18] This argument is—not surprisingly—often made by trained historians that work in Africana Studies departments. For a review of some of the more prominent arguments, see the work of historian Pero Dagbovie, "History as a Core Subject Area of African American Studies: Self-Taught and Self-Proclaimed African American Historians, 1960s-1980s," *Journal of Black Studies* 37 (May 2007): 602-629.

[19] James Turner, "Foreword: Africana Studies and Epistemology: A Discourse in the Sociology of Knowledge," in *The Next Decade : Theoretical and Research Issues in African Studies,* ed. James Turner (Ithaca, NY: Africana Studies and Research Center, 1984), ix-x; Maulana Karenga, *Introduction to Black Studies* (Los Angeles, CA: University of Sankore Press, 2010), 65-66.

[20] Capitalized here to denote the distinctly professional pursuit as opposed to the broader ideal of a theory or understanding of the past. It is necessary to distinguish the two, absent a more appropriate term. The difficulties in conceptualizing this distinction our outlined by Ashis Nandy, who argues, "Enlightenment sensitivities, whether in the West or outside, presume a perfect equivalence between history and the construction of the past; they presume that there is no past independent of history." See his "History's Forgotten Doubles," *History and Theory* 34 (May 1995): 44-66.

[21] On the constructions of historical knowledge in the United States and challenges

to these constructions, see inter alia, Peter Novick, *That Noble Dream: The "Objectivity Question" and the American Historical Profession* (Cambridge, UK: Cambridge University Press, 1988).

[22]In outlining a tradition of Black historiography, Kim Butler states: "Professional history had ignored or misrepresented the Black subject, compelling African descendants to rely on their own inscriptions and interpretations of their past," Kim Butler, "Clio and Griot: The African Diaspora in the Discipline of History," in *The African Diaspora and the Disciplines,* ed. Tejumola Olaniyan and James H. Sweet (Bloomington, IN: Indiana University Press, 2010), 25. Butler's essay argues that the formal conventions within disciplinary History are difficult to reconcile with "the multiplicity of expressive languages with which African peoples have encoded, remembered, and recovered their experiences…" Ibid, 21. In her estimation, Africana Diaspora History provides an opportunity to perhaps deal with the absences and misinterpretations ascribed to historical interpretations of Africans, if it could reconcile these discordant traditions. Greg Carr's forthcoming contribution to the next edition of The African World History Project of the Association for the Study of Classical African Civilizations in large part attempts to deal with this query. Ashis Nandy has also raised the importance of conceptualizing the ways in which human beings know the past beyond the strictures of history. Nandy asserts that some human beings exist "outside history" not to suggest that they have no past, but in order to critically interrogate "the idea of history itself" as an Enlightenment derived intellectual project complicit in the hegemony of the West. See his "History's Forgotten Doubles," 51.

[23] For a recent discussion on nationalism and history, see Kenneth Pomeranz, "Histories for a Less National Age," *American Historical Review* (February 2014): 1-22.

[24] See Lawrence Reddick, "A New Interpretation for Negro History," *Journal of Negro History* 22 (January 1937): 17-28; Harding, *Beyond Chaos;* Anderson Thompson, "Developing an African Historiography," in *The African World History Project: The Preliminary Challenge,* eds. Jacob H. Carruthers and Leon C. Harris, 9-30 and Jacob H. Carruthers, "An African Historiography for the 21st Century," in Ibid, 47-72. See also the appendices, Ibid, 327-361.

[25] Greg Carr, "What Black Studies is Not,"180.

[26] Greg Carr is the leading thinker arguing for the articulation of a historical memory divorced from Western strictures and guided by African ways of knowing, grounds from which to construct a distinct approach to Africana Studies. See his "You Don't Call the Kittens Biscuits": Disciplinary Africana Studies and the Study of Malcolm X," in *Malcolm X: An Historical Reader,* eds., James L. Conyers, Jr. and Andrew P. Smallwood (Durham, NC: Carolina Academic Press, 2008), 364-368 and "Black Consciousness, Pan-Africanism, and the African World History Project: The Case of Africana Studies for African Cultural Development," in *African American Consciousness: Past and Present,* ed. James L. Conyers (New Brunswick, NJ: Transaction Publishers, 2012), 13-16.

---

[27] This concept stems from the early years of the Temple graduate program in African American Studies and is meant to indicate a sense that the disciplines that scholars were initially trained in were less important than the need to flesh out something new, that which came to be known as Africology. See Molefi Asante, *An Afrocentric Manifesto* (Malden, MA: Polity Press, 2007), 103.

[28] This, of course, can be said about most historical thinkers of African descent. See Novick, *That Noble Dream*, 472-491. While she was not discussed in August Meier and Elliot Rudwick's seminal *Black History and the Historical Profession* (Urbana: University of Illinois Press, 1986), historian of African American historiography, Pero Dagbovie, has mentioned her in his work. See his "Black Women Historians from the Late 19th Century to the Dawning of the Civil Rights Movement," *The Journal of African American History* 89 (Summer 2004): 251.

[29] Thompson, "Developing an African Historiography," 21-22.

[30] See inter alia, Wilson Jeremiah Moses, *The Golden Age of Black Nationalism* (New York: Oxford University Press, 1978), 156-161 and Stephen G. Hall, *A Faithful Account of the Race* (Chapel Hill, NC: University of North Carolina Press, 2009), 53-61.

[31] Arturo A. Schomburg, "The Negro Digs Up His Past," in *The New Negro*, ed. Alain Locke (New
York: Touchstone, 1997), 231-237; Arturo A. Schomburg, *Racial Integrity: A Plea for the Establishment of a Chair of Negro History in our Schools and Colleges, etc.: Negro Society for Historical Research Occasional Paper No. 3* (New York: August Valentine Bernier, 1913).

[32] See W.E.B. Du Bois, "The Propaganda of History," in his *Black Reconstruction in America, 1860-1880* (New York: Free Press, 2000), 711-729 and Reddick, "A New Interpretation for Negro History." Reddick's article was a paper prepared for Woodson's Association for the Study of Negro Life and History. This organization was largely responsible for the popularizing of Black history and for the training of Black historians. Though it is known that Woodson's relationship to the academy was not the most amiable, the relationship between the association writ large and academic History bears more research. See inter alia, Pero Dagbovie *The Early Black History Movement, Carter G. Woodson, and Lorenzo Johnston Green* (Urbana, IL: University of Illinois Press, 2007).

[33] On Woodson's and Du Bois's relationship to Africana Studies, see Talmadge Anderson and James Stewart, *Introduction to African American Studies: Transdisciplinary Approaches and Implications* (Baltimore: Inprint Editions 2007), 17-18 and James B. Stewart, "The Legacy of W.E.B. Du Bois for Contemporary Black Studies," *Journal of Negro Education* (Summer 1984): 296-311. On the centrality of James and his work, *Stolen Legacy* (1954), which is similar in some respects to Houston's *Wonderful Ethiopians*, see Carr, "The African-Centered Philosophy of History," 312.

[34] See Martin Delany, *Principia of Ethnology: The Origins of Race and Color, With an Archaeological Compendium of Ethiopian and Egyptian Civilization* (Philadelphia: Harper and Brothers, 1879), 80-81.

---

[35] Houston, *Wonderful Ethiopians*, 9. Further references will be cited in-text.

[36] I am referring to Oswald Spengler's seminal *The Decline of the West* (New York: Alfred A. Knopf, 1932). See also Arnold Toynbee's *A Study of History* (New York: Oxford University Press, 1972) for similar ideas. The catastrophic impact of The Great War, or World War I, is well documented in recent and contemporary works. For a recent take that is centered on "the how" of the conflict see Christopher Clark, *The Sleepwalkers: How Europe Went to War in 1914* (New York: Harper, 2013) and on its ramifications, David Reynolds, *The Long Shadow: The Legacies of the Great War in the Twentieth Century* (New York: W.W. Norton and Co., 2014).

[37] See Du Bois's seminal essay, "The African Roots of War," *Atlantic Monthly* (May 1914): 707-714.

[38] This included both a materialist construction and a theoretical construction, so that the West is also an intellectual posture predicated on denying humanity (history) to non-Western persons. See Walter Rodney, *How Europe Underdeveloped Africa* (London: Bogle-L'Ouverture Publications, 1972) and inter alia, Nandy, "History's Forgotten Doubles," 53-56.

[39] See Novick, *That Noble Dream*, 440-445.

[40] See Ibid, 523-524. For Kwesi Otabil's "agonistic imperative" which argues for a "rational" construal of the African-centered movement and its contribution to a new world-nexus, see his *The Agonistic Imperative: The Rational Burden of Africa-Centeredness* (Bristol, IN: Wyndham Hall Press, 1994).

[41] See among many others, Cedric Robinson's discussion in *Black Marxism*, 121-122; 179-184.

[42] On Hansberry in relationship to Houston, see James G. Spady, "Tri-Muse: The Historiography of Joel A. Rogers, Drusilla Dunjee Houston, and William Leo Hansberry," *Y'Bird* 1 (1978): 98-115. On Hansberry generally, see Joseph E. Harris, "William Leo Hansberry, 1894-1965: Profile of a Pioneer Africanist," in *Pillars in Ethiopian History: The William Leo Hansberry African History Notebook, Volume One*, ed. Joseph E. Harris (Washington, DC: Howard University Press, 1974), 3-30.

[43] W.E.B. Du Bois, "Whither Now and Why?" in *The Education of Black People: Ten Critiques, 1906-1960*, ed. Herbert Aptheker (New York: Monthly Review Press, 1973), 151.

[44] W.E.B. Du Bois, "On the Conversation of Races" 491.

[45] See G.W.F. Hegel, *Philosophy of History* (New York: Colonial Press, 1899), 99.

[46] Issued on March 26, 2000. A copy is in the author's possession.

Women without Men: African American Widows in Post-Emancipation Maryland

Arlisha Norwood

In 1855 enslaved Sophia Jones married John H. Chambers, a free man in Baltimore, Maryland. John Chambers was mustered into the 30th Regiment of the United States Colored Troops on March 18, 1864.[1] While in service, illiterate John asked several of his friends to help him write letters to his wife. On October 16, 1864 while in a camp near Petersburg, Virginia, he wrote:

> Dear Wife, with much plusher [sic] I take my pen in hand to inform you that I am well and I hope wen these few lines reches [sic]you it may fine you the same. Ples [sic] wright to let me know if you got the letter with the $20.00 in it that that I sent you ten days ago.[2]

Sophia, also illiterate, used her neighbor's aide to communicate with her husband. She responded in November of 1864 stating:

> Dear Husband, I like the pleasure of answer you letter dated and was glad to see you was enjoying good health fore my part I am enjoyin [sic] the same. I think the letters wish you sent me with twenty dollars must been lost as I can't get any new from it.[3]

The couple continued correspondence throughout the war until John was finally mustered out in Baltimore, Maryland on December 10, 1865. Once he returned to civilian life, John was unable to work due to a "hacking cough" and back pain which caused him to walk with a stick.[4] His "acquaintances noticed his change in appearance and often helped him walk from one place to another."[5] Sophia worked where she could, cleaning

177

offices and performing other "odd jobs" around town.[6] Unfortunately, in 1867 John Chambers suddenly died. Sophia, now a struggling widow filed for a pension in 1877.[7] For reasons unknown, she was denied. Sophia, undeterred, filed again in 1880. The Chambers pension file spans 200 pages and explores Sophia's difficulties in widowhood.

Sophia was around 45 years old when she applied for her second pension. She hired a local attorney, Chad G. Gartill for a fee of $25.00 to advocate on her behalf and more importantly, deal with the bureaucracy of the Civil War pension system.[8] In January of 1882, Sophia was informed that the Pension Bureau would begin a special examination on her case due to several discrepancies in her deposition. The main point of contention was her assertion that her deceased husband contracted a disease while in service.[9] The Pension Bureau assigned Special Examiner, A. Ferguson to carry out a thorough investigation on the application and encouraged him to collect the testimonies of "family, doctors and neighbors who were well acquainted with solider until discharge and during each year till death."[10] In her second deposition, Sophia claimed that her husband worked at an Oyster House before his enlistment. She testified that he was a very "able bodied and healthy man" before he entered the Union Army. She could recollect only one instance in which he experienced illness "it was the year the smallpox was so bad and that was 1858 or 1859."[11] Upon his return she stated that, "he was complaining of his left side hurting him." John Chambers appeared very ill by 1867, and he was so weak he could not work, Sophia recalled a time when he tried to return to his place of employment, "he went to the Oyster House once and came back and said he could not stand it."

Special Examiner Ferguson, explicitly inquired about Sophia's private life, continuously questioning her about past sexual relationships and former friendships. She chose to answer the questions with hopes that she would be approved for the pension. Ferguson, also performed a thorough investigation of the community members who corroborated Sophia's testimony. Henry Gray, a neighbor and carriage maker testified that the deceased Chambers "was a fresh, healthy, young man that was in 1855" he then went on to assert "that when he came out of the army he was all broken up."[12] The special examination continued with several testimonies from various neighbors, old friends and doctors. By the end of his investigation Ferguson concluded that Sophia Chambers should be denied the claim based upon the testimonies of a doctor who stated that John Chambers contracted the disease after his service.[13]

No more documents appear in the case until 1890. Apparently, Sophia, still determined to receive her rightful pension, hired a new lawyer Allan Rutherford.[14] She attempted to make her final case with several new testimonies from John's former acquaintances. While the claim reveals much about the communities veterans constructed after the Civil War. The documents also expose the hardship Sophia had to survive after her husband's death. On April 11, 1890 Sophia made a plea to the Pension Bureau to expedite her approval. In the affidavit she argued "that she has filed more than sufficient evidence to complete her application." The testimony continued by stating her present condition, "she is a great sufferer from rheumatism all crippled up with it-also from asthma and heart tremble also with kidney disease-that her condition is all broken down and suffering with a hacking cough-that her physical condition is such that she is in fear of and danger of an immediate death." The document went on to

179

discuss Sophia's present economic troubles, "she is a great poorly and completely disabled from doing any work. She has a little boy who gives her two dollars per week and her only income besides that is three dollars per month, other than this she has no means and is also the recipient of charity from her friends."[15]Her affidavit was supported with a letter from her doctor who stated the same conditions.[16] Moreover, several testimonies allude to Sophia's life in poverty as one of her neighbors declared, "his wife is in a bad need."[17] After ten years Sophia was approved for a pension of $8.00 per month after evidence showed that her husband died from exposure to consumption while in service.

Sophia's story is not an anomaly. Her life of struggle, strife and negotiation permeated the experience of many African American widows after the death of a spouse. Without partners, the difficult transition from bondage to freedom could present the black widows with economic and social dilemmas. Sophia's interaction with the Pension Bureau also provides insight into the numerous complications black widows confronted when filing a pension claim. Their stories prove that seeking economic compensation was often an invasive, tedious process that required persistence.

In recent years there has been an increase in the usage of African American Military Pension Bureau files in Civil War and Reconstruction era scholarship. A recent work on the subject, Freedom's Promise: Ex-Slave Families and Citizenship in the Age of Emancipation by scholar Elizabeth Regosin utilizes the claims to symbolize the determination of African American widows, parents and guardians to gain the rights of citizenship after the Civil War.[18] Her work also explores the complexities of black familial relations in the post war era. Furthermore, Donald Schafer's work

After the Glory: The Struggle, explores the experiences of USCT veterans.[19] Many other Emancipation and Reconstruction scholars rely on the claims to illuminate the world of transition experienced by African Americans who moved from bondage to freedom.[20] Unfortunately, the claims have not been used to examine the hardship of African American widows after the death of a spouse. Widowed African American females suffered great difficulties, which they chose to communicate vividly in their pension claims. This work will examine the pension claims of several African American women in Maryland. Using their personal testimonies as evidence, this paper will prove that widowhood for black women often meant a consuming battle to literally "survive the peace."[21]

Maryland works as a convenient location for this study because the state lacked considerable intervention from Federal Government agencies following the Civil War.[22] Prior to the War, the state held a large amount of both enslaved and free African Americans, making the border territory a contested space for much of its history.[23] Maryland remained loyal to the Union during the War. As a result, during and after the Civil War, African Americans were left to navigate a peculiar space where they received little assistance but were forced to sustain households and families. USCT widows proved themselves worthy of the challenge, they remained adamant and asserted their presence by applying for pensions. Through their pursuit of pensions we are able to further understand what black widowhood looked like.

For African American widows their interaction with the Civil War pension system was a daunting yet necessary undertaking. The Pension Act of July 14, 1862 granted pensions to soldiers who were disabled from wounds or injuries incurred during their time in service.[24] Furthermore, the act also stipulated that widows, children or dependents could receive a pension if a soldier died from a result of any injury acquired during the war. In 1864 the Federal Government amended the act to include the marriage of slaves which had not been legally recognized before the war, the amendment declared: "the widows of colored soldiers who lived in states could not marry needed only to prove by testimony that they lived as man and wife."[25] The act was revised two more times before congress decided to wholly place the decision of legitimacy of slave marriages in the hands of individual pension commissioners.[26] The act also granted back pay to both widows and children who could prove evidence of a legitimate relationship with the deceased or injured soldier.

Another condition of the Pension Act required that the widow of deceased soldier or veteran remain unmarried. Republican/free labor ideology believed the presence of male figure meant that the widow no longer required support or relief from the Pension Bureau.[27] A large number of USCT widows navigated the Civil War pension system with hopes of receiving some sort of relief. Unfortunately, the commissioners and the widows often held contradicting ideals of marriage.[28] In bondage, African Americans created complex and varied relationships which represented a marital union. The pension files are filled with testimonies from both men and women who adhered to vastly different concepts of marriage. This contestation could be problematic for widows who were forced to legitimize their union to Special Examiners who were not familiar with cultural customs. In the case of Sophia Chambers she was questioned several times about her marriage ceremony even after providing documentation. [29] Many times when both soldier and widow were enslaved obtaining documentation could be impossible, therefore, the legitimacy of the marriage had to be solidified in the testimonies of friends, family and sometimes former owners. The path to retaining a pension was even more burdensome for those who were illiterate or uninformed about the qualifications. African American widows often hired lawyers on their behalf. This decision could aid or hinder their application process. Even with all the obstacles, the relief of a pension could rescue many of the widows from a life of perpetual poverty. The pension meant guaranteed income for those who lived in unstable economic conditions. Widows with children could expect an increased pension for every child which was born during the union. The single mothers who appear in the pension claims elucidate on the troubles of sustaining a household without an additional income from a spouse.

Susan Ann Webb married James Moore on May 8 1852. At the time they were both enslaved in Talbot County, Maryland. Rev. James Massey married the couple in Maryland, and provided no "marriage certificate nor was the marriage ever recorded in the church record."[30] The couple had six children during their marriage. James Moore enlisted in the Union Army on March 31, 1864.[31] He wrote a letter from Freedmen's Hospital in Alexandria, Virginia. He addressed his wife, expressing his uneasiness about her late response. "I have not received any letter to answers my letters I sent July 3rd I am very uneasy about it indeed."[32] He then spoke of sympathy for his wife's current condition stating, "I don't know if it was your opportunity to or not my heart and mind is always drawn out to hear from you my dear though it may be a little difficult for you to git [sic] paper by having no body to tend to your business."[33] He concluded the letter by proclaiming his love for his children and he informed his wife " ples dont forgit [sic] what I told you to rease [sic] them in fear of the Lord."[34]

James Moore died from remittent fever in a hospital located in New Bern, North Carolina on August 20, 1865.[35] Susan Moore applied for widow's pension in 1868. The commissioner procured the testimonies of William Moore, the deceased's brother and Horace Jones another U.S.C. T. veteran from the same neighborhood. They both stated that James Moore had been a healthy man before entering a service and before his death he recognized Susan as his wife and all of the children as his own.[36] Apparently there were some discrepancies in Susan's claim about the ages of her children. Susan Moore submitted her testimony two more times with hopes of proving her claim, she asserted:

permit me to offer the following as an answer, as the mother of the children. I have given very correctly the names and the months of their ages, but I am very sure I could give the date of the same. I have abandoned none of them, they are all under my care and except what they can give, which is not much, I have to work very hard to obtain a scanty livelihood.[37]

Susan was approved for a claim in 1868. She also requested an increase in her pension in 1879. The Pension Bureau responded with, "Clerk informed that she has been allowed all the law provides." [38]

African American widows in the pension files appear very transparent in their claims. They are open to sharing their current struggles and past memories with government officials. Unfortunately, their transparency came with a price. Standing amid the judgment of bureaucrats and strangers they chose to confront serotypes, racism and patriarchy head-on. Moreover, after being rejected they displayed resistance by persistently demanding they receive [39]compensation that they believed rightfully belonged to them.   After the Civil War, African American widows in Maryland emerge eager to construct and maintain new lives in freedom, no matter the obstacles. Their pension files show their resilient and forceful voices, intent on being heard even as they are struggling to survive.

---

[1] The Maryland State Archives Present: Legacy of Slavery in Maryland, Legacy of Slavery Project, Internet, available from
http://mdhistory.net/msa_sc4126/msa_sc4126_04/html/msa_sc4126_33-0059.html accessed 2 February 2014.

[2] Ibid,,.http://mdhistory.net/msa_sc4126/msa_sc4126_04/pdf/msa_sc4126_33-0036.pdf.

[3] ibid., http://mdhistory.net/msa_sc4126/msa_sc4126_04/pdf/msa_sc4126_33-0038.pdf.

[4] Ibid, http://mdhistory.net/msa_sc4126/msa_sc4126_04/html/msa_sc4126_33-0115.html.

[5] See testimonies of John Trusty and Chad O Gallanier
http://mdhistory.net/msa_sc4126/msa_sc4126_04/html/msa_sc4126_33-0117.html
http://mdhistory.net/msa_sc4126/msa_sc4126_04/html/msa_sc4126_33-0135.html

[6] Ibid,.

[7] Ibid,http://mdhistory.net/msa_sc4126/msa_sc4126_04/html/msa_sc4126_33-0009.html.

[8] Chad O Gartrill signed in the space designated for claimant's attorney:
http://mdhistory.net/msa_sc4126/msa_sc4126_04/html/msa_sc4126_33-0013.html

[9] See
document:http://mdhistory.net/msa_sc4126/msa_sc4126_04/html/msa_sc4126_33-0110.html

[10] See documents:
http://mdhistory.net/msa_sc4126/msa_sc4126_04/html/msa_sc4126_33-0097.html

[11] Ibid,http://mdhistory.net/msa_sc4126/msa_sc4126_04/pdf/msa_sc4126_33-0113.pdf-
http://mdhistory.net/msa_sc4126/msa_sc4126_04/pdf/msa_sc4126_33-0113.pdf

[12] Ibid, http://mdhistory.net/msa_sc4126/msa_sc4126_04/pdf/msa_sc4126_33-0140.pdf,

[13] http://mdhistory.net/msa_sc4126/msa_sc4126_04/html/msa_sc4126_33-0107.html

[14] See documentation which holds the signature of Allan Rutherford in space designated for claimant's attorney
:http://mdhistory.net/msa_sc4126/msa_sc4126_04/html/msa_sc4126_33-0050.html

[15] Ibid,http://mdhistory.net/msa_sc4126/msa_sc4126_04/html/msa_sc4126_33-0049.html.

[16] Ibid,http://mdhistory.net/msa_sc4126/msa_sc4126_04/html/msa_sc4126_33-0091.html.

---

[17] Ibid,http://mdhistory.net/msa_sc4126/msa_sc4126_04/html/msa_sc4126_33-0066.html.

[18] Regosin, Elizabeth,Freedom's Promise:Ex-Slave Families and Citizenship in Age of Emancipation. (Charlottesville: University of Virginia Press,2002).

[19] Schaffer, Donald.After the Glory: The Struggles of Black Civil War Veterans.(Lawerence, University of Kansas Press,2004).

[20] Also see, Frankel, Noralee. Freedom's Women:Black Women and Families in Civil War Era Mississippi (Bloomington:Indiana University Press,1999).
Kaiser, Mary Farmer. Freedwomen and the Freedman's Bureau:Race, Gender and Public Policy in the Age of Emancipation (New York:Fordham University Press,2010) 27

[21] Schwalm,Leslie. A Hard Fight For We (Chicago:University of Illnois Press,1997)149.

[22] Sharita Jacobs." Competing Realities:Black Southern Marylanders and Their Quest to shape Freedom in "Loyal" Maryland 1860-1880" (Phd Diss, Howard University, 2009.

[23] Fields Barbara. Slavery and Freedom in the Middle Ground:Maryland during the Nineteenth Century. (New Haven: Yale University Press,1984).

[24] Glasson, William. Federal Military Pensions in the United States.(London: Oxford University Press,1918) 123-175

[25] Regosin, Elizabeth, Freedom's Promise: Ex-Slave Families and Citizenship in Age of Emancipation. (Charlottesville: University of Virginia Press,2002) 83.

[26] Ibid, 83-85.

[27] Ibid.

[28] For more on African American concepts of love, marriage, femininity and masculinity see the following works:
Frankel, Noralee. Freedom's Women:Black Women and Families in Civil War Era Mississippi (Bloomington:Indiana University Press,1999).
Deborah Gray White, Ar'n't I a Woman? (New York,W.W Norton & Company,1985).
Gutman, Herbert, The Black Family in Slavery and Freedom 1750-1925 (New York, Vintage Press, 1977).

[29] The Maryland State Archves Present: Legacy of Slavery in Maryland,Legacy of Slavery Project, Internet, available from
http://mdhistory.net/msa_sc4126/msa_sc4126_04/html/msa_sc4126_33-0059.html accessed 2 February 2014.

[30] The Maryland State Archves Present: Legacy of Slavery in Maryland,Legacy of Slavery Project, Internet, available from
http://mdhistory.net/msa_sc4126/msa_sc4126_05/pdf/msa_sc4126_52-0006.pdf accessed 5 February 2014.

[31] Ibid,.

[32] Ibid.,

[33] Ibid.

---

[34] Ibid,.

[35] Ibid,http://mdhistory.net/msa_sc4126/msa_sc4126_05/html/msa_sc4126_52-0003.html.

[36] See testimonies of William Moore and Horace Jones
http://mdhistory.net/msa_sc4126/msa_sc4126_05/html/msa_sc4126_52-0003.html

[37]Ibid, http://mdhistory.net/msa_sc4126/msa_sc4126_05/html/msa_sc4126_52-0006.html.

[38] Ibid, http://mdhistory.net/msa_sc4126/msa_sc4126_05/html/msa_sc4126_52-0023.html.

[39]

Building Bridges Between Black America and the World: Dr. Mary McLeod Bethune's 1949 Trip to Haiti

Ashley Robertson

One of the most influential and recognized slave revolts was the Haitian Revolution, and after the successful battle for freedom, Haiti became a symbol of success for African people throughout the Diaspora. Immediately it became a model for enslaved people across the western hemisphere that were looking to achieve what Haiti's enslaved African's had− Freedom. During the United States occupation of Haiti (1915-1934), African Americans were watchful of the conditions in Haiti and often attempted to intervene in any way possible. Influential African American leaders including James Weldon Johnson, and Walter White, along with Black newspapers including *Chicago Defender* and the *Pittsburgh Courier* spoke out against the United States military's unfair treatment of Haitians. They also utilized media outlets to highlight the rich culture and history of Haiti, which was under attack as a result of the occupation. The solidarity that emerged out of the Haitian Revolution and sustained itself throughout the occupation was the foundation on which Dr. Mary McLeod Bethune was able to build upon during her 1949 trip to the country. During her ten day visit she traveled through the countryside engaging in meaningful conversations with local community members, met with key political figures and received the nation's highest award. Upon her return she wrote "I Love Haiti! I Love Her People!" [1]

At the turn of 1948 on the 144th anniversary of the independence of Haiti, Bethune took part in celebrations with Haitians in Washington, D.C. Invited by Joseph D. Charles, United States Ambassador of Haiti; she attended a celebration at the Haitian Embassy. A month later in February she hosted Ambassador Charles, along with Minister Charles D. B. King of Liberia, in a reception at the headquarters of her organization, National Council of Negro Women (NCNW), in Washington, D.C. As the organization's president, Bethune pushed for greater international programming and cultural exchange. During the reception she stated "Here in a hotbed of international relationships, we as citizens of a leading world power have a special responsibility to begin building a bridge to peace through understanding."[2] Both leaders were moved by Bethune's sincere efforts to solidify mutual understanding and dedication to peace. Hundreds of people attended including Howard University faculty members, *Chicago Defender* staff and State Department officials to help Bethune in honoring the diplomats of Haiti and Liberia.

1949 marked the 200th anniversary of the founding of the Haitian capital of Port-au-Prince. In celebration of the anniversary President Dumarsais Estimé, created the Haitian International Exposition to showcase the culture of Haiti to the world. Haitian artists and performers showcased their talents to a worldwide audience during the Exposition. In recognition of the achievements of people of African descent, the Haitian Medal of Honor and Merit was awarded to Bethune as a part of the Exposition. For years to come she was seen wearing the Medal proudly and she also displayed it in her home for visitors to see.

The Journey to Haiti

On June 9, 1949 Bethune received an official invitation from Joseph D. Charles, the ambassador of Haiti. Written in French, Mr. Joseph wrote: It gives me great pleasure to convey to you officially the invitation of my government has come to visit Haiti will be happy to welcome and receive one of its congeners whose value and personal merits are great.[3] She accepted the invitation and on July 12, 1949 she left Florida for a ten day trip to Haiti. Stopping over in Montego Bay for a layover she connected with local Jamaicans inquiring about how many people of African descent lived on the island and what the main employment industries were.[4] She reached Port-Au-Prince in the afternoon and began her journey throughout Haiti.

Much of the time Bethune spent in Haiti was dedicated to increasing her cultural and political awareness while she also sought to connect with the people of Haiti on a personal level. On her second day in Haiti, July 13, 1949, she spent the day with the nation's First Lady Madame Estimé. The pair talked for hours on end about unity and the issues faced by the people of Haiti. Bethune expressed her purpose for coming, stating that she wanted "to try to bring about a better understanding and inspire the women of Haiti to work with her in trying to bring about peace and unity."[5] She discussed the possibility of establishing a Haitian section of NCNW and explained the organizations core values to the First Lady Estimé. NCNW had been quite successful in creating one united voice for women of color and Bethune wanted the women of Haiti to be a part of the movement. It was her goal to make the organization one that would reach women in all parts of the world. By the end of the conversation Madame Estimé was honored to be considered to lead a Haitian council and she took the first step by becoming a lifetime member. For the NCNW and Bethune, this was a major step in expanding the influence of the organization and in uniting women across the globe all facing similar issues as women of color.

The day did not end with the long discussion with Madame Estimé;

William E. DeCourcy, American Ambassador to Haiti, also hosted Bethune. Having been appointed as U.S. Ambassador in 1948, United States Vice Consul in Cairo (1924-26), Marseille (1926-28), Paris (1928-34) and Cape Town (1935-36), DeCourcy had seen much of the world and was intrigued by Bethune's point of view. Ralph Bunche, who had been a member of the Black Cabinet, and worked alongside Bethune during her tenure as the Director of Negro Affairs in the National Youth Administration, had been a part of her topic of discussion with DeCourcy.[6] She told DeCourcy that she was impressed that Bunche had done "a fine thing to demonstrate the whole spirit of democracy"[7] in his refusal to accept the position of Secretary of State. President Harry Truman offered Bunche the position but he declined the offer in protest of Washington, D.C.'s segregated housing policies. Ending their discussion around noon Bethune had once again laid foundations for a working relationship with a leading advisor on foreign affairs.

On July 14, 1949 on her third day in Haiti, Bethune spent it learning more about Haitian culture and its role as the first Black Republic. Haiti's Minister of Foreign Affairs hosted Bethune, which gave her the opportunity to interview him and gain a better understanding of Haiti's history. She was deeply concerned about the welfare of the masses in Haiti and expressed her concern to the Minister. In turn he told her about his desires to improve education in Haiti and that he was looking forward to working with Bethune to make some of the goals he set for the country to come to pass. The sharing of ideas and their visions for betterment of the race would forge a vital connection between Bethune and Monsieur Timelson Brutus, Minister of Foreign Affairs.

During the meeting, Bethune also asked tough questions regarding the status of women's rights in Haiti. As the leader of the largest African American women's organization in the United States, Bethune was a staunch advocate for women's equality. Having been a part of the women's suffrage movement as a member of National Association of Colored Women (NACW), Bethune wanted to ensure that the women of Haiti had the same rights; however, by the time she arrived in 1949 they had yet to gain suffrage. In her conversation with Minister of Foreign Affairs she asked if women had gained suffrage. Unsatisfied with the Minister's answer, she pressed for more information about when they would gain those rights asking, "How far removed are they?"[8] It was her conversation with Monsieur Brutus that led her to introduce the issue of Haitian women's suffrage to African American's when she arrived back in the United States.

Thursday July 14, 1949 would prove to be one of the highlights of Bethune's voyage to Haiti. It was the day she met President Dumarsais Estimé. His term as president lasted from 1946-50 and he was the first Black president to serve after the 1934 ending of the United States' occupation. The United States was yet to have an African American president and Bethune was overjoyed to be in the presence of the young leader of Haiti stating "As I look on you I have the realization of the prayers and yearning of the Black republic of the world. I feel like I am on my own soil."[9] Having worked with in advisory positions to President's Calvin Coolidge, Edgar Hoover and Franklin D. Roosevelt, sitting down with President Estimé was her first interaction with a Black president. During their conversation she expressed her desire to help improve conditions in Haiti, she pledged to do all that she could to strengthen the country. Bethune, who had always had a relationship with Haitians and its people from afar, gave her word to its leader that she was now one with its people. Given her influence in the States as "First Lady of Negro America," Bethune as an ally was a major development for Haiti.

Connecting with the Masses

Bethune's love for people and desire to understand the shared plight of people of African descent throughout the diaspora was expressed throughout her journey in Haiti. Although much of her time was spent meeting and connecting with political leaders, she also made sure that connecting with the masses in Port-Au-Prince and surrounding areas. On Friday July 15, 1949 during her Haiti visit, she traveled to Ecole République d'Argentine, a local elementary school where she met nearly 475 students and 20 teachers. As an educator and an advocate for young people Bethune was overjoyed by the friendly welcome she received from the elementary students.

From 1917 to 1924, while also establishing her school, Bethune served as President of the Florida Federation of Colored Women. It was in her position as president that she would also establish the Delinquent Home for Colored Girls in Ocala, Florida. On the fifth day of her visit to Haiti, she met the children of the Sunshine Orphanage, and her heart ached for them just as it had for the children she set up homes for in Florida. She was overwhelmed by the children's malnourished bodies and the poorly kept space, yet encouraged by their desire to overcome and succeed. She made a donation to the orphanage before she left, and was humbled by the visit. A few days later Madame Estimé showed Bethune the orphanage she was building, which she later financially committed to assisting with.

In the short visit Bethune did her best to build as many meaningful relationships as possible. On July 20, 1949 she met teachers at the School

Republique of Venezuela during her trip where she shared the story of how she built her school and the struggles she had to overcome throughout her life. She made the pledge that she would "do all she can to help Haiti when and while every opportunity presents itself."[10] Later that afternoon she attended a meeting with the Women's League of Equal Rights (*Ligue Feminine d'Action Sociale*), a women's organization concerned with women's rights and the equality issues faced by Haitian women. Formed in 1934, *Ligue Feminine d'Action Sociale* was Haiti's first feminist organization. Hearing and discussing issues with the league, Bethune encouraged the women to become affiliates of NCNW and pledged that the NCNW will back their efforts to gain suffrage. The next day she was introduced to the impoverished conditions at the rural training centers for women, which pushed her to think about what she could do to help the situation. On the last day of her trip she reflected on all that she had experienced and how much work she would like to contribute to the restoration of Haiti. Bethune connected with youth, women's organizations, and those in need just as she did in the States and took time to understand the issues they faced while assessing how she could best work to bring about solutions.

On July 21, 1949, Bethune became the first female recipient of the country's highest award, known as the Haitian Medal of Honor and Merit. The night included a ceremony honoring Bethune and her many achievements and life's work. In a speech honoring Bethune on the night of the award, one of her presenters stated, "her works for mankind had changed the face of the world."[11] From her work as an educator, to her position as the Director of Negro Affairs fighting for African Americans to be a part of President Franklin D. Roosevelt's "New Deal" programs, Bethune had led a life in which she fought tirelessly for the inclusion of

Black people and now her efforts were being celebrated outside of the United States.

Renewed Dedication to Haiti

Before her July 1949 trip, Bethune developed a relationship with Haiti mostly through Ambassador Joseph D. Charles, but once she visited Haiti for herself her relationship became a more personal one. Nearly two years prior to her visit, Ruth Clement Bond had written to Bethune requesting her assistance in building orphanages in Haiti, but it was not until after seeing a firsthand account of the devastation in orphanages in Haiti that she became active in the program. Calling on all of her networks, particularly the members of the NCNW, she began the work of rallying support for financial assistance to build orphanages. In a letter to her assistant Constance Daniel she requested for her to write a letter stating:

> Send out a statement as to the great needs of the orphans of Haiti and our desire as American women, to help Madame Estimé in the gigantic task she has undertaken. For that sacrificial service I am asking all men and women of ALL races, and creeds—not in any organized form, but any individual that might like to help to complete this shelter for the orphans in Haiti.[12]

In her pleas for assistance Bethune called on anyone who was willing to help her meet the goal of assisting Haiti. She also made plans to send volunteers to assist First Lady Estimé and a committee to go back to Haiti to present the funds collected. In preparation for an article being written, Bethune was eager for Ms. Daniel to highlight the success of the Sunshine Orphanage and its leader, Ms. Doris Burke. During Bethune-Cookman College's 1949 Southeastern Conference, which was themed "Working Towards World Peace and Prosperity," Bethune addressed women from 12 states and 150 Cubans on international affairs including raising funds for the Refuge Home for Orphan Children in Haiti.[13]

Upon returning to the United States she assumed the task of advocating for Haitian women's right to vote. While in Haiti she met with *Ligue Feminine d'Action Sociale*, led by Madame Augustine Garoute to discuss women's rights and suffrage. The organization was one of Haiti's leading advocates for women's voting rights. Having fought tirelessly against the disenfranchisement of African Americans in Daytona Beach, Florida, Bethune stood behind women in Haiti to gain voting rights. As early as the 1920's she stood against the Ku Klux Klan when the organization threatened Black voters in an attempt to keep them from the voting polls. In a June 1950 article of the *Chicago Defender* in regards to the suffrage practices in Haiti, she stated "Women astute enough to drive a hard bargain in the market place, are astute enough to drive another at the polls!"[14] By addressing the issue of voting in the well-known *Chicago Defender* newspaper Bethune utilized her position to make African Americans aware of the similar challenges being faced by Haitian women. Still struggling against poll taxes and violence against voters, African Americans understood what it was like to be denied the right to exercise their rights to vote. In 1950 Haitian women gained the right to vote with the stipulation that they had to have their husband's approval and in 1957 they received full voting rights.

Bethune not only shared the issues of Haiti with those in the United States, but she also conducted an analysis of the country and offered solutions to President Dumarsais Estimé. In her analysis she outlined the four main needs of Haiti to be: employment, health, housing, and education.[15] In an effort to increase employment and a more stable economy she advised the President to consider producing bananas to export to the United States, while also encouraging more focus on agricultural development. Another business she recommended was selling handcrafted furniture as an export item. Having enjoyed the food on her visit immensely, according to her descriptive diary entries, she also promoted the creation of a cookbook with authentic Haitian recipes as an export product. To increase the interactions and exchange between African Americans and Haitians she also suggested sending African American newspapers to Haiti and vice versa to "bridge the information gap between them."[16] Summing up her analysis with a pledge of direct assistance, she had taken on a role of responsibility in the building of Haiti's economy.

In her analysis of the needs of Haiti, Bethune offered advice to President Estimé out of the wealth of knowledge she'd gained through her own experiences. She was very resourceful in the building of her school and often utilized agriculture and farming as a fundraiser, growing sugarcane and making sweet potato pies to sell to the local Daytona Beach community. As the Director of Negro Affairs in the National Youth Administration, Bethune also assured that African Americans benefited from programs that provided training opportunities to rural farmers. The NYA vocational training programs featured "centers focused primarily on training young men in modern farming techniques and offered young women instruction in dairying, raising poultry and food preservation."[17]

She advised Estimé to explore similar methods for economic development in Haiti. Having understood America's desire for coffee and Haiti's initial development of the crop, she gave Estime very practical advice stating "It seems to me very wise that more stress is now being placed on the increased cultivation of this crop."[18] Given Bethune's work with the Committee on Farm Tenancy under President Roosevelt's administration she also suggested that the country "study the advantages of large acreages, privately developed, and of combined small acreages cooperatively developed."[19] Offering the example of the successes of cooperative farming methods in the rural south she tried to show Estime that the methods had worked in favor of African American farmers.

In her analysis to the president she addressed women's suffrage under the theme of "The Franchise for All." She utilized the example of women's right advocate and former United States Minister Resident and Consul General to Haiti, Frederick Douglass, to provide a clear visual for the role that men had played in the United States during the struggle for women's suffrage. On the subject of democracy, she wrote that Douglass had "called also for the broader application of the term, to include all women."[20] In the midst of reminding Estime of their conversation about possible franchise for women she also praised the Women's League for Equal Rights and upheld them as a model example of Haiti's potential voters. Essentially she called attention to a vital right and persuasively pressed for its extension to women further demonstrating her commitment to equality.

Throughout her life Dr. Mary McLeod Bethune was a proponent for African American solidarity with Africans throughout the Diaspora. She utilized her position as a leading political figure to create awareness and cultural exchange with the people of Haiti, while she also called on her networks to support Haiti both politically and financially. In the spirit of Anna Julia Cooper (who worked for colonial reform at the Pan-African

Conference in London), Ida B. Wells (who traveled to England to bring attention to the lynching of Black men in America), and Amanda Smith (who broke gender barriers evangelizing in India, Liberia and Sierra Leone) Dr. Bethune was an international civil rights activist who spent her life works dedicated to the cause of liberation.

[1] Mary McLeod Bethune, "The People, The Land, The Economy of Haiti A Revelation," *Chicago Defender*, 6 August, 1949, p. 6.

[2] "Haiti and Liberian Diplomats Honored," *Chicago Defender,* 28, February, 1948, p. 2

[3] Charles to Bethune, 9 June 1949, Mary McLeod Bethune Foundation Papers, National Archives for Black Women's Records, Washington, D.C.

[4] Bethune Diary, 12 July 1949, Mary McLeod Bethune Foundation Papers, National Archives for Black Women's Records, Washington, D.C.

[5] Bethune Diary, 13 July 1949, Mary McLeod Bethune Foundation Papers, National Archives for Black Women's Records, Washington, D.C.

[6] For more information on federal records that exam Bethune's Tenure with the National Youth Administration please see: Debra L. Newman, *Black History: A Guide to Civilian Records in the National Archives* (Washington, D.C.: National Archives Trust Fund Board, 1984).

[7] Bethune Diary, July 1949, Mary McLeod Bethune Foundation Papers, National Archives for Black Women's Records, Washington, D.C.

[8] Ibid.

[9] Ibid.

[10] Bethune Diary, 20 July 1949, Mary McLeod Bethune Foundation Papers, National Archives for Black Women's Records, Washington, D.C.

[11] Bethune Diary, July 1949, Mary McLeod Bethune Foundation Papers, National Archives for Black Women's Records, Washington, D.C.

[12] Bethune to Daniel, 8 August 1949, Mary McLeod Bethune Foundation Papers, National Archives for Black Women's Records, Washington, D.C.

[13] Bethune to Daniels, 18 August 1949, Mary McLeod Bethune Foundation Papers, National Archives for Black Women's Records, Washington, DC.

[14] Mary McLeod Bethune, "Constructive Action in Haiti Depends on Unity Among People," *Chicago Defender*, 3 June, 1950, p. 6.

[15] Bethune to Estimé, 15 September 1949, Part 2, Mary McLeod Bethune Foundation Papers, National Archives for Black Women's Records, Washington, DC.

[16] Bethune to Estimé, 15 September 1949, Mary McLeod Bethune Foundation Papers, National Archives for Black Women's Records, Washington, DC.

[17] Joyce A. Hanson, *Mary McLeod Bethune and Black Women's Political Activism* (Columbia, MO: University of Missouri Press, 2003), 145.

[18] Bethune to Estimé, 15 September 1949, Mary McLeod Bethune Foundation Papers, National Archives for Black Women's Records, Washington, DC.

[19] Ibid.

[20] Ibid.

Clara Burrill Bruce: An Aristocrat in the African American Freedom Struggle

Crystal R. Sanders

A February 1947 issue of the Baltimore *Afro-American* ran the headline "Final Rites Held in Washington for Wife of Roscoe C. Bruce."[1] The obituary title was in no way fitting for Clara Burrill Bruce, a published poet, an accomplished attorney, and a sought after speaker. Her marriage to Roscoe Bruce, the son of the first elected black United States Senator to serve a full term, overshadowed her own many achievements. Clara Burrill Bruce was the third African American woman to attend Radcliffe College. In 1925, the wife and mother of three became the first African American editor-in-chief of a law review in the United States. Armed with a law degree and a passion for uplifting the race, Bruce sought out opportunities throughout the 1930s and 1940s to improve black life.

Over the past thirty years, historians have pushed back against the scholarly trend to treat black women as historical subjects "only if they were attached to a man, an institution, or an organization."[2] In doing so, scholars have cited African American women's resistance during slavery, clubwomen's efforts to uplift the race, and black women's "bridge leadership" during the 1960s civil rights movement. Collectively, this scholarship demonstrates that black women have made meaningful contributions to the nation in general and black communities in particular.[3]

This essay aims to contribute to existing literature on black women's history by considering the political work of a black woman aristocrat in the early twentieth century. For the purposes of this study, the words aristocrat and black elite are used interchangeably to define African Americans who had high social status at the turn-of-the-century because of education, income, or membership in black independent institutions such as churches and social clubs.[4] While much work has been done to disprove the notion that members of the black elite served only their own interests before and after Emancipation, scholars are still discovering the many ways in which affluent black women assumed race leadership within the constraints of normative gender roles.

John Henry Burrill, a longtime State Department employee and his wife Clara, gave birth to Clara Washington Bruce (née Burrill) on June 25, 1880 in the nation's capital. Young Clara Bruce came of age in a comfortably middle-class black household. She and her family worshipped at the Fifteenth Street Presbyterian Church whose pastors included black abolitionist and orator Henry Highland Garnet and National Association for the Advancement of Colored People (NAACP) co-founder Francis Grimké. Fifteenth Street had long been the place of worship for the most prominent black families in Washington, D.C.[5] The Burrill family was connected to African American aristocrats not only though church, but also through civic organizations. John Burrill served as the Most Worshipful Grand Master of a local Prince Hall Masonic lodge, an affiliation that put him in contact with other members of Washington's black elite including hotel owner and operator James. A. Wormley and attorney and future federal judge Robert H. Terrell.[6]

The Burrill family's relative wealth afforded Bruce access to the best educational institutions. She attended M Street High School, which was the first public high school for blacks in the nation. After graduating from M Street in 1897, Bruce received further training at the Miner Normal School, an institution for teacher preparation. She spent the 1899-1900 academic year at Teachers College, Columbia University and then studied at Howard University the following year where she specialized in advanced French, German, and mathematics.[7] Bruce's higher education pursuits set her apart. In 1900, a little more than 2,000 blacks in the United States had earned college degrees with 390 receiving their education from white institutions.[8]

The year 1901 brought significant changes for Bruce. Her father died in May. Four months later, she moved to Cambridge, Massachusetts, and began study at Radcliffe College. Radcliffe, Harvard College's coordinate institution for female students, was established in 1879. Before Bruce's admission, only two other African American women had attended the institution. During her tenure at Radcliffe, Clara was the only black student among a student body of approximately 450.[9]

While Bruce did not publicly speak about her time at Radcliffe, the experiences of black men at adjoining Harvard offer some clues. Harvard had begun accepting black men in 1865, but there were never more than two or three in each class. W.E.B. Du Bois, who attended Harvard from 1888 to 1891, remarked about his tenure, "I was in Harvard, but not of it...most of my classmates I knew neither by sight nor name."[10] While black students had access to one of the most prestigious institutions in the world, a color-caste stymied their full inclusion.

Relocating to Cambridge allowed Bruce to continue her romantic relationship with Roscoe Bruce. Roscoe, the son of former United States Senator Blanche K. Bruce, attended Harvard. The couple had known each other since grade school and began dating during their teenage years. They met often in Cambridge, although their joint tenure in the city was short. Roscoe graduated from Harvard in 1902 and accepted a job as the director of Tuskegee Institute's academic division.[11]

Sacrificing the opportunity to earn a degree from one of the best women's colleges in the nation, Clara withdrew from Radcliffe in May 1903 in order to marry Roscoe Bruce. The couple exchanged vows the following month in a ceremony whose guest list included Richard Greener, Harvard first's black graduate and Booker T. Washington, Tuskegee Institute's founder. After the wedding, the newlyweds departed for Tuskegee, Alabama, where they remained for three years.[12] Clara's early departure from Radcliffe and her subsequent relocation to the Deep South demonstrate the hard personal choices black women of her stature often made in the early twentieth century. She neglected her own impressive academic abilities to help support her husband. Once in Alabama, Clara taught Tuskegee students from 1903 until 1906.[13]

Bruce learned to balance her classroom duties with familial responsibilities. She and her husband welcomed their first child, Clara Jr., in March 1904. Two years later, she bore a son, Roscoe Jr. By remaining in the workforce with two small children at home, Bruce certainly gave her detractors something to talk about. Those who had opposed her union to Roscoe Bruce had asserted that she was "too intellectual to make a good wife." Having already passed on the opportunity to become the third African American graduate of Radcliffe College, Clara refused to allow motherhood to limit her teaching opportunities.[14]

The Bruce family returned to Washington, D.C. during the fall of 1906 because Roscoe Sr. had grown tired of Tuskegee's industrial education focus. Despite disagreeing with Booker T. Washington about the best education for blacks, the Tuskegee founder helped Roscoe Sr. to secure a job as a supervising principal in the District of Columbia schools. The following year, he became the Assistant Superintendent of colored schools in the District. He faced many controversies and investigations during his fourteen-year tenure as Assistant Superintendent. At various times, some of the most powerful African Americans in Washington called for his firing.[15] Certainly, Clara Bruce worried about Roscoe Sr.'s ability to continue being the family's breadwinner. The Bruces now had a third child, Burrill. For the three Bruce children to have similar educational opportunities to the ones afforded their parents, Roscoe Sr. needed to maintain his well-paying supervisory position.

Despite the employment concerns, the Bruces maintained an active social life. Clara Bruce attended theme parties where she interacted with Mary Church Terrell and other elite black women. In 1911, Bruce's husband became one of seventeen charter members of the Washington D.C. chapter of Sigma Pi Phi Boulé alongside historian Carter G. Woodson. Roscoe Sr.'s membership in the Sigma Pi Phi Boulé, an invitation-only social club for prominent black men, solidified his and his family's standing in upper middle-class black society.[16]

Membership in the District's elite black organizations was no shield from discrimination. While Bruce and her children could visit public museums and libraries in the district's theaters, parks, and social clubs practiced segregation. Moreover, President Woodrow Wilson had implemented an unprecedented level of Jim Crow policies in the federal government during his tenure between 1913 and 1921. Black federal job seekers found their opportunities curtailed and those blacks who were employed in government positions found themselves physically separated from their white counterparts.[17]

The entrenchment of racial segregation at the same time that the United States fought to make the world safe for democracy was not lost on Clara Bruce. In 1918, *Crisis* magazine, the NAACP's official media outlet, published a poem that she wrote titled "We Who Are Dark." In the piece, Bruce exposed the contradictions between American ideals of freedom and equality and African American's reality of racial discrimination. The poem asserts, "we bravely march...to victory, bearing aloft to foreign lands a freedom sweet that's not our own."[18]

After World War I, Clara turned her attention to a battle raging much closer to home. Washington black elite's calls for Roscoe Bruce's removal from his position as Assistant Superintendent of colored schools became louder. He resigned during the 1921 spring in spite of his precarious financial situation. His children's lofty educational goals came with costly tuition payments. Roscoe Jr. was at Exeter and Clara Jr. planned to enter Howard University that fall. Desperately needing income, the family patriarch accepted a job as principal of Browns Creek District High School in West Virginia. Clara Bruce joined her husband the following year and worked as the head of the English Department at Browns Creek.[19].

The two oldest Bruce children followed in their parents' educational footsteps. Clara Jr., who attended Howard during the 1921-1922 academic year, had taken a year off before entering Radcliffe College in September 1923. Her matriculation at Radcliffe gave the Bruce family the distinction of being the first black mother-daughter pair to attend the institution. Roscoe Jr. entered Harvard in 1926. Only a new exclusionary policy at Harvard meant that Roscoe Jr.'s tenure would be much different from his father's.

In 1922, Harvard enacted a new policy that prohibited first-year black students from living in freshman dormitories. Roscoe Sr., who had lived in Harvard housing for three years, wrote to Harvard President A. Lawrence Lowell in 1923 to secure a housing reservation for Roscoe Jr. Lowell asserted that Harvard could not provide Roscoe Jr. with first-year housing because it was not possible "to compel men of different races to reside together." In what became a very public feud between the elder Bruce and Lowell that was covered by several national media outlets, Harvard professors and alumni and black activists took sides in the college discrimination controversy. After much negative publicity, Harvard's board of overseers overruled Lowell and banned discrimination.[20]

Clara Bruce did not speak publicly about the Harvard dormitory crisis but it surely troubled her. It was firsthand proof of the racial discrimination that she had alluded to in the poem she published in *Crisis* magazine. She could take some comfort in the fact that she was equipping herself with the skills to dismantle the very racism that prevented her son from living in a Harvard residence hall. Bruce successfully applied for admission to Boston University Law School in May 1923.[21]

Bruce was an untraditional law school student in every sense of the word. She was black, female, a wife, and a mother. Moreover, she did not possess a college degree. In pursuing a legal career, she joined a small group of black women pioneers. As late as 1941, there were only fifty-seven black women practicing law in the United States. Black women attorneys often faced discrimination in the law school classroom and in the courtroom.[22]

Sadie Alexander, a black woman attorney and economist in Philadelphia, was Bruce's peer. Alexander's experience sheds light on some of the obstacles that Bruce may have faced as a law school student. Alexander entered the University of Pennsylvania's Law School in 1924, the first black woman to do so. At Penn, Alexander experienced much discrimination. Law school dean Edward Mikell refused to call on her during class or speak to her in the halls. He even tried to deny her membership on the law review, one of the highest academic achievements for law students.[23]

While no two experiences are the same, it is highly likely that Bruce experienced some of the same slights as Alexander. For much of the twentieth century, women struggled to gain entry into the legal profession. Many American law schools, including Harvard Law, excluded women. At Boston University Law School, Bruce not only defied the male exclusivity of the legal profession, but also, she excelled in the classroom. Her high academic marks earned her election to the *Boston University Law Review* in 1924. While that was a feat in itself, the wife and mother made history in 1925 when she was unanimously elected editor-in-chief of the law review. The honor made Bruce the first woman editor of the *Boston University Law*

Review and the first African American in the nation to serve as a law review editor-in-chief. As editor, she published four articles and oversaw a team consisting of six associate editors who were all white men.[24]

Clara Bruce's stellar law school grades put her at top of the 1926 graduating class. She qualified scholastically with six men in a class of 175 for the Woolsack key that the law school awarded for high scholarship. Unfortunately, her sex kept her from receiving it. She did receive the Leila J. Robinson Award given to the woman with the highest scholastic record. She was one of five and the only woman in the class to graduate cum laude.[25]

On October 27, 1926, Bruce became the third black women admitted to the Massachusetts bar. Armed with formal educational training and a bar membership, she set up a private practice in the Bay State, which was no easy task in the early twentieth century.[26] No matter the type of legal practice, the opportunities for black women lawyers were more limited than those of their white counterparts. African American clients' tendency to prefer white lawyers exacerbated the problem. While Alexander was able to practice in her husband's established Philadelphia law firm, Bruce was compelled to build her own legal brand from the ground up.[27]

Physical limitations stymied Bruce's attempt to operate a successful law practice in Massachusetts. On December 8, 1926, three months after passing the bar, Bruce entered a downtown Boston department store elevator and plummeted five flights. The elevator's malfunction caused bones in her legs and hips to shatter. She remained in the hospital for fourteen weeks. The extent of her injuries necessitated that she use a cane for the rest of her life.[28]

Adding insult to injury, Bruce received very little support from her husband as she recovered in Cambridge. Roscoe Sr. had moved to New York in 1925. Not only did he visit his wife infrequently, but also, he socialized regularly with Harriet Shadd Butcher, a single black socialite. The two spent evenings and weekends together in Harlem clubs, theaters, and restaurants. While Bruce had forsaken a Radcliffe degree for Roscoe Sr., she was not on his social calendar.[29]

Bruce relocated to New York in 1927 to be with Roscoe Sr. who had accepted a job as the resident manager of the Paul Laurence Dunbar Apartments. She became his assistant and once again found herself giving up her goals to remain at Roscoe Sr.'s side. Like other early twentieth century women lawyers, Bruce found her legal passion to be in conflict with her familial obligations. She chose to focus on the latter. Sadie Alexander faced the same conundrum. She wrote:

It is a hard job trying to be a mother, a lawyer, and a good wife. I am not at all too certain that the three can be successfully combined. At times I think it is impossible and that I must devote my entire time to my husband and children; then I think of the sacrifice my mother made to train me and of the number of clients who seem to depend upon me. I then try to find strength to serve all the interests.[30]

Bruce could certainly relate to Alexander's dilemma. John and Clara Burrill had provided her with a first-class education that she cut short for love. She gave up the chance to practice law in Massachusetts when she relocated to be with her husband.

Despite the pattern of sacrifice, Bruce found a way to reconcile her responsibilities as a wife and mother with her own intellectual and community pursuits. She used her legal training to improve African American life outside of traditional legal practice. In 1930, she spoke before the Harlem Housewives League where she encouraged black women to wield influence as consumers. She reminded league members that one of the best ways to help the race was to demand that local stores with black clienteles hire black workers. Two years later, Bruce spoke before the group again and made black purchasing power the subject of her address. She pointed out that black purchasing power in seventeen U.S. cities was in excess of total purchasing power in Mexico and several South American countries. In promoting the retention of material resources in black communities, Bruce worked to help African Americans survive the Great Depression.[31]

Bruce made a name for herself as a sought-after speaker. She shared a stage with historian Carter G. Woodson where she spoke about the African American need for more opportunity to achieve economic parity with whites. The NAACP featured her as a speaker alongside executive secretary Walter White and special counsel Charles Hamilton Houston in a luncheon to garner support for the proposed federal anti-lynching bill. She sounded the alarm for better housing for African Americans when she shared a dais with the chairman of the Washington, D.C. Committee on Housing.[32] While she was not practicing law, Bruce found ways to advocate for the race.

In 1933, Bruce's racial advocacy led her to engage in a very public debate with a New York newspaper reporter about racial epithets. In a feature story about the opening of Radio City Music Hall, Edward Angly, a

New York *Herald Tribune* reporter, used condescending language to describe the Tuskegee Institute Choir that performed at the event. Angly wrote, "The dish of German talent was then replaced with an importation from London, Kirkwhite, and Addison, dancers. They gave way to the singing darkies of Alabama—the first appearance of the Tuskegee Choir in New York." Bruce objected to the word "darkies." In a letter to the managing editor of the *Herald Tribune* she wrote, "it ill becomes a great newspaper to permit any members of its staff to refer in its columns to the members of the renowned Tuskegee Choir as 'the singing darkies of Alabama.' I note that your correspondent does not characterize Italian artists as 'singing wops," the Jewish as 'singing sheenies' and so on." The derogatory description aroused Bruce's anger not only because she had professional ties to Tuskegee, but also, because the word had ties to slavery and minstrelsy. When the reporter argued that "darky" was a term of endearment for African Americans that he had used to describe his "mammy" with no complaints, Bruce shot back like a skilled prosecutor. She asserted:

> I have a most friendly feeling toward my dog, but nevertheless my attitude toward the poor brute is fundamentally different from my attitude toward a person. Now, it is probable that the American Negro resents the application to him by any white man of the word 'darky' because he senses the implication that the white man is thinking of him as perhaps superior to the dog but still distinctly below the level of human personality. A word as to that 'darky mammy' of yours. What her reactions were to be called a darky mammy, of course, I don't know. But neither do you. In her breast there may have been a slumbering resentment against the indignity. But knowing where her bread and butter came from, she was too keen a diplomat to let 'her white folks know the truth.'[33]

The back and forth between Bruce and the editor not only resulted in a public pledge that the newspaper would never again use the word "darky" to describe African Americans, but also, it gave voice to African Americans' often masked pain during the age of Jim Crow.

In the same year as her dispute with the newspaper reporter, Bruce published a poem in the *Saturday Evening Post* titled "What Would I Be?" The poem told of her devotion to an unnamed lover that was probably Roscoe Sr. or her three children. In many ways, the poem was a ballad of what Bruce had lost. She left Radcliffe for a man who publicly consorted with another woman. She was a consummate caretaker for her three children who proved to be disappointments. Clara Jr. performed poorly in the classroom and failed to graduate from Radcliffe after four years of study. Roscoe Jr. dropped out of Harvard because of dismal grades. He entered the City College of New York in 1929 to finish his bachelor's degree and eloped the same year. Youngest child Burrill Bruce entered New York University in 1930. In later years, both sons faced criminal charges.[34]

Despite familial setbacks, Bruce remained committed to using her voice and skills to uplift the race. In the late 1930s, she became the Fusion Party's nominee to represent the Nineteenth Assembly District in the New York State Senate. Bruce was especially active in the National Council of Negro Women (NCNW) and in 1937, two years after the organization's founding, she became its executive secretary. In 1938 Bruce chaired an NCNW committee that studied black women's representation in federal bureaus and presented the committee's findings to Eleanor Roosevelt during a White House meeting. The committee, going head-to-head with white federal supervisors who were present, recommended the placement of black women in all federal departments that involved black women and children.[35]

Clara Burrill Bruce was an aristocrat in the African American freedom struggle. Although her education and marriage sheltered her from many of the harsh living conditions of her working-class peers, by tackling bread and butter issues such as decent housing and black employment, Bruce concerned herself with the advancement of the entire race. Thirty years after Bruce's death in 1947, Patricia Roberts Harris became the first black woman to hold a cabinet position in the federal government. In 2014, black women serve in a variety of prominent federal government roles including as the United States Surgeon General and as the Commissioner of the Food and Drug Administration. The present-day integration of black women in all ranks of federal government administration has antecedents in Bruce's NCNW work to increase black women's presence in the federal government. Many of the black women currently engaged in federal civil service are doing so because of appointments from President Barack Obama who cut his political teeth as the first African American president of the *Harvard Law Review*. In demonstrating African American law students' ability to lead a student-run law journal sixty-six years before Obama's editorship at Harvard, Bruce paved the way. Her achievements and activism weakened white supremacy and contributed to the development of African American life.

---

[1] "Final Rites Held in Washington for Wife of Roscoe C. Bruce," *Afro-American*, February 8, 1947, 11.

[2] Darlene Clark Hine, *Speak Truth to Power: Black Professional Class in United States History* (New York: Carlson Publishing, 1996), 98.

[3] For example, see Deborah Gray White, *Ar'n't I A Woman: Female Slaves in the Plantation South* (New York: W.W. Norton, 1999); Tera W. Hunter, *To Joy My Freedom: Black Women's Lives and Labors After the Civil War* (Cambridge, MA: Harvard University Press, 1998); Stephanie J. Shaw, *What a Woman Ought to Be and Do: Black Professional Women Workers during the Jim Crow Era* (Chicago: University of Chicago Press, 1996); Belinda Robnett, *How Long? How Long?: African American Women in the Struggle for Civil Rights* (New York: Oxford University Press, 1997); Chana Kai Lee, *For Freedom's Sake: The Life of Fannie Lou Hamer* (Urbana: University of Illinois Press, 2000); Unita Blackwell with JoAnne Prichard Morris, *Barefootin': Life Lessons from the Road to Freedom* (New York, : Crown, 2006); Katherine Mellen Charron, *Freedom's Teacher: The Life of Septima Clark* (Chapel Hill: University of North Carolina Press, 2009); Bettye Collier-Thomas, *Jesus, Jobs, and Justice: African American Women and Religion* (New York: Knopf, 2010).

[4] For more on the definition of black elites, see Jacqueline M. Moore, *Leading the Race: The Transformation of the Black Elite in the Nation's Capital, 1880-1920* (Charlottesville: University of Virginia, 1999), 3. Existing studies on elite black women include Beverly Washington Jones, *Quest for Equality: The Life and Writings of Mary Eliza Church Terrell, 1863-1954* (New York: Carlson Publishing, 1990); Anna Julia Cooper, Charles C. Lemert, and Esme Bhan, *The Voice of Anna Julia Cooper: Including A Voice from the South and Other Important Essays, Papers, and Letters* (Lanham, MD, 1998); A'Lelia Bundles, *On Her Own Ground: The Life and Times of Madam C.J. Walker* (New York: Scribner, 2001).

[5] Willard B. Gatewood, *Aristocrats of Color: The Black Elite, 1880-1920* (Fayetteville, AR: University of Arkansas Press, 2000), 286; Moore, *Leading the Race*, 73-75.

[6] "A Prominent Citizen Dead," *Washington Bee*, May 18, 1901; "Masonic," *The Colored American*, March 25, 1901; Moore, *Leading the Race*, 180. John Burrill was a member of Pythagoras Lodge, No. 9.

[7] "Clara Burrill Bruce Has Received Many Honors," *New York Amsterdam News*, November 14, 1928; "The M Street High School, 1891-1916, *Records of the Columbia Historical Society, Washington, D.C.* 51 (1984), 129; Joseph J. Boris, editor, *Who's Who in Colored America: A Biographical Dictionary of Notable Living Persons of Negro Descent in America* (New York: Who's Who in Colored America Corporation 1927), 29.

[8] "Key Events in Black Higher Education," *The Journal of Blacks in Higher Education*, http://www.jbhe.com/chronology/.

[9] "Black Graduates at Radcliffe Arranged by Class," Folder 36, Radcliffe College Afro-American Students, Radcliffe College Archives, Cambridge, MA; "Clara Burrill Bruce."

216

[10] Werner Sollors, Caldwell Titcomb, and Thomas A. Underwood, eds., *Blacks at Harvard: A Documentary History of African-American Experience at Harvard and Radcliffe*, (New York: New York University Press, 1993), 75-77

[11] Lawrence Otis Graham, *The Senator and the Socialite: The True Story of America's First Black Dynasty* (New York: Harper Collins 2006), 194-214.

[12] Graham, *The Senator and the Socialite*, 244; *Evening Star*, June 4, 1903, 5.

[13] Clara Bruce's teaching experience listed in her Admissions Application to the Boston University School of Law.

[14] Graham, *The Senator and the Socialite*, 236.

[15] Moore, *Leading the Race*, 99-111; Graham, *The Senator and the Socialite*, 268-298.

[16] Moore, *Leading the Race*, 53; Graham, *The Senator and the Socialite*, 280-281.

[17] Moore, *Leading the Race*, 52, 203.

[18] Clara Burrill Bruce, "We Who Are Dark," *Crisis*, December 1918, 67.

[19] Graham, *The Senator and the Socialite*, 298-300; Boston University Law School Admission Application for Clara Bruce Burrill.

[20] Sollors, Titcomb, and Underwood, *Blacks at Harvard*, 195-227.

[21] Boston University Law School Admission Application for Clara Bruce Burrill.

[22] Kenneth Walter Mack, "A Social History of Everyday Practice: Sadie T.M. Alexander and the Incorporation of Black Women into the American Legal Profession, 1925-1960," *Cornell Law Review* 87, no. 6 (2002): 1416-1420.

[23] Mack, "A Social History of Everyday Practice,"1419-1420.

[24] Mack, "A Social History of Everyday Practice," 1421; J. Clay Smith, Jr., *Emancipation: The Making of the Black Lawyer, 1844-1944* (Philadelphia: University of Pennsylvania Press, 1999), 39; "Clara Burrill Bruce."

[25] "Clara Burrill Bruce."

[26] Smith, *Emancipation*, 111.

[27] Mack, "A Social History of Everyday Practice," 1424.

[28] Graham, *The Senator and the Socialite*, 337.

[29] Graham, *The Senator and the Socialite*, 337-339.

[30] Mack, "A Social History of Everyday Practice," 1432.

[31] Bank Head Talks to Housewives League," *Chicago Defender*, March 8, 1930, 11; "Colored Purchasing Power is Enormous," *Afro-American*, February 27, 1932, 11.

[32] "Happy Race Teaches Lesson—Woodson," *Afro-American*, April 23, 1932, 11; "Perhaps She's Rights," *New York Amsterdam News*, January 31, 1934, 6; "400 Fete Educator," *New York Amsterdam News*, November 21, 1936, 13; "Women Important Factors in Solution of Two Major Problems," *New York Amsterdam News*, July 23, 1930, 11; "Campaign Is Started: Speakers Favor Fight Against Lynching," *New York Amsterdam News*, February 5, 1938, 8; "Better Housing Conference Meets at Miner College," March 28, 1936, 21.

[33] "If Darky, Why Not 'Sheeny' or 'Wop'?", *Afro-American*, January 14, 1933, 7.

[34] Clara Burrill Bruce, "What Would I Be?" *Saturday Evening Post*, April 22, 1933, 71; Graham, *The Senator and the Socialite*, 304, 354-361, 367-377; "Roscoe Bruce, Jr. Marries After 3 Week Courtship," *Afro-American*, November 2, 1929, A2. Clara Jr.

secretly married Barrington Guy, a black actor three years her senior, in 1922, but she did not live with him until she left Radcliffe. By the 1930s, Clara Jr. and Barrington occasionally allowed people to think they were white in order to have more successful careers.

[35] "Clara Bruce is Picked for Post in State Senate," *New York Amsterdam News*, August 1988, 2. Rebecca Stiles Taylor, "What The Women Did When They Met in Washington," *Chicago Defender*, April 16, 1938, 17; "Women Seek More Federal Positions," *New Journal and Guide*, April 16, 1938, 10.

"I'm 'Gon Die with my Boots On:" Hattie Williams, The Oakland Study Center, and her Fight to Mother a Community

Jermaine Scott

On October 14, 1963, the Coordinating Council of Community Organizations (CCCO) designated October 22nd as Freedom Day. The CCCO requested that parents keep their children out of school in protest against Superintendent Benjamin Willis and the racist elements of the Chicago school board.[1] The CCCO was a Chicago-based organization that brought together civic and religious organizations to "fight for equality and the elimination of discrimination."[2] The boycott kept 225,000 students home on "Freedom Day" and the school board lost $470,000 in just that one day.[3] However, the boycott did not change the attitude of the Superintendent of Chicago Public Schools Benjamin Willis.

The CCCO garnered support from a group of mothers from the South Side of Chicago called the Parents Council for Integrated Schools (PCIS). A few days before the boycott, the PCIS announced that they supported the CCCO and the protest.[4] One of the founders of the PCIS was Hattie Williams. Williams served as the president of the Parents and Teachers Association (PTA) of Forrestville North Upper Grade Center, and was a mother who had a vested interest in the boycott. Forrestville North was one of the schools where Benjamin Willis installed the infamous and notorious "Willis Wagons." The black schools in Chicago, particularly on the South Side, operated under a double shift school system and resulted in severe overcrowding. Consequently, instead of integrating all of Chicago's schools, Benjamin Willis established mobile classrooms at specific school sites. Parents and community activists dubbed these mobile classrooms "Willis Wagons" and became the symbol for the racial inequality that characterized the Chicago school system.

Civil rights groups like the PCIS and the CCCO protested the "Willis Wagons" in the summer of 1963 and into the school year. Days after the beginning of school, Hattie Williams appeared at the school board along with her committee, the Kenwood-Oakland-Grand Boulevard Emergency Schools Committee, comprised of more than 50 parents. They demanded drastic improvements to the poor education that their children suffered. After meeting with the associate and assistant superintendent, Williams felt dissatisfied with their response. When a *Defender* reporter asked her what their group was going to do as a result of their demands being unmet, she replied, "we will open an emergency school at Ebenezer Church in our neighborhood."[5] This emergency school would grow into The Oakland Study Center (TOSC) and would serve hundreds of children on the South Side of Chicago.

The existing literature on the southern civil rights movement is vast. Less studied however, is the movement that took place up north, and Chicago in particular. Historians James R. Ralph and Robert McKersie have contributed in depth studies of the civil rights movement in Chicago. Their analyses however, focus on the work of the popular civil rights organizations, such as Martin Luther King's SCLC and the CCCO.[6] These organizations demanded assistance from federal, state and local governments and used traditional forms of protest politics such as picketing, sit-ins, and marches. While this account is critical in understanding the ways in which marginalized groups resisted the racial and social order, it trivializes the more local movements and their indigenous leaders that engaged with less conventional forms of protest. Dionne

Danns shifts the focus to the parents and community members who conducted an equally potent struggle. Surprisingly however, the organization and leadership of Hattie Williams remains obscured.[7] Williams adhered to the accustomed forms of protest politics, but also created her own techniques and institutions to challenge racial inequality in Chicago.

Williams captured the essence of what Nancy Naples coined, an "activist mother." This concept "highlights how political activism formed a central component of the community workers' motherwork and community caretaking."[8] She claims that activist mothering not only encompassed "nurturing work" for those outside one's family, but also involved "all actions, including social activism that addressed the needs of their children and community."[9] Historian, Francoise Hamlin cautions not to confuse "mothering as liberating and empowering and mothering as oppressive, caught in biological determinism and directing rigid gender roles."[10] I argue that Hattie Williams took on the role of an activist mother and strove to improve her community with her organizing abilities, nurturing spirit for her community and its children, and her attentiveness to issues that violated a politics of respectability.

By examining Williams through a lens of "community caretaking," we can gain a greater appreciation for the role that women played in the development of their communities. This paper focuses on two aspects of Williams' life, her role as founder and director of The Oakland Study Center, and her contribution as a mentor to the community but specifically to the young mothers. Illuminating these capacities shed new insight on the black freedom struggle and how communities, particularly in the north, organized grassroots campaigns to rally around issues specific to their community.

Born on December 7, 1922 in Chicago, Illinois, Hattie Williams was a life-long resident of the city. She was deeply involved in her Roman Catholic Church and accepted God at an early age. She met her future husband Bernard Williams, Sr., at the age of thirteen and got married after he returned from fighting in WWII. They had five sons and one daughter, who all attended Chicago's public schools.[11] From 1961-1963, Hattie Williams served as the PTA president of Forrestville North Upper Grade Center. Before Chicago's schools opened their doors in 1963, Williams along with other black parents held a meeting with the school board and Ben Willis. They protested the installment of "Willis Wagons" at Forrestville North, as an extension of DuSable High School. She reported that over 600 students recently graduated from Forrestville North, a junior-high school, and were kept there as ninth graders because of the overcrowding at DuSable High. The group demonstrated urgency, frustration, and personal initiative when they "announced that parents of some 600 children plan to picket" Forrestville North for three days.[12] Nevertheless, Willis and the school board rejected the parents' demands and left black students in a "jim crow game of musical chairs."[13] Dissatisfied but not defeated Williams, with the help of other parents, opened an "emergency school" at Ebenezer Baptist Church.[14]

Williams immediately organized support for TOSC. A student organization at the University of Chicago provided needed assistance. The Student Woodlawn Area Project (SWAP) delivered tutoring services to the children on the South Side of Chicago and covered a number of topics from reading, science and mathematics.[15] Williams' son, Bernard, recruited the two leaders of SWAP, Ann Cook and Herb Mack, to help with TOSC. The relationship with SWAP however, did not last. At first, the relationship between SWAP and TOSC appeared healthy. *Ebony Magazine* explained that SWAP served as tutors and serviced 150 children with 300 on the waiting list.[16] According to Bernard, SWAP attempted to "co-opt" TOSC and take over the operations of his mother and the other parents.[17]

For the first year and a half, TOSC served the community without any difficulties. The *Chicago Defender* hailed it as the "brainchild of Mrs. Hattie Williams" but recognized the community effort behind the project.[18] Mothers, fathers, college and high school students all tutored the younger kids. Parents were particularly pleased with improvements in their children's reading scores. One mother reported that "her child's reading score was raised by a full year" while a father expressed that his "boy is relaxed and confident in school because he's learned how to read."[19] Opposition towards TOSC came from white school principals who feared that high school tutors were incapable of teaching the pre-school kids. The parents responded that "the proof of the pudding is in the reading-and the kids are definitely learning how to read."[20] As TOSC established success in the community, however, tension emerged between TOSC and SWAP.

In a letter to SWAP, Williams expressed her dissatisfaction with Ann Cook and Herb Mack. She expressed that "SWAP completely dominates the program." She accused them of thwarting "community leadership," and "undermining all attempts by parents to establish a real community based program."[21] Williams refused to let SWAP or any other organization interfere with the progress of the study center. The *Chicago Defender* discussed the conflict between the two parties. Williams proclaimed that the "mothers were caught in the middle" after SWAP intervened, and that they eventually "became just figure heads." Williams expressed that SWAP minimized the mothers' involvement and "all they let us do was play games with the children when they wanted publicity pictures."[22] Williams, however, faced more powerful opposition.

Individuals and organizations who disagreed with Williams called her everything from a communist to an Uncle Tom.[23] Mayor Daley's democratic machine, which Alderman Claude Holman represented in the fourth ward, continued to try and subvert the intentions and goals of the center. Holman was the alderman of the ward in which Williams lived. He was one of six black aldermen in Chicago, dubbed the "silent six," who strongly supported Mayor Daley. The group received the name because of their lack of initiative in civil rights issues and their silence over Mayor Daley's power politics.[24] Once Williams and TOSC established a considerable influence in the community, political workers approached some of the mothers "asking them not to get involved in the project." According to Williams, some of the supporters of the study center "began turning away requests with apologetic shrugs." The mothers group, declared the *Defender*, "had committed the only unforgivable sin in the ghetto;" they had set down their own initiative and organized something to improve their neighborhood "without approval or sponsorship by the right organization."[25]

The Oakland Study Center expanded in the summer of 1964. The Eleanor Roosevelt Memorial Foundation awarded Williams and TOSC the Eleanor Roosevelt Community Award worth $800.[26] The award was supposed to help purchase more supplies for the operations of the program, and Williams had even temporarily changed the name from The Oakland Study Center to The Eleanor Roosevelt Oakland Study Center. TOSC suffered an unexpected loss in the upcoming winter when the TOSC building mysteriously burned to the ground.[27] According to Hattie's son, Bernard, local gang members burned it the ground at the request of

Alderman Holman. Williams was a republican and opposed Mayor Richard Daley's democratic machine. According to Bernard, after they received the award money from the Eleanor Roosevelt Foundation, Holman wanted them to name the study center after him. However, when they named it after Mrs. Roosevelt, he had members of a local gang burn down the establishment in revenge.[28]

Williams, however, remained dedicated to her community work in the face of different obstacles. Hattie Williams opened TOSC in 1969 for its sixth consecutive year.[29] By this time Williams had already undergone her first of four brain surgeries. She had her last one in 1988. The doctors diagnosed her with a brain tumor and she spent a considerable time in the hospital in her older adult life. Williams believed in "modern day miracles," and "although critically ill, she continued her volunteer service as a community and social worker through the years."[30] Her son Bernard took care of her after the first surgery, and advised that she take a break from TOSC. Williams replied determinedly "I'm 'gon die with my boots on."[31] This captures the resilient nature of Williams and demonstrates her dedication to improve the social welfare of her community.

A critical feature of TOSC's operations was Williams' organizing efforts. Williams regularly solicited local businesses for supplies and organizations donated materials. She never hesitated to ask the churches in her community to assist as tutors and to donate whatever they could. Williams organized across racial and religious lines to contribute to her efforts.[32] For example, members of the Prairie Shores B'nai B'rith lodge, a white Jewish organization, delivered "carloads of old books" to Williams for the study center's library and tutoring program.[33] Due to financial pressures, however, TOSC closed its doors in the early 1970s.[34]

Williams strongly believed in local grassroots struggles and sought unconventional methods to advance the community. Still, she engaged with traditional avenues to local reform as well. In November 1973, Williams ran for the 4th Ward Alderwoman against Timothy Evans.[35] However, there are two critical points about campaign for alderwoman. Even though she identified as a republican during the 1960s, she ran as an independent in 1973. She campaigned on a platform of "community involvement and responsive government." Furthermore, "more than 100 of Chicago's most prominent black women" endorsed her campaign.[36] Her independent political affiliation reflected her commitment to a political platform that emphasized the improvement and involvement of her community. Another critical endorsement of Williams' campaign was from Al Raby, president of United Teachers of Chicago and a past leader of the CCCO. Raby explained that he and Dr. Martin Luther King were called the leaders of the Civil Rights Movement in Chicago during the middle 1960's. However, he declared, "the real leaders were people like Hattie Williams."[37] Those words from Al Raby suggest the importance of Hattie Williams in Chicago's struggle for racial justice. His statement also demonstrates the patriarchal dominance of the civil rights movement and highlights the "real" leadership of local black women leaders. Williams lost the election, but never neglected the needs of the community, especially as it related to women's concerns.

Her role as an activist mother is further demonstrated in her capacity as a mentor to the young mothers in the Oakland-Kenwood neighborhood. From her experience as the president of multiple PTA's, she established and maintained numerous relationships with the mothers of the children. The mothers were the main volunteers at the study center. Betty Davenport, a mother who volunteered at TOSC remembered when she would baby-sit, sometimes for money, "twenty five dollars or something like that; nothing big at all."[38] Williams also drove the mothers around the city and taught them how to solicit "milk and cookies" from the neighborhood businesses. As an activist mother, with years of community organizing experience, she provided them with life lessons and encouraged them to continue their community service.[39] According to Linnie Woods, a mother who volunteered at TOSC, six of the mothers became teachers and two became doctors.[40]

Shortly after the close of TOSC, she became a vocal advocate for rape victims that lived in her neighborhood. In 1978, the Chicago Sun-Times invited Williams to publish two articles on the problem she described as an "urban epidemic." Williams, as "a woman and as an Afro-American" was primarily concerned with "the number of pregnancies in very young girls."[41] Williams discussed the taboo issue of rape in the black community and local authority's response. She accused the police for not doing anything to solve the problem. According to Williams, when they girls reported the rape, the police chastised the young girls about how they dressed, "especially to the black girls." Williams admitted to not having the one answer but suggested that "one approach is to improve the spiritual life of people in the community."[42] Williams' articles reflect her devout Christian faith and her critiques about Chicago's legal structures.

In 1978, Williams testified in front of the Rape Crisis Study Commission. In her testimony she presented alarming statistics of rape in her community. The geographical area she focused on consisted of 98,441 individuals and had "the highest illegitimate birth rate in the city of Chicago." Her presentation featured three examples of rape victims that she personally interviewed. She displayed the "dehumanizing process" that rape victims often suffer in the hospital emergency rooms by doctors and police.[43] Williams shamed the police departments and hospitals. For example, Williams presented a case of a 19 year old nursing student who was raped by "2 men with guns." She reported that the "doctors were reluctant to treat her" and that the "police wanted to know repeated details." Another instance was a 16 year old girl who "was raped and then carried to Michael Reese Hospital for emergency treatment." Yet when the doctors arrived, they shouted such questions at her as "did he ejaculate?"[44] Williams brought awareness to the problem of rape in her community and abandoned a politics of respectability. While most civil rights organizations steered away from such topics because they were not "respectable" issues to rally around, Williams "shed new light on the growing problem of rape, and the abysmal lack of sensitivity" with which hospitals and police departments treated rape victims nationwide. Her testimony demonstrates that she would openly criticize authorities of power to protect the rights of black women.

To the very last years of her life, Hattie Williams strove to improve the educational conditions of her community. Her leadership of TOSC demonstrates the ways in which she captured the essence of an activist mother. In her role as PTA president she organized parents and encouraged a sense of community empowerment and self-sufficiency. She created, directed and maintained The Oakland Study Center for more than five years. She funded the center with grants, donations and community fund-raisers, and mobilized a local grassroots movement that attended to the needs of the community children. While she engaged in traditional forms of protest politics, she also created her own methods to gain racial and economic justice. Her capacity as a mentor, role model and advocate for the women in her neighborhood demonstrates that activist mothers were influential not just to the community children but also to their young parents. In all of her contributions, Hattie Williams displayed that black women possess a certain degree of power to affect change in their neighborhoods. She was faced with a number of different obstacles, including subversive attacks from local politicians and SWAP. Moreover, in her later adult life, she faced life threatening medical concerns. Through all of these roadblocks, Williams committed herself to the improvement of life in Chicago's South Side neighborhoods. She is remembered by friends and family as a woman who tirelessly worked for her community. Fittingly, the Washington D.C.-based Caring Institute recognized Williams, with twelve other people, as "being the most caring people of 1988."[45]

1 "Oct. 22 School Boycott Planned As Protest Against Ben Willis," *Chicago Daily Defender*, October 14, 1963.

2 Dionne Danns, *Something Better for Our Children: Black Organization in the Chicago Public Schools, 1963-1971* (Great Britain: Routledge, 2003), 1.

3 "School-by-School Story of Boycott," *Chicago Daily Defender*, October 23, 1963.

4 "Oct. 22 School Boycott Planned As Protest Against Ben Willis," *Chicago Daily Defender*, October 14, 1963.

5 Ted Coleman, "Parents' Walk-In At Board Gets Nowhere," *Chicago Daily Defender*, September 5, 1963.

6 See, James R. Ralph, *Northern Protest: Martin Luther King, Jr., Chicago, and the Civil Rights Movement*, (Cambridge, MA: Harvard University Press, 1993); Robert B. McKersie, *A Decisive Decade: An Insider's View of the Chicago Civil Rights Movement During the 1960's*, (Carbondale, IL: Southern Illinois University Press, 2013).

7 Danns, *Something Better for our Children*

8 Nancy Naples, *Grassroots Warriors: Activist Mothering, Community Work, and the War on Poverty* (New York: Routledge, 1998), 111.

9 Ibid, 113.

10 Francoise Hamlin, *Crossroads at Clarksdale: The Black Freedom Struggle in the Mississippi Delta after World War II*, (Chapel Hill: The University of North Carolina Press, 2012), 60-61.

11 Bernard Williams, Jr., interview by author, Chicago, IL, October 27, 2013. Mr. Williams is the oldest son of Hattie Williams. It is important to note here that this paper would not be possible without the assistance and generosity of Mr. Williams. Not only did he provide fascinating detail to his mother's activism but he also had in his possession important primary documents related to her story that was extremely useful.

12 Ted Coleman, "School Board Facing New S. Side Troubles," *Chicago Daily Defender*, August 27, 1963.

13 "'Spotlight on Schools' On Forrestville No. Today," *Chicago Daily Defender*, April 15, 1964. This article features a report from the CCCO that explained the situation at the Forrestville schools. The students in kindergarten through 3rd grade at Forrestville South were sent to a housing project for classes, the students at Forrestville North were sent to Forrestville South, and the ninth graders at DuSable High School used the space at Forrestville North, hence the reference to a game of musical chairs.

14 Ted Coleman, "Parents' Walk-In At Board Gets Nowhere," *Chicago Daily Defender*, September 5, 1963.

15 David Sookne, phone interview by author, Chicago, IL, November 14, 2013. David Sookne was a volunteer for SWAP who tutored four African American children in junior-high mathematics.

16 "That They Might Learn: Chicago College Students' SWAP Program Offers Tutoring Help to Children of Ghetto Schools," *Ebony Magazine*, March 1965, 93.

[17] Bernard Williams, Jr., interview by author, Chicago, IL, October 27, 2013.

[18] "Why Don't 'They' Help Themselves? 'They' Do At The Oakwood Study Center," *Chicago Daily Defender*, May 14, 1964.

[19] Ibid.

[20] Ibid

[21] Hattie Williams to SWAP, correspondence, Hattie Williams Papers, in author's possession (hereafter, Willams Papers). Prior to this study, there have been no attempts to account for Hattie Williams' story and therefore all of her personal papers have yet to be processed. Her son, Bernard Williams, Jr. allowed the author to make copies of her papers. Attempts are being made to archive her personal papers at the Vivian G. Harsh Research Collection of Afro-American History and Literature at the Chicago Public Library.

[22] "Mother Fights to Upgrade Ghetto Life," *Chicago Daily Defender*, December 7, 1967.

[23] "Mother Fights to Upgrade Ghetto Life," *Chicago Daily Defender*, December 7, 1967.

[24] David K. Fremon, *Chicago Politics, Ward by Ward*, (Indiana: Indiana University Press, 1988), 40.

[25] Ibid

[26] Eleanor Roosevelt Memorial Foundation, award letter, July 23, 1964, in author's possession.

[27] "Oakland Center Gives Poor Youths Hope," *Chicago Daily Defender*, December 9, 1967.

[28] Bernard Williams, Jr., interview by author, Chicago, IL, October 27, 2013. It is important to note that the author did not find any written document that supports this account of how TOSC was set ablaze.

[29] Mozella Anthony, "Oakland Study Center Opens 6th Session," *Chicago Daily Defender*, September 30, 1969.

[30] Copy of Hattie Williams' obituary, Williams Papers, in author's possession; Copy of Williams' funeral program, Timuel D. Black, Jr. Papers (hereafter Black Papers), Box 153, Folder 26, Vivian G. Harsh Research Collection of Afro-American History and Literature (hereafter Harsh Collection), Chicago Public Library.

[31] Bernard Williams, Jr., interview by author, October 27, 2013.

[32] For more information on the role of religion in black women's lives, see, Bettye Collier-Thomas, *Jesus, Jobs and Justice: African American Women and Religion*, (New York: Knopf, 2010); and for more information on the role of the Roman Catholic Church's activism in Chicago, see, Suellen Hoy, *Good Hearts: Catholic Sisters in Chicago's Past*, (Champaign, IL: University of Illinois Press, 2006).

[33] "Lodge Collects Library Books," *Chicago Tribune*, July 11, 1965.

[34] Bernard Williams, Jr., interview by author, October 27, 2013.

[35] Ted Watson, "Ward Battles Heat Up," *Chicago Daily Defender*, Oct. 15, 1973.

[36] "Women Endorse Hattie," *Chicago Defender*, Nov. 24, 1973.

[37] Al Raby, support advertisement for Hattie Williams' campaign for alderwoman,

Williams Papers, in author's possession.

[38] Betty Davenport, phone interview by author, Chicago, IL, October 30, 2013. 4040 Oakenwald was the last location of The Oakland Study Center.

[39] Ibid

[40] Linnie Woods, phone interview by author, Chicago, IL, October 30, 2013.

[41] Hattie Williams, "Urban Epidemic: Babies Having Babies," *Chicago Sun-Times*, August 29, 1978

[42] Hattie Williams, "The Children of God in Apartment X," *Chicago Sun-Times*, August 30, 1978.

[43] Hattie Williams, transcript of her testimony to the Rape Crisis Study Commission, October 9, 1978, Williams Papers, in author's possession.

[44] Ibid

[45] "13 Receive Awards as Most Caring in '88," *Bangor Daily News,* Dec. 7, 1988.

Founding Mother, Confounding Narratives: Harriet Wilson's Past & Present New England

Cait Vaughan

Harriet E. Wilson's autobiographical novel *Our Nig; Or, Sketches from the Life of a Free Black*—the first by a Black American to be published in North America, in 1859—provides an incisive literary expression and examination of a biracial Black woman's experiences living and laboring in antebellum New England. Wilson deployed and subverted the traditions of sentimental fiction in order to document the life of a house servant girl, Frado. By doing this she exposed the abuses and inner workings of her white family of employ, The Bellmonts, who are based on the real-life Hayward Family of Milford, New Hampshire. The novel was also an economic enterprise for Wilson, who hoped to earn enough money to help save her ill son's life. Beyond the significance of being a literary 'first', *Our Nig*'s greatest impact is due to the force with which Wilson challenged the entrenched anti-slavery tropes of her time. Her subversive rendering of domestic fiction eviscerated the myth that a gradual, legal end to slavery in New England necessarily resulted in the absence of servile conditions and racist treatment for free people of color. She also exposed the inefficacy of liberal Christian piety divorced from moral action to improve the living conditions of free Black workers in the region. Perhaps her most rebellious literary maneuver is achieved via Frado's strategic navigations of Mrs. Bellmont's domestic authoritarianism, wherein Wilson underscored the primary role of white *women* in upholding white supremacy. Wilson's tale endures as a powerful rupturing of myths and master narratives about New England's regional identity and legacy of racism, inviting an honest reckoning with the past in order to foster an anti-racist future.

In order to fully comprehend Wilson's tenacity, one must consider the socio-political moment in which she penned *Our Nig*. While Northern abolitionists in the mid-nineteenth century were devoted to educating their Southern brethren about the evils of chattel slavery, Wilson chose to focus on the remnants of gradual emancipation in the Northeast, where she experienced an oppressive climate of anti-Black racism and economic disparity. Historian Joanne Pope Melish explains that the antebellum "triumphant narrative" of New England nationalism and moral authority over a 'backwards' slave-holding South neglected to account for the historical existence and treatment of people of African descent; rather, the popular narrative dismissed free Black folks as "permanent, unaccountable strangers" in the mythically all-white region (655). While the Bellmont family absorbed Frado as "a permanent member of the family" who was "quite indispensable," Mrs. B unrelentingly placed barriers in the way of Frado's education, religious practice and her basic bodily autonomy (Wilson 30). Wilson carefully delineated Frado's deepening understanding of the contradictory political convictions of her abolitionist neighbors, "who didn't want slaves in the South, nor niggers in their own houses, North" (129). Her work bolsters Melish's assertion that People of Color were "active participants in the evolving discourse of race" during the antebellum period, who "struggled mightily" to "fashion their own racial identity as strategies of resistance" (660). It is from the distinctive position of intimate stranger within her own community that Harriet Wilson wrote her forceful rebuttal to the Northern abolitionist movement's master narratives.

Seven years prior to Wilson's publication of *Our Nig*, another well-known Harriet published *Uncle Tom's Cabin*. It is this other Harriet whose story has endured, while Wilson's novel was lost for over a century, until its rediscovery in 1983 by Professor Henry Louis Gates, Jr. There is no doubt that Wilson encountered Stowe's book. One of her primary maneuvers of self-invention in the literary marketplace was to turn on its head what James Baldwin later identified as Stowe's sentimentalist "catalogue of violence" in the Southern states, in order to excavate white Northerners' fear of proximity to free Black people (10). Stowe's sentimental anti-slavery novel promoted the world-changing powers of Christian piety, sympathy and compassion to overcome the extreme evils of slavery. Wilson responded to Stowe by revealing the failure of sympathetic characters within the Bellmont Family to shield Frado from harm or create circumstances that would foster her economic self-sufficiency.

Wilson participated in and perpetuated the African American women's tradition of resistance via counter narrative, unmasking Stowe's saccharine-coated depiction of a moral universe wherein mere white sympathy toward individual Black people could foster conditions of equity. Wilson engaged the same literary genre and affective tools to interrupt Stowe's "ostentatious parading of excessive and spurious emotion" that abolitionists had quickly adopted to fight slavery in the South (Baldwin 10). While both authors magnified Black suffering in the tradition of sentimental fiction, Wilson also dared to magnify the white female abuser's *pleasure* in equal measure to Frado's experiences of pain and torment. By focusing the reader's attention to the other half of the abuse experience, Wilson rendered a gruesome image of Stowe's original distortion of white female passivity and martyrdom offered in *Uncle Tom's Cabin*.

It is useful to explore the ways in which Wilson detailed the active and sadistic nature of Mrs. B's white womanhood as it is co-constructed simultaneously with Frado's Black femaleness. Wilson achieved early on something which many in this present moment still struggle and often fail to do: she truly accounted for and reckoned with the interdependent constructions of white and Black womanhood that have far-reaching effects and consequences for Black women's self-invention and economic security. Scholar Cassandra Jackson explains that Wilson's portrayal of Mrs. Bellmont "vehemently professes" how "the notion of a blissful coalition between abolition and feminism is mythical" (162). We can take this further to say that Wilson subverted the conventions of sentimental fiction in order to reveal how white women in antebellum America, particularly 'mistresses of the house', performed much of the heavy lifting of white supremacy, enforcing economic and physical control of Black workers with nearly unanimous community approval.

Once orphaned by her mother's economic necessity, Frado is acquired by the Bellmont family to perform the labors of a servant girl and a farm boy. Frado's existence in the Bellmont household serves as a class status symbol for the family, and Mrs. B "felt that her (Frado) time and person belonged solely to her (Mrs. B)" (Wilson 41). At best, Frado is treated like an entertaining pet, called "our Nig" and "Nig" affectionately by the more sympathetic members of the Bellmont household. When her real name is spoken, it bears a too-close resemblance to her one true companion, Fido the dog. At worst, Mrs. B and the youngest Bellmont daughter, Mary, beat and torture Frado, at times threatening to kill her. Wilson not only cataloged Mrs. B's overt violence, but also detailed Frado's exhaustion of the solutions, faux salvation and precarious emotional shelter provided by the more 'sympathetic' Bellmonts; she thereby exposed the inefficacy of an abolitionist model that focused on condemning slavery without condemning racism or transforming economic realities for free

People of Color. The communal ownership and responsibility implied in the use of an appellative like *"our* Nig" proves to be a hollow contract. Frado's time, labor and body are accessed by the whites of Singleton whenever they deem fit, but when as an adult Frado falls ill, she is subject to the "unpleasant charities of the public," which keep her health in an increasingly poor state—finally forcing her to relate her tale in literary form (Wilson 124).

Returning to the question of proximity, one can apply recent scholarly insights proffered by critical race studies scholar Sharon Patricia Holland who argues, "regardless of how much we intend to understand race as being had by everyone, our examples of racial being and racist targets are often grounded in black matter(s)...the Black body is the quintessential sign for subjection, for a particular experience that it must inhabit and own all by itself" (4). Holland urges us to consider the place of desire and the erotic when dealing with the black/white binary, as this sheds light on some of the reasons for racism's staying power, interpersonally and institutionally. When examining closely Frado's encounters with Mrs. B, one notes how Wilson focused both on Frado's suffering *and* Mrs. B's psychic and physical experience of beating her—not requiring Frado's black body to solely inhabit the meanings of such abuse. In one passage, Mrs. B catches Frado seated at work in the kitchen and orders her to stand; Frado replies that she is too ill to work on her feet. The narrative describes Mrs. B as "angry that she (Frado) should venture a reply to her command" (Wilson 82). For Frado to step outside the prescribed boundaries of hierarchy established in the home and infringe upon Mrs. B's claims to her body is so maddening that Mrs. B gets "excited by so much indulgence of a dangerous passion," and is unrestrained in her malicious beating (Wilson 82).

Through such embellished descriptions, Wilson exposed the brutal daily practices of control required for the construction and maintenance of racialized gender lines.

Cassandra Jackson has examined the sexual tones of Mrs. B's abuse, and argues that the strategic silences Wilson places throughout the novel allude to female rape, an experience for which Wilson's contemporary society possessed no language. Jackson understands these sexual assaults as "motivated by hatred of the object rather than lust" (159). However, Holland's work helps us to understand that hatred and lust are not mutually exclusive, particularly when it comes to relations across the black/white color line. Indeed, while Jackson explores the sexual and abusive, she does not deal with the erotic nature of these encounters; which is to say, she does not acknowledge, as Holland might and as I agree, "the erotic as a possible harbinger of the established order" (9). Wilson's uncomfortably graphic and sexualized accounts of Mrs. B's abuse arrest our attention and force us to focus on what Holland points out as "the everyday system of terror and pleasure that in varying proportions makes race so *useful* a category of difference" (6, emphasis mine).

Mrs. B's relief and pleasure in torturing Frado is recounted in detail throughout the book. Its moral perversity is made clear by the narrator, and yet it is weathered by the supposedly more enlightened members of the Bellmont family, as well as the other residents of Singleton. Wilson shows us that Mrs. B's beatings do not just cause Frado suffering, but evoke passion and pleasure from the "malevolent matriarch" (Kete 118); these interactions seem to strengthen her and give her grounding in the domestic environment. As it is once recounted, no matter the stress Mrs. B was enduring "a few blows on Nig seemed to relieve her" (Wilson 41). With the nation on the verge of Civil War, Wilson wrote from the vantage point of a Northern state 75 years removed from the start of gradual emancipation, bringing a critical eye to the brutal interpersonal dynamics and economic consequences attendant to maintaining rigid categories of racial difference outside the parameters of formal slavery.

Wilson portrayed Mrs. B as a "right she-devil" and unrepentant handmaiden to a white male power structure, one that required a clear line of difference between white and Black, and between poor and owning classes (Wilson 17). White womanhood could not be passive when the boundary between white and Black—or of property and poverty—needed distinguishing and maintenance. As Holland asserts, "Racism transforms an already porous periphery into an absolute, thereby making it necessary to deny all kinds of crossings" (6). Mrs. B denies the racial crossings evidenced in Frado's light complexion and enviably pretty hair, forbidding Frado "to shield her skin from the sun," so as to distance her color from that of daughter Mary Bellmont (Wilson 39). Wilson's novel focused attention on the need for genuine accounting of white womanhood's particular, quotidian, and intimate racist practices towards Black women, which constitute the very social and bodily material of gender, womanhood and racial formation in the United States—especially in the New England situation. Wilson exposed the comingling pleasure and pain of white woman's labor to hold the line between One and Other. At this antebellum moment, women's bodies were a primary site for reproduction of racial meanings and their futurity. Thus, white women of any property were on the front lines of reproducing and rearing children capable of sustaining a hold on capital, as well as the difference upon which the uneven accumulation of said capital depended.

Mrs. Bellmont serves as the axis for the domestic power structure, which is a necessary condition and essential building block for the larger economic and political power structure. Her tirades are frequently described in terms of forces of nature—as storms and winds, which the sympathetic Bellmonts—such as James, Aunt Abby and Mr. Bellmont—must avoid provoking, or if already occurring then seek shelter, leaving Frado vulnerable to endure them alone. Wilson anthropomorphized and then magnified the workings of the white power structure in the character of Mrs. Bellmont, operating within the generic parameters of sentimental fiction. Mrs. Bellmont is the climate surrounding and determining everyone's movements. Her constant cruelty prompts Frado to run away more than once. The searches for Frado, which employ Fido—her one true companion—mimic in an eerie way the classic hunt for a runaway Southern slave. In this moment, Wilson posed the question: Where does a free Black woman in the abolitionist North run when faced with abuse and degradation at the hands of her employer? Frado—like the author herself—reached and lived along the limits of Black Northern freedom in the antebellum period.

In the progression of Frado's story, the embattled protagonist develops knowledge of her own labor power and identity as a worker and free person in a system stacked against her. Frado eventually claims spiritual and moral autonomy. After being tutored by Aunt Abby and James, she rejects her former longing to join a Heaven that would ever permit Mrs. B's entry, and studies the scripture privately instead. Wilson also shows us a series of strategies Frado deploys in order to navigate Mrs. B's storms, including a climactic moment wherein she famously withholds her labor as a way of staving off an unjust beating. Ultimately, Frado exhausts all white-proffered options for illusory 'shelter' or 'salvation', and the real-life Wilson instead produced the autobiographical novel as an indictment of the impossible conditions of her existence in the economic arrangement of a supposedly free North. Both Jane and Jack Bellmont's actions to secure their own economic stability leave Frado worse off and less sheltered from their mother's storms than ever before. Wilson thereby connected the domestic and economic dots of white accumulation and management *of* capital to Frado's subjection *as* capital.

Wilson appropriated the sentimental genre in order to highlight its limitations, as well as those of an abolitionist strategy motivated by sentimentality and seeking white catharsis. In wielding narrative authority, she disrupted regional and political categories of identification and practiced a mode of resistance, whereby she overpowered the "cruel author of her misery" (Wilson 83). In her greatest maneuver, the novel's final line, Wilson warns that Frado "will never cease to track them till beyond mortal vision" (131). This eerie closing recasts the racial, gendered and class arrangement wherein Frado is subject to surveillance and control, instead investing her with the power of the ultimate gaze.

Thanks to recent scholarly research, we know that the real-life Frado reinvented herself professionally and economically a number of times. And yet, she was never able to break out of the imposed conditions of poverty that were tied to her race and years of ruthless labor under the Hayward Family. Her book's failure to be an economic success was due in no small part to her indictment of abolitionist New England, despite its packaging in the widely popular sentimental fiction genre. Scholar Eric Gardner has pointed out that many "would have felt it (*Our Nig*) could hurt the abolitionist efforts given that its depictions of suffering free Blacks in the North echoed texts like the pro-slavery novels written in response to *Uncle Tom's Cabin*" (10). New England's liberal whites were not ready to receive Wilson's subversive truth-telling, thus, while her self-invention plaid out on the page, her lived experience beyond the margins of the story could not forge a viable path to wellness and peace for her and her son. The book's re-emergence in the late 20th century, and ongoing academic queries into why it failed to gain critical acceptance compared with other abolitionist writings, invite one to ask if present day New England is *yet* ready for Wilson's unapologetic soothsaying.

Despite its long period in the shadows of obscurity, a contemporary analysis of Wilson's life and novel is critical to understanding the development of African American culture, because it is truly a root of the Black American literary tradition. The canon is built upon practices of coding subversive meanings within traditional or seemingly apolitical forms, while simultaneously transforming white dominated writing genres into vehicles for liberating expression and political resistance. Harriet Wilson's *Our Nig* honors the complexity of Black self-invention in predominantly white-populated spaces like Northern New England, thereby providing a fuller picture of Black American women's experiences of identity, belonging and creative labor in both the past and present.

Works Cited

Baldwin, James. *Notes of a Native Son*. New York: Bantam, 1968. Print.

Gardner, Eric. "Of Bottles and Books: Reconsidering the Readers of Harriet Wilson's Our Nig." *Harriet Wilson's New England: Race, Writing, and Region*. Ed. JerriAnne Boggis, Eve Raimon, and Barbara A. White. Durham: U of New Hampshire, 2007. 3-26. Print.

Holland, Sharon Patricia. *The Erotic Life of Racism*. Durham: Duke UP, 2012. Print.

Kete, Mary Louise. "Slavery's Shadows: Narrative Chiaroscuro and Our Nig." *Harriet Wilson's New England: Race, Writing, and Region*. Ed. JerriAnne Boggis, Eve Raimon, and Barbara A. White. Durham: U of New Hampshire, 2007. 109-22. Print.

Melish, Joanne Pope. "The "Condition" Debate and Racial Discourse in the Antebellum North." *Journal of the Early Republic* 19.4, Special Issue on Racial Consciousness and Nation-Building in the Early Republic (1999): 651-72. *JSTOR*. Web. 22 May 2014. <http://www.jstor.org/stable/10.2307/3125137?ref=search-gateway:70a2a4f41ec5fb66252a69de5786d0f4>.

Wilson, Harriet E. *Our Nig: Sketches from the Life of a Free Black*. Mineola, NY: Dover Publications, 2005. Print.

In Defense of Black Womanhood and Femininity in Slavery

Jervette R. Ward

In "Looking Back from Zora, or Talking Out Both Sides My Mouth for Those Who Have Two Ears," P. Gabrielle Foreman writes, *"Black womanhood* is an oxymoronic term. Black *womanhood*, indeed Blacks' very humanity in this era [slavery], is anything but presumed. Black femininity, then, has to be forcefully asserted" (651). During slavery, black women forcefully asserted their womanhood and femininity. They were neither passive nor submissive in their enslaved roles as they fought not only for their personal freedom, but also for the freedom of their loved ones. Slavery provided the justifying means of stripping black women of their inherent womanhood; however, the essential feminine nature of the enslaved women could not be repressed. Black women demanded not only their God-given personal freedoms, but also claimed their freedom as women in direct opposition to the unrealistic Cult of True Womanhood, a controlling mechanism for the subjugation of women to men that is also known as the Cult of Domesticity. The provisionary, nurturing, and sexual nature of black women directly supports their innate black femininity and womanhood, which could not be stripped from them.

Black womanhood was manifested in many different ways. First, returning to the foundation of their existence, black women are descendants of agricultural women who provided food and sustenance for their families. They were providers, but often not in the glossed simple preparation of meals that was lauded in European society. They endured the hard labor of not only preparing food in the kitchen, but also of planting, sowing, and harvesting the food before it ever made it to the kitchen. Black women were nurturers, of not only their own children, but also often for a community of children, whether white or black. In addition, black women were sexual creatures, separate from and in opposition to the sexual nature defined by white men. The love of both themselves and their families supported their natural femininity. The Cult of True Womanhood was a controlling mechanism for the subjugation of women to men; just as white slave owners manipulated Christianity to control slaves, so did men use the Cult of True Womanhood to control women. The criteria of piety, purity, submissiveness, and domesticity were used to unfairly evaluate the femininity of black women.

To uphold their perceived racial superiority, white society created the Cult of True Womanhood that excluded black women. White males were able to strip black women of their status as women by holding up a standard that was nearly impossible for an enslaved individual to meet. Laura F. Edwards details the plight of the Southern Black in *Scarlett Doesn't Live Here Anymore: Southern Women in the Civil War Era*. Edwards writes, "White slaveholders considered their own gender roles inapplicable to slaves, whom they placed in a category fundamentally different from elite white men and women. Many slave women thus performed hard, physical labor alongside their menfolk from sunup to sundown, through bone-chilling winters and sweltering summers. In many areas, the majority of field laborers were actually women" (57). By placing black women in the field next to men, white southern men were in essence placing black women on the same level as black men. In "African Women in the Atlantic Slave Trade," Herbert S. Klein writes:

> All recent studies reveal that planters showed little or no sexual preferences in labor use, with women performing all the basic unskilled manual labor tasks that men worked at. Women in most American plantations were, in fact, overrepresented in all the brute force field hand labor occupations, and in mature plantation areas they tended to be the majority of actual field gang plantation workers. (72).

This lack of distinction was simply another way to prevent the womanhood of the black female from being manifested.

As the black woman was degraded, the white woman was upgraded. In *Woman: Gender Discourses in Caribbean Slave Society* Henry McD Beckles writes:

> White women described as "ladies" were not expected to labour in the field or perform any demeaning physical task. This was clearly a class position since the thousands of female indentured servants imported from Europe between 1624 and 1680 worked on the cotton, tobacco, and sugar plantations in gangs alongside their male counterparts, as well as with enslaved Africans. It was not until the late seventeenth century that English planters, in particular, thinking of gender more in terms of race than class, implemented the policy that the white woman was not to work in sugar plantation labour gangs. (7)

Placing white women on a pedestal allowed white men to create a social order that appeared to place white women on top, then white men, then black men, and lastly the black woman. However, this chapter will not address the cage the Cult of True Womanhood created for white women, which allowed them a pedestal only in theory. Yet, returning to the idea of removing white women from the field, white women in essence became the support for white supremacist ideas. Beckles continues, "This ideologically driven initiative to isolate white womanhood from plantation field work, however, had much to do with the social needs of patriarch to idealize and promote the white woman as a symbol of white supremacy, moral authority, and sexual purity" (7). The rise of the white woman from the field of servitude, led to the downfall of the black woman because the empty spaces in the field had to be filled.

The justification for the placement of black women in the field of labor was inherently tied to the preconceived notions surrounding the female body. Colonial slaveholders argued that the black female body was inclined towards heavy labor. Beckles explains:

> The black woman was ideologically constructed as essentially 'non-feminine' in so far as primacy was placed upon her alleged muscular capabilities, physical strength, aggressive carriage, and sturdiness. Pro-slavery writers presented her as devoid of the feminine tenderness and graciousness in which the white woman was tightly wrapped. (10)

By stripping the black woman of the basic "charms" that were readily bestowed upon the white woman, proponents of slavery were able to find a justification for their cruel and barbaric system:

> The defeminisation of the black woman, recast as the 'Amazon', (sic) allowed slave owners to justify within the slavery discourse her subjugation to a destructive social and material environment. It was said that she could 'drop' children at will, work without recuperation, manipulate at ease the physical environment of the sugar estate, and be more productive than men. (Beckles 10)

The black female body was born for physical labor, according to the logic of the slaveholder. This same concept was carried over to black motherhood. The ability of the black woman to work all day, birth a child, and return to the field supported the slaveholder mentality of careless motherhood.

Slave owners perpetuated the idea that black women were inherently bad mothers who did not care for their children as a white mother did. Beckles writes:

> Slave-owners spoke instead about black women's disregard for motherhood and nurturing, and explained this as further evidence of their brutishness and lack of femininity. Since it was 'natural', (sic) they argued, for women to desire motherhood, black women's apparent low fertility within the context of an *alleged sexual promiscuity* (italics my own), suggests a certain kind of moral underdevelopment rather than physical inability. (11)

The domestic world of motherhood was not available to the black woman because the opportunity to manifest it was never presented to black women. Black women were expected to submit (another aspect of the Cult of True Womanhood) to the demands of their enslaver; however, they often resisted, but their resistance was forcefully met with punishment. The abuse of black women's sexuality was even manifested in their hindrances in trying to escape from slavery. Black women who were always subject to the sexual demands of their owners in a time that predated birth control. Slave women often found themselves in "the family way" after sexual assaults: "Women were less likely to do so (flee) because of the difficulties of transporting and supporting those (children) on their own" (Edwards 104). Motherhood became another tool for the master to deepen her ties to slavery.

The white male society created the hypocritical social veil of disgust with the lack of black femininity to justify their base sexual assault on black females. By erecting the pedestal of white womanhood, white society was able to create an ideal of beauty that was unobtainable for black women.

This unobtainable nature aided the cementing of the double standard involving black and white womanhood. Yet in the midst of this double standard, Edwards writes, "Slave women were particularly vulnerable to the advances of their white masters, many of whom demanded female slaves' sexual favors as a matter of course" (61). Yet, even as black womanhood was attacked, it was still promoted in the lives of black women due to the sexual resistance of slave women like Harriet Jacobs, writing as Linda Brent in *Incidents in the Life of a Slave Girl*, who avoided her sexual predator, Dr. Flint/Dr. James Norcom, for years by hiding in a near box like room attached to her grandmother's house. Even in the midst of the debasing nature of slavery, black women were not only able to claim their right as free people, but also as simply women. Beckles writes, "Plantation owners…maintained that slave women were generally promiscuous, and pursued sexual relations with white males for their own material and social betterment" (26). Even as white men criticized and belittled black women for their assumed sexuality, white men used them as an outlet for their own debasing activities: "White elite males possessed a sexual typology in which white women were valued for domestic formality and respectability, coloured women for exciting socio-sexual companionship, and black women for less-structured covert sexual adventurism" (Beckles 32). Ironically, the question arises of how can one strip a woman of her womanhood and femininity when she is labeled as a hypersexual being? The sad dichotomy is that the sexuality of the black woman was equated to a bestial or barbaric innate tendency that in essence robbed her of her femininity and branded her as little better than a dog in heat. Beckles writes, "The circuitous route of capital accumulation within the slave system, furthermore, recognized no clear distinction between the slave-based production of material goods, and the delivery of sexual services. Production and reproduction oftentimes were indistinguishable with the market economy of slavery" (22-23). The slave owner made "sexual services" his right. However, this sexual exploitation was rooted in stereotypes. Slave owners equated fertility with sensuality. This stereotype created a cycle of exploitation and mulatto/a children. The chastity of slave women was always in question in direct opposition to the assumed purity of white women. Ironically, resistance to race and sexual abuse often led to punishment. Yet, the double-edged sword of this experience was the brand they received of being labeled a "loose" woman if they simply gave into the sexual exploitation.

The ability of physical labor that was capable in black women was quickly recognized by white slave owners: "Planters also took advantage of women's domestic skills, giving raw supplies to families with the expectation that women would turn them into clothes and meals" (Edwards 58). However, in an effort to promote their own womanhood, black slave women took this evil and turned it into good. Slave women exalted their womanhood by taking pride in their domestic labor which is one of the key components of the Cult of True Womanhood: "Slave women resented their masters' demands, but they took pride in the work itself. They saw their strength and skills as a positive affirmation of their womanhood" (58). Barbara Welter fully explains the criteria for meeting the Cult's standards in her essay, "The Cult of True Womanhood: 1820-1860," and she argues that the cult was a standard by which "a woman judged herself and was judged by her husband, her neighbors and society" (152). By taking the evil plan of the slave master and flipping the plan, black slave women were able to manifest and to meet one of the criteria of the Cult of

True Womanhood.

The labor of slave women was one of the first areas that were used to strip them of their inherent femininity. All work done by black slave women was the property of their masters. Field labor and child labor alike benefited slave masters: "Anything that slaves used or produced, including their children, belonged to their masters" (Edwards 50). In addition, the body of the slave, whether male or female, did not belong to the individual slave, rather the body of the human soul it surrounded belonged to a white master: "If another person assaulted a slave, the law considered it a crime against the owner. Sexual assault was not a crime at all, since slaves had no legally recognized power to give or withhold consent" (50). Ironically, this same legal concept was contradictory in practice because a slave was responsible for his or her own actions if he or she committed a crime and would be punished for the crime: "Masters were not held responsible for criminal acts committed by their slaves, who had to answer for their crimes just as free whites did" (50). The hypocritical system of slavery recognized and denied the innate individual when it was convenient for white slaver holders. This same dual system both manipulated and exploited slave women.

Even as slavery sought to strip slave women of their innate rights, both black men and women attempted to reaffirm their roles as humans. Edwards writes, "Working against the odds, slaves managed to construct families both strong enough and flexible enough to withstand the instabilities of the slave system" (52). These family ties allowed slave women to create worlds where their femininity was recognized as wives, mothers, sisters, and daughters. Even when families were torn apart due to death, sale, or other external forces, slave families and slave women still

251

fought to create some sort of family system: "Necessity also combined with African cultural patterns, making extended kin and community networks central to slaves' lives" (53). The family ties also extended to individuals not necessarily related by blood: "Slaves recognized people as mothers, fathers, sisters, brothers, grandmothers, grandfathers, aunts, uncles, nieces, nephews, and cousins even if they were not actually related to them by blood" (54). This family role directly supported the family-focused, domestic aspect of the Cult of True Womanhood.

Even as their sexualized stigma led to rape and sexual exploitation, black women found a way to assert their femininity in the product of these liaisons. Through their relationships and interactions with their children, often born of a slave master, black women were able to assert their femininity in the realm of motherhood. Slave women placed a high priority on the raising of their children in the midst of a system that often kept them from their offspring:

> Painfully aware of their children's status, slave mothers harbored no illusions about childhood. Even with the expectation of community involvement in childrearing, the mother-child bond was very strong among slaves. Some historians have argued that slaves invested this relationship with more social importance than the tie between husbands and wives. (Edwards 56)

For Jacobs, slavery was a far greater ill for slave women than for slave men, for not only was the physical female body enslaved, but so also was the sexual body of the female. A slave, in essence, was property in a patriarchal system that lauded white womanhood and belittled black womanhood. That property, or slave, was subject to the total will and desire of the slave master. The burden of the female slave was the master's demand for physical or sexual labor, or sometimes both. Ironically, patriarchy, which argues for a male head of the family with traditional primogeniture, existed in a skewed manner in the slave households. Patriarchy was blatantly obvious in the southern white households; however, for the slave system, it was hypocritically manifested. Relationships and family lines were not passed through the male line. Jacobs' children, just like the children of other slave women, were slaves and had little or no ties to their paternal line. While Jacobs was ill following the birth of her premature baby, her master reiterated the known fact concerning her son and her son's ignored bloodline: "Dr. Flint continued his visits, to look after my health; and he did not fail to remind me that my child was an addition to his stock of slaves" (66). Even though the white Mr. Sands was the father of Jacobs' children, his lineage was denied because Jacobs was a slave and subject to the will of her master, Dr. Flint, which is in complete contrast to the white rules of patriarchy.

In addition to their own daily toils, black women asserted their roles as wives and as mothers in their willingness to work "after hours." Edwards writes, "They worked evenings and Sundays in their own garden plots to supplement their families' meager rations and sat up long into the night to sew, mend, and quilt" (57). This domestic role at the end of long hours of field labor was a way for the domestic nature of the black woman to be manifested in support of her feminine nature. Unlike black men, whose work day was often over once field labor was complete, black women continued to their second job once the day's field work was complete: "They expected slave women to work a full day in the fields and then stay up late into the night to produce basic necessities that owners could not or would not purchase" (102). Black women were also forced into the fields to work in even greater numbers once both black men and white men were recruited into the Civil War. However, unlike the outrage surrounding white women who had to take to the field due to shortages[1], the plight of the black women was largely ignored: "White southerners were accustomed to seeing black women work in the fields. They expected it. They did not even seem to notice they had dumped the primary burden of feeding their families onto African American women" (102). By creating a beast of burden out of the black woman, the entire black race was allowed to suffer due to the overworked nature of the black woman.

In the chapter, "For the Freedom of the Colored People," Edwards writes, "In 1861, for instance, one South Carolina planter gave the men on his plantation pants, but no coats. The women got nothing at all" (101). The Civil War brought shortages to all, but the already overworked and starved slaves were hit even harder, especially the women: "Shortages had particular implications for slave women. When planters began to produce more food and clothing, most of the extra labor fell to female slaves. Not only were many already skilled in these areas, but also planters considered the labor to be 'women's work'" (101-102). However, this "women's work" was race specific. The work was "women's work" for black women, yet white women had the luxury of delegating the work to slaves or performing very little of it themselves: "To be sure, planter-class women took on more domestic production as well, but they supervised and delegated, just as they had done before the war. It was slave women who did the heavy labor" (102). Just as before the Civil War, even during Emancipation, black women were seen more as beasts of burden and not as women to be protected and cherished as white women were. The hard

---

[1] Think of the famous scene in the movie adaptation of *Gone With The Wind* when Scarlett O'Hara works in the fields to the shame of her family.

labor was thoughtlessly tossed upon them.

Piety, morality, and purity were all traits desired in a woman. Both Jacobs and her grandmother, at times, defined morality, in the same way. Initially they both held the moral standards that were often expressed in white society that upheld the Cult of True Womanhood. Even though, they lived in a slave world, where social norms were not always observed, "good slaves" were still expected to cling to the Christian values that their white slave masters espoused. Jacobs recognized the hypocrisy of the slave system. Slave marriage was not legally recognized and even if a slave "married" that slave was still subject to the will of the master, who could sell, punish or even take the slave woman as his sexual partner. Jacobs recognized this fact and sought her own justice in the arms of another white man. Both Jacobs and her grandmother were ashamed of her pregnancies; however, Jacobs justifies her actions by explaining that they would have never happened outside of the morally corrupt slave system. Her grandmother was not able to reach the same level of justification because she strongly clung to the slave infused Christianity of white slave owners.

During the Civil War, black women sought continuous employment as they fled slavery; however, steady job opportunities were unavailable to them. Yet, in the midst of slim options, black women were criticized for their plight: "Inconvenienced by women's presence, blind to their problems, and indifferent to their desires, northern officials could not see the inadequacy of the available economic options. Often, they blamed the women themselves: if they were cold and hungry, it was because they were lazy and irresponsible" (112). Black women were neither protected nor provided for, yet when their limited means did not result in provisions for them or their families, they were labeled and belittled for their shortcomings. Unlike white women, it was expected that black women would take care of themselves and their families. White women had the luxury of living under the financial protection of husbands, fathers, and families. Black women on the other hand struggled to survive in a system that saw them as not as people, and especially not as women. White womanhood and femininity was protected through a code of chivalry while black womanhood was completely ignored.

Jacobs is brilliantly able to create space for herself morally, sexually, and physically, when to all norms there was no space for any of the aforementioned realms. Jacobs, like many slaves created her sense of morality in the midst of a morally lost culture. Even though many slaves clung to the slave infused Christianity of their masters, which provided them with some sense of hope, it also created a sad standard of morality that was very unrealistic in their slave world. In the mind of Dr. Flint, Jacobs would have been performing her Christian duty if she had submitted to his sexual desires. Jacobs would have been submitting to the will of her master, just as slaves were told the Bible commanded them to do. By refusing her master's advances and choosing her own sexual alliance, Jacobs broke from the hypocritical morality of her master and created her own moral standard. In addition, this breach allowed Jacobs to create her own definition of the Cult of True Womanhood. This new sense of morality was intricately tied to Jacobs' sexual freedom. Jacobs manifested her sexuality by forming a longstanding sexual alliance with a white man, Mr. Sands. Jacobs did not allow the hypersexual stigma to prevent her from reveling in her own sexuality as a woman. Instead of allowing her sexual acts to be controlled by the sexually depraved Dr. Flint, Jacobs made a choice to give her body to another white man when and how she pleased. Jacobs was able to choose her sexual partner and was able to have two children by him. Her children were not free; they were the property of her master, but they were not the blood of her master, living proof of her sexual freedom. The physical freedom that Jacobs created for herself, could arguably be said was not real freedom. Jacobs spent seven years hiding in a boxlike enclosure attached to her grandmother's house. For some, this space was an enclosed prison, yet for Jacobs, this space was her freedom. The enclosure became her freedom from Dr. Flint's sexual advances and eventually led her to complete physical freedom in the north. By clinging to her own definition of womanhood, Jacobs was able to broadcast her humanity and femininity, and in Jacobs one can find a compelling representation of the inherent womanhood and femininity of all black women.

Works Cited

Beckles, Hilary McD. *Centering Woman: Gender Discourses in Caribbean Slave Society.* Oxford: Ian Randle, 1999. Print.

Edwards, Laura F. *Scarlett Doesn't Live Here Anymore: Southern Women in the Civil War Era.* Urbana: University of Illinois, 2000. Print.

Foreman, P. Gabrielle. "Looking Back from Zora, Or Talking Out both Sides My Mouth for Those Who have Two Ears." *Black American Literature Forum* 24.4, Women Writers Issue (1990): 649-66. Print.

Jacobs, Harriet. *Incidents in the Life of a Slave Girl.* New York: Signet, 2000. Print.

Welter, Barbara. "The Cult of True Womanhood: 1820-1860." *American Quarterly* 18.2, Part 1 (1966): 151-74. Print.

About the Editors

Lopez D. Matthews, Jr., PhD, Lopez is an Archivist in the Howard University Archives, a division of the Moorland-Spingarn Research Center.

Kenvi C. Phillips, PhD, Kenvi is the Prints and Photographs Librarian for the Moorland-Spingarn Research Center.